Quality Web Systems

Quality Web Systems

Performance, Security, and Usability

Elfriede Dustin

Jeff Rashka

Douglas McDiarmid

ADDISON–WESLEY

Boston • San Francisco • New York • Toronto • Montreal
London • Munich • Paris • Madrid
Capetown • Sydney • Tokyo • Singapore • Mexico City

Many of the designations used by manufacturers and sellers to distinguish their products are claimed as trademarks. Where those designations appear in this book, and Addison-Wesley, Inc. was aware of a trademark claim, the designations have been printed with initial capital letters or in all capitals.

The authors and publisher have taken care in the preparation of this book, but make no expressed or implied warranty of any kind and assume no responsibility for errors or omissions. No liability is assumed for incidental or consequential damages in connection with or arising out of the use of the information or programs contained herein.

The publisher offers discounts on this book when ordered in quantity for special sales. For more information, please contact:

Pearson Education Corporate Sales Division
One Lake Street
Upper Saddle River, NJ 07458
(800) 382-3149
corpsales@pearsontechgroup.com

Visit Addison-Wesley on the Web: www.awl.com/cseng/

Library of Congress Cataloging-in-Publication Data

Dustin, Elfriede.
    Quality web systems : performance, security, and usability / Elfriede A. Dustin,
Jeff Rashka, Douglas McDiarmid.
        p.   cm.
    Includes bibliographical references and index.
    ISBN 0-201-71936-3
    1. Web site development. 2. Web sites—Quality control. I. Rashka, Jeff.
II. McDiarmid, Douglas. III. Title.
    TK5105.888 .D88 2001
    005.2'76—dc21   2001034329

0-201-71936-3
Text printed on recycled paper
1 2 3 4 5 6 7 8 9 10—HT—0504030201
First printing, August, 2001

Contents

Foreword

This book addresses an important niche for the software industry, specifically the need for deploying quality Web systems. At a time when the successful development and deployment of Web-based systems is pivotal to the survival of both public and private organizations, the *Quality Web Systems* book steps up to fill the need for solid guidance on how to ensure that key Web system success factors have been satisfactorily implemented. The book brings together, in one place, important instructions on how to deliver a usable, accessible, compatible, secure, and high-performing Web system.

The amount of business being conducted via the Web has experienced phenomenal growth, and organizations are struggling to deploy and update Web system content ahead of competition. Many systems have been deployed prior to satisfactory assurances that system success factors, such as usability and security, have been adequately addressed. *Quality Web Systems* provides today's Web professionals with the insights needed to understand all the things that can go wrong for a system when quality is not built in as the system is developed and when systems are not tested before being deployed. The book further outlines the system assurance activities necessary to help prevent potential catastrophe.

The book articulates technical issues that can create compatibility problems for system end users. Since users insist that a system be able to refresh a screen or return a query within a very limited amount of time, system performance and scalability are two of the predominant system success factors. The authors outline test strategies that provide assurance in these areas and also provide guidance on how to interpret performance measures. Similarly, their book addresses Web system usability issues at a level that is complementary with the host of information that has been published to date on these subjects.

In the early days of e-commerce, some companies rushed sites into production without sufficient attention to quality. Most of these sites are dead now. In any case, to the extent that it may ever have been possible to cut a few corners on quality in the early days, this is certainly not possible any more.

In recent years, malicious attacks on flagship e-commerce systems brought these Web sites down and cost the affected companies millions of dollars. The U.S. federal government has also released studies that have highlighted the prevailing problem across the software industry with regard to the vulnerability of Web-based systems to malicious attack. The *Quality Web Systems* book provides extensive technical guidance on sources of security problems and how to proceed to conduct tests to verify whether security issues exist for a Web system.

With the *Quality Web Systems* book, Elfriede Dustin and her coauthors are providing timely and necessary material that allows responsible parties to implement a quality Web system. Without quality, both individuals and organizations are at risk of deploying systems that fail in any one of the key Web system success factors. Once you have read this book, you will never view the Web system development life cycle in the same way again.

Jakob Nielsen, Ph.D.
Author of *Designing Web Usability: The Practice of Simplicity*
www.useit.com

Preface

Quality Web Systems addresses the challenge for today's Web software professionals engaged in the development of Web sites and Web-based applications—products that support the business of an organization. These professionals working to develop and to deploy Web systems are under pressure to complete development efforts and to incorporate upgrades to systems ahead of the competition. Deployment delays often translate into the loss of revenue and reputation for the organization and can result in the loss of market share, which may be vital to the future of the organization. Similarly, the deployment of troublesome or error-prone Web systems can result in disgruntled customers, loss of revenue, and loss of market share. Web customers are seeking Web systems that serve them in a reliable fashion, that are secure and usable, and that provide quick and easy service.

Often overlooked during the effort to quickly deploy a Web system are the many necessary aspects that make up a successful system. Among these key success factors are proper functionality, ease of use, compatibility with a variety of browsers, security of the site's components and content, and system performance and scalability.

The Web has brought many changes to the way that systems are built and deployed. Software engineers attempting to build these sites face a multitude of new concerns, most of which have arisen over just a few years. Many systems are deployed with flaws that pose serious problems for the site, such as security holes and the inability to cope with user load. These issues have the effect of placing one or more of the key success factors at risk. This book provides a technical examination of these issues, outlines appropriate implementation techniques, and describes the problem areas in technical detail.

Delivering a quality Web system, however, does not rely merely on the merits of having a grasp of the potential problems and the knowledge of how to fix them. A critical component of any Web development project is the proper use of testing techniques, which are necessary for verifying that the site addresses these concerns and delivers the required functionality to the end users. Therefore, in addition to the technical discussion of each problem area, we also provide detailed testing strategies.

The starting point for exploring these issues and the first step toward ensuring that key Web system success criteria have been addressed during the development of the Web system is the capture and analysis of the site's intended functionality. One of the most effective and popular techniques for requirements capture is known as *use case* analysis, a technique for specifying system functionality precisely. Use cases are the basis for further analysis and design of the system. The study of use case analysis is a large topic, and it can be undertaken in several ways, depending on the size of the project and the people involved. The use case approach presented here, known as RSI (requirement-service-interface), is a specific way of *engineering the functionality* of a system and includes definition of system requirements, modeling of the high-level system services, and specification of the user interface.

RSI use cases are also an excellent starting point for test case definition, providing an appropriate level of detail for black-box and gray-box testing activities. This book does not attempt to cover all the possible implementation techniques and functional issues that may be encountered but rather concentrates on the engineering of system functionality, a critical factor in Web system quality and success. This effective approach to engineering system functionality supports the development of thorough tests that help to ensure proper operation of the system. The specification of system functionality occurs throughout the project life cycle, with the majority of the work being performed in the earlier phases. The specification of system functionality is an activity that warrants special attention by software professionals and project managers, and it should be regarded as one of the keys to delivering a quality Web system.

Another critical activity pertains to the early phases of architecture definition, system design, and implementation. These activities are also performed iteratively throughout the life of the project. Some decisions that are made early in these processes will be difficult, if not impossible, to reverse at a later time should a major flaw be discovered in the system's ability to perform in accordance with defined nonfunctional requirements—security, performance and scalability, and so on. Unfortunately, much of the guidance necessary to avoid these issues and to be able to deliver a system that properly addresses the key Web system success criteria has not been readily available and, in particular, has not been provided in one source.

Quality Web Systems addresses in detail the key success factors—security, performance and scalability, compatibility, usability, and the specification of functionality—that have a profound effect on the acceptance and use of the Web system by the end user. Engineering these factors into the system during the architecture, design, and implementation phases enables the Web site to be constructed with proper consideration for these concerns. In addition to the engineering of the key success factors into the Web system, software professionals need to apply the testing samples and guidance provided in the book in order to verify the successful implementation of the key success factors.

As an aid in helping to more completely outline the concepts addressed within the book, a single case study system, the Technology Bookstore, is portrayed throughout. In each chapter, relevant examples from the case study system are examined to provide concrete examples for the implementation concerns and test procedures.

Audience

This book focuses on the pragmatic concerns for Web system architecture and development: the Web enabling of applications, the establishment of Internet and intranet Web sites, and the development of Web applications supporting enterprise information portals. Thus, this book is valuable for *Web architects* and *Web developers*, who require detailed technical information on Web architectures and the proper implementation of site components to provide a site that is secure, scalable, compatible, and usable. The book also supports *software test engineers* seeking a more comprehensive technical understanding of Web systems. In addition, each success criterion is accompanied by step-by-step testing strategies for the test engineer. The book supports *project managers* by providing them with greater technical insight into the key Web system success factors.

Conventions

This book uses the following conventions to help the reader.

- Code samples, log entries, commands, and other captures are represented in a special type font: `// this is a code sample.`

- Important terms and ideas are highlighted with *italicized* text.

Organization

Chapter 1 provides an overview of Web systems and technologies. The chapter outlines the paradigm shift that has occurred, associated with the movement of modern business and commercial software applications to the Web, and discusses how this shift has introduced new system development issues. Architectural approaches and Web system components are addressed, as well as the languages and products that are used to create Web systems. Basic terms used throughout the book are introduced.

Chapter 2—explains how to capture system behavior, or functionality, at the appropriate levels of detail through use case analysis using the RSI approach. The application of RSI use cases as an excellent starting point for test case definition is addressed.

Chapter 3—covers a multitude of security and privacy concerns for any Web system. The chapter focuses on security issues pertaining to the Web server, the database server and browser, and content security of custom components of a Web system.

Chapter 4—provides an in-depth discussion about the ability of the system to perform and scale. The chapter also explains how to identify and correct performance and scalability problems. The need for capacity planning is addressed as it pertains to the process of determining the resource require-ments necessary for the Web system to be able to handle future load within an acceptable response time.

Chapter 5—details the challenges of providing service in an acceptable way to users with various operating systems and Web browsers. Guidance is provided on the implementation of standards and the development of a compatibility test matrix to aid in defining the proper scope of compatibility tests, given the extremely large possible number of test combinations.

Chapter 6—examines the suitability of the site's interface and end user expe-rience relative to the intended user base. The Web system must be logical and intui-tive and must provide a unique and pleasant shopping experience. Tests need to be applied to the system to provide assurance that an adequate level of usability has been implemented.

Chapter 7—outlines the various kinds of tools that are available to assist with the issues described in the previous chapters. Finally, Appendixes A–C provide supplementary information: Web testing checklists, a test tool evaluation matrix, and the Technology Bookstore case study.

Note that Chapters 3–6 provide not only an in-depth technical discussion of the material applicable to Web architecture and Web development audiences but also step-by-step guidance for the performance of tests applicable to both Web development and software testing. In addition and where applicable, references to additional sources of information are provided.

About the Authors

Elfriede Dustin has worked as a computer systems analyst/programmer developing software applications and utilities. She has experience supporting system application development projects on health, financial, logistic, and enterprise information management systems. She has also been responsible for implementing the entire development life cycle: requirements analysis, design, development, and automated software testing.

Elfriede is the principal author of the software testing book *Automated Software Testing* and has been a speaker on automated software testing at numerous conferences. She has been a test manager and a lead consultant guiding the implementation of automated testing on many projects. Because of her expertise in automated testing, she has had a personal hand in the modification of capabilities represented in industry test tool products, providing use and feedback on test products.

Jeff Rashka has managed a multitude of significant information system and systems integration projects in such areas as worldwide transportation asset management, data warehouses/data marts, enterprise information management, financial management, configuration management, bar-coded inventory management, and shipboard information systems. Jeff also has experience in process improvement management: implementing the ISO-9001 standard and the guidelines contained in the Software Engineering Institute's Capability Maturity Model (CMM).

Douglas McDiarmid is a consultant specializing in the architecture and development of distributed Web systems. Douglas is proficient in the latest architecture and development technologies: component-based development, *n*-tier architectures, and design patterns. He has been responsible for the full life cycle of Web-based systems, which has involved use case modeling with UML (Unified Modeling Language), as well as definition and verification of system requirements. He has worked on a variety of traditional and Internet-based enterprise systems, including sales force automation, medical bill auditing, and financial management.

Acknowledgments

Thanks to a great number of software professionals in the areas of e-commerce, system security, Web development, and system performance who have helped support the development of this book. We are especially grateful to all the individuals below whose reviews, contributions and other support were invaluable. We also wish to thank BNA Software's General Manager, David Wilkes, and Project Manager Jim Broomfield for allowing us to use experiences gained at BNA Software in the writing of this book.[1] Although we have not been able to list everyone who helped on the book, we are appreciative of all your help.

AJ (Amjad) Alhait
Christina Anzaldua
Simon Berman
Mark Collins-Cope
David Daish
George Exarhacos
Julie Ferron
Jennifer Graham
Diane Hagglund
Gerald Harrington
Dawn Haynes
Terry Horwath
Albert Hsieh

Jenny Jones
Capers Jones
Marie Joppich
Richard Jussaume
Bruce Katz
Kirk Knoernschild
Thomas McKearney
Don Magie
Norm Moreau
Carl Nagle
Jeff Nyman
Roland Petrasch
John Paul

Cristian Radu
Geoff Raines
Glenn Reemes
Jonathan Rende
Marcia Robinson
Robert Sabourin
David Seibert
Danya Schumaker
Kevin Sturgeon
Andy Tinkham
Tim Van Tongeren
Paul Woods

[1] For more information about BNA Software, see its Web site: http://www.bnasoftware.com.

chapter 1

Overview of Web Systems and Technologies

Today's new business models, new technology, and Web-based economy impose new technological challenges for the Web professional.

1.1 Quality Web Systems

Web systems are the new business model of companies and organizations seeking to take advantage of the worldwide network known as the Internet. The Web business model is a major expansion area for most businesses. The translation of business plans incorporating Web objectives into concrete actions has brought business executives and software professionals together as partners in the new Web-based economy.

Why is the Web so attractive to today's business leaders? The Web business model offers the potential of cost savings by reducing sales and distribution overhead associated with traditional storefront retail sales. The new business model also represents an opportunity for an organization to expand its market share and to extend its customer base. For example, Barnes & Noble research indicates that online book shoppers buy five to ten times as many books as do traditional book buyers (Kalakota 2001, p. 15).

Companies are eager to excel in promoting their products and services through the Web, but multitudes of their competitors are seeking to do the same. Successful organizations must be able to create and to modify Web-based information with great speed and need to do so in a manner that is well received by the end user. To do so, an organization's Web-based system must exhibit the success criteria described in the next section.

1.2 Success Criteria

The solutions to the challenges introduced in the previous section can be categorized into several key *success criteria*. The focus of this book is on exploring the necessary success criteria of a Web system, detailing the problem areas and providing information on how to deliver a system that exhibits the success criteria. In addition, strategies are provided to ensure that the Web system properly addresses those criteria and continues to do so from one release to the next.

- *Functionality:* The primary factor the customer values is the Web system's functionality. The requirements defined for a Web system will be manifested in the application components and the Web pages that are produced as a result of the development effort. Each component and Web page will have specific functions that it must perform in order to fulfill one or more of the system requirements, such as presenting catalog information or gathering user payment data. The engineering of system functionality through use case analysis is addressed in detail in Chapter 2.
- *Security and privacy:* Web sites must be resistant to malicious attacks by Internet users, safeguarding both site and user confidential data. The Web system's end users must have confidence that they can use the system without unauthorized users accessing transactions or personal information stored and used by the Web system. Of particular concern for end users is the safeguard of credit card and other personal information. Web system security and privacy are addressed in detail in Chapter 3.
- *Performance and scalability:* A Web system must be designed so that it can handle a large number of users accessing the system at the same time with an acceptable response time and server resource usage. The system must also gracefully handle an *overload* condition, rejecting additional users instead of encountering application and transaction errors. It is important to analyze the behavior of the Web system under load and to plan for the expansion of the site when the required user load increases. System performance requirements and the evaluation of performance and scalability behavior are outlined in Chapter 4.

- *Compatibility:* The Web system must operate properly with all the potential end user configurations, for which browser and operating system compatibility are of paramount concern. If the system is expected to be accessed by Internet users through a browser, together with a desktop or a laptop computer, the user interface must be compatible with a combination of browsers, operating systems, and video settings. Compatibility concerns are addressed in detail in Chapter 5.
- *Usability:* Web system user interfaces need to be logical, accessible, and intuitive. If users abandon the system as a result of the nonintuitive features of the interface, the problem cannot be labeled as simply cosmetic. The system needs to provide the customer with a pleasant and efficient experience. Usability engineering represents the effort to make the Web system understandable and usable by each customer who visits the site. In addition, accessibility by disabled users is an important consideration for any Web system. Web system usability is discussed in Chapter 6.

1.3 Assigning Priorities Based on Risks

Although the criteria described in the previous section are important factors for the success of any Web system, it may not be feasible for all of them to be addressed in full, given time, costs, and other constraints of a Web project. For example, creating the most secure Web system possible will have an impact on the performance and scalability of the site. Making a site compatible with every known combination of browser and operating system may require the simplification of the site's functionality or, if that is not acceptable, duplicate or complex implementations, resulting in performance problems and cost and time overruns.

As a result of these interrelationships among the success criteria, it is useful to prioritize them, based on a risk analysis of the Web system under development. Each Web system will have different risk-determined priorities, owing to functional, project, and business constraints, and each of the success criteria should be weighted on the basis of these priorities. During the definition of the functional and non-functional requirements and the implementation of the system, the weighted priorities must be considered.

Certain types of Web systems have inherent risks. E-commerce sites, for example, must regard security as high risk, given the handling of confidential user information. In addition, performance and scalability are high priorities for an e-commerce site, as the potential for lost revenue is high if customers cannot complete their transactions. Other types of sites may choose to place usability and compatibility higher on the list of risks if, for example, they have a low number of expected users and do not deal with sensitive data.

In addition to prioritizing success criteria according to risks, the evaluation of site functionality should also be prioritized. Although it is desirable to test every site function, or use case, for each of the success criteria, the reality of time and budget constraints may make this infeasible. Therefore, it is necessary to select the functions to be evaluated in each area, based on risk. For example, in an e-commerce system, it is imperative to evaluate the security and the performance of the payment transaction interfaces and components, as they pose the largest risk to the site. Other functions have a lower risk to the site and so perhaps may not be tested, owing to project scheduling and budget issues.

1.4 Web System Engineering

The effort to address the success criteria for a major Web system requires adequate planning and preparation. Many of these issues run quite deep in the architecture, design, and implementation of a system's components and therefore must be addressed continuously throughout the development life cycle, as well as during the maintenance phase. Proper specification of system requirements is a primary element of successful Web system development.

Proper analysis and documentation of the functional requirements for a Web system are difficult tasks that have been described in a multitude of books and methodologies over the years. One of the more recent approaches to documenting functional requirements is known as *use case analysis*. Use cases seek to describe the functionality of the system in a formal, precise manner, in concert with object-oriented analysis and design principles. The results obtained from proper use case analysis provide the entry point for the design of system components. Use cases also support the generation of *test cases,* which serve to explicitly list the steps necessary to exercise the Web system in order to determine whether it has properly addressed the success criteria.

The application of use cases and test cases represents an important approach to quality, which helps drive the analysis of each of the success criteria. Given the importance of this concept, an introduction to use case analysis is provided in Chapter 2, along with the steps needed to formulate a test case from a use case.

1.5 Web System Architecture

A Web system consists of an Internet-connected group of computers that support the retrieval of information and the implementation of services, usually in support of a business or commerce venture. The typical Web system is distributed across three or more tiers: a front-end presentation layer, middle tier consisting of application business logic and a back-end tier managing the data. All tiers are joined and supported by a hardware and network infrastructure. Smaller Web systems may merge some or all of these tiers onto a single machine. In contrast, larger Web systems may require more tiers to support background processing, integration with legacy databases, and so on. For this reason, modern distributed architectures are generally referred to as *n-tier.*

Collectively, the Web system consists of the application components together with the supporting hardware and network infrastructure, as illustrated in Figure 1-1. Keep in mind that this is a "generic" Web system diagram; most Web systems will have variations on this basic theme to accomplish their tasks. Although a Web system generally consists of application components together with the supporting hardware and network infrastructure, the specific elements of the system can be further defined. A Web system can be constructed from a variety of components, such as application servers, databases, and Web servers, as well as such network devices as routers, firewalls, load balancers, and switches.

Most Web systems are built using the *n*-tier approach, allowing for excellent scalability through optimal distribution of application activity across the client, middle, and database tiers.

Client Tier

This tier, responsible for hosting the end user application components, consists primarily of a Web browser, such as Microsoft Internet Explorer or Netscape Navigator. Most major browsers support extensions to provide additional functionality, such as plug-ins, applets, and client-side scripting. These components provide interaction with the user for capturing input, displaying output, and, potentially, performing some level of processing. The client typically interacts with the middle-tier components over HTTP (HyperText Transfer Protocol) or HTTPS (Secure HyperText Transfer Protocol).

The following list describes some of the more common technologies that exist on the client tier:

- *HTML/XHTML.* The primary language for displaying pages on a browser is HTML (HyperText Markup Language). HTML provides a rather large set of tags for separating Web documents into sections, displaying data in a table, embedding audio, and so on. Generally, if a browser is displaying a page, HTML is involved somewhere. XHTML (Extensible HTML), poised to take over the role that HTML once served, is the next-generation markup language for Web sites, allowing a more "pure" approach to separating the document's content from the document's appearance. This separation will further the access of Web information by devices other than PCs with graphical browsers, such as handheld devices, and by the disabled.

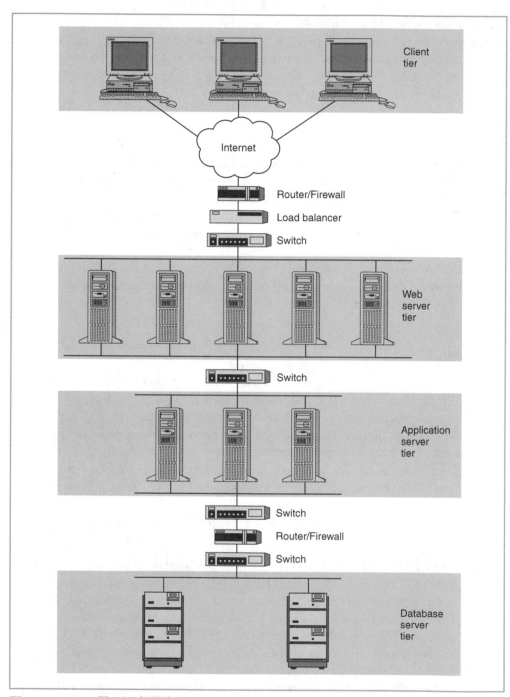

Figure 1-1   Typical Web System Architecture

- *CSS.* For most of the early years of the Web, HTML tags were used to produce the graphical display of a document. When new display features were added to a browser, the HTML language was extended by adding new tags or overloading existing HTML tags. This led to some serious browser compatibility issues, and eventually a new mechanism was created to handle the graphical display of content: CSS (Cascading Style Sheets). CSS allows a Web developer to specify the position, size, and other attributes of an element on a Web page separately from the content of the document. Most major browsers support CSS, although the level of support varies.

- *Client-side scripts.* One of the more common ways that Web pages are made interactive is the use of client-side scripts. Client-side scripting allows a Web developer to write code that executes on the client machine and interacts with the elements on the Web page. This interaction is enabled by the browser's DOM (Document Object Model), which exposes page elements and browser functions as scriptable elements. ECMAScript, which is essentially standardized JavaScript, is the scripting language recognized by most major browsers. Some browsers have additional script language capabilities, such as VBScript.

- *XML/XSLT.* Although HTML/XHTML is quite suitable for Web-based distribution of documents, it is not well suited for the distribution of pure *data.* HTML has no mechanism for enforcing the structure of a list of names and phone numbers, for example. XML (Extensible Markup Language) is ideal for working with data, as it allows the structure of the data to be described and validated as necessary. XSLT (Extensible Stylesheet Language: Transformations) is used to convert the XML data into another format, such as HTML or XHTML.

- *Plug-ins.* At times, a Web site may wish to provide a non-HTML document to the user. One way to allow the user to view a non-HTML document is to provide a plug-in, which is a binary component that extends the user's browser with the capability to view a certain type of document. For example, a PDF document requires the Adobe Acrobat Plug-In. A plug-in is platform specific, so a version must exist for the user's operating system.

- *ActiveX controls.* Similar to plug-ins, ActiveX controls are binary components that provide a high level of functionality on the client machine. ActiveX controls, embedded inside a Web page, can be used to display specialized content, such as high-quality audio, or enhanced user interaction. Only Microsoft Internet Explorer supports ActiveX controls, but plug-ins for other browsers allow them to display some ActiveX controls.

- *Java applets.* Similar to ActiveX controls, applets allow enhanced functionality on the client side. Applets are not binary, however; they exist as platform-neutral bytecode. Any browser that supports applets—through the use of a JVM, or Java Virtual Machine—can display an applet.

Middle Tiers

The middle tiers provide the business and system processing power of the application; application services are implemented through the various components of the middle tiers. Application duties are distributed over multiple middle-tier nodes, including Web servers and application processing servers, which host transactional, nontransactional, and entity objects.

Web servers, such as Microsoft Internet Information Server (IIS), iPlanet Web Server, and Apache, are the main components of the middle tier in a Web system. Web servers typically interact with clients with a request/response cycle, meaning that the client requests a page or a piece of information from the Web server, and the server returns it and disconnects. The next time it requires information from the server, the Web client connects again and makes another request.

A server may process a request in many ways. The client may simply need a static Web page, which the server will read from disk and return it, untouched. In other cases, the client may request a dynamic page, requiring the server to read it and, potentially, execute code contained in the page prior to returning the response to the client.

Following are some of the technologies for middle-tier components:

- *CGI programs.* The earliest mechanism for dynamic content, the Common Gateway Interface (CGI) program is an external program that is invoked by the Web server in response to a client request. CGIs can be written in pretty much any language, as long as the server can execute it and pass some parameters. The CGI approach suffers from a few limitations that make it inefficient for large sites; thus, CGIs are typically not used in high-volume Web systems.
- *Dynamic pages.* In addition to static HTML pages, Web servers have the ability to deliver dynamic pages, which can retrieve data or perform other operations prior to being returned to the user. Examples of dynamic pages are Microsoft Active Server Pages (ASP), Java Server Pages (JSP), and PHP Hypertext Pages (PHP). These technologies are much more efficient and have replaced CGI as the preferred approach to dynamic content on large sites.
- *Web server extensions.* Most Web servers support a low-level extension mechanism, which allows developers to extend the server itself with another binary component. This approach is not very common but can offer a high degree of performance at the cost of maintainability. ISAPI (Internet Server

API) and NSAPI (Netscape Server API) are two examples of this mechanism.

- *Application components.* Typically, a Web system must perform some kind of business processing, such as retrieving data from a database or computing an invoice. Rather than perform this work in a dynamic page, these operations are encapsulated into application components, which may run on the Web server or on an entirely separate group of machines. Examples of application components are COM+ (on Microsoft platforms), Java Servlet, and EJB (Enterprise JavaBeans) components.

Database Tier

The database tier provides data management services for the application. This tier is responsible for reliable, scalable, high-volume transaction processing of application data. This tier hosts the database management system, database file stores, and any database-side processing components used in handling the system's data transactions. Microsoft SQL Server and Oracle 8i are two of the more commonly used databases in Web systems.

1.6 Chapter Summary

- ▲ A Web system consists of an Internet-connected group of computers that support the retrieval of information and the implementation of services, usually in support of a business or a commerce venture.
- ▲ Web systems are popular with today's business leaders for a number of reasons. The business model offers the potential of cost savings by reducing sales and distribution overhead. The Web also represents an opportunity for an organization to expand its market share and to extend its customer base.
- ▲ Several factors are key to successful Web system implementation. The Web system needs to be secure, reliable, available, and usable and must meet customer functional and performance expectations.
- ▲ The success criteria must be prioritized, based on the needs of the Web system, from functional, project, and business perspectives.
- ▲ Web systems are typically *n*-tier, meaning that the functionality of a system is divided among distinct components that may execute on several machines.

1.7 References

1. Kalakota, Ravi. 2001. *e-Business: Roadmap for Success,* 2d ed. Reading, Mass.: Addison-Wesley, 2001, p 15.

chapter 2

Web Engineering Using the RSI Approach

In the early days of e-commerce, some companies rushed sites into production without sufficient attention to quality. Most of these sites are dead now. In any case, to the extent that it may ever have been possible to cut a few corners on quality in the early days, this is certainly not possible any more.

Jakob Nielsen[1]

The quality of a e-commerce, functionality is the primary factor the customer values. Engineering functionality into a system begins with the proper definition of system requirements. As the Standish Group reports, the most significant factors for producing a successful Web system are requirements related.[2] Use cases are a common method for capturing requirements in an object-oriented development environment. Although remarkably well suited for capturing requirements, use cases can be difficult to implement, owing to their somewhat subjective nature. When engineers first undertake use case analysis, a number of issues are often raised, including the following.

---

[1]Jakob Nielson, extracted from the Foreword of this book.

[2]For more information, see the Standish Group Web site: http://www.standishgroup.com.

- How does user interface design fit into the use case analysis process?
- Should user interface dynamics be included?
- What is the appropriate level of granularity (size) and abstraction (detail) for use cases?
- Should large-grained use cases be decomposed into "lower-level" use cases?
- If so, at what point should this decomposition stop, and how should these sub–use cases be used?
- What are the "relationships" between these use cases?
- How should this decomposition be approached from a process perspective?
- How are use cases related to object models? Should the *things* referred to in use case descriptions be cross-referenced against object models?

Similarly, software test professionals facing the results of use case analysis have their own concerns, as follows.

- How can test cases be derived from the use cases?
- How can user interface elements be properly incorporated into test cases?
- How do we determine the sequence of test case steps, especially when faced with complex use case models?
- When executing test cases, how do we verify that the components did what they were supposed to do?

A Web system needs to perform as expected and in accordance with organization standards and end user requirements. System functionality needs to be verified against specified system requirements or defined use cases. The Requirement-Service Interface (RSI) approach provides a framework for analyzing and understanding potential use case deliverables and their interrelationships, with a view to answering questions such as those just detailed. The RSI approach to use case analysis was developed by Mark Collins-Cope.[3] This chapter explores the definition of use cases to capture functional requirements for a Web system and the application of those use cases to support the development of test cases.

2.1 Use Case Analysis

Use case analysis as a technique for requirements capture is most often used in the early stages of object-oriented and component development projects. The technique was introduced by Ivar Jacobson et al. (1992). The description of use case analysis

---

[3]RSI approach used with permission of Mark Collins-Cope. "The RSI Approach to Use Case Analysis," Ratio Group Ltd., at http://www.ratio.co.uk.

presented in that book has been interpreted in many different ways. Therefore, no two use case analysis projects ever deliver the same information. Broadly speaking, the generation of use cases supports the definition of functional requirements. A sample use case diagram is portrayed in Figure 2-1, which consists of the following elements:

- A bounding box, which depicts the scope of the system under specification
- Actors, the stick figures used to represent the categories of users or systems that interact with the system under specification
- Use cases, the ovals representing system functions, or processes, that are provided or supported by the system
- Interactions depict the interaction between an actor and one or more use cases

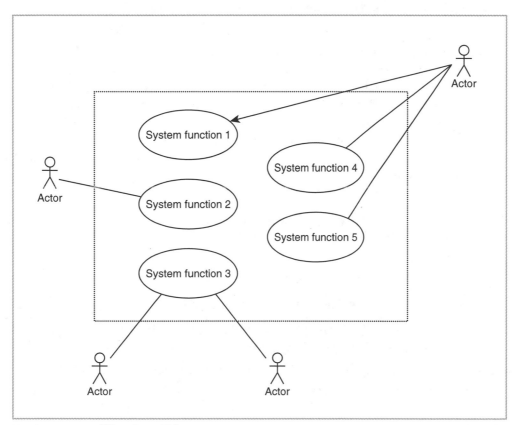

Figure 2-1   Use Case Diagram

Requirements use case modeling can generally be performed at either the *business* or the *domain* level (Jacobson, Booch, and Rumbaugh 1999, pp. 119–127). Business use cases are typically used to model an organization's business processes, regardless of automation, and are useful for gaining an understanding of the business problem at hand. Domain use cases, or system use cases, are used to model functionality in the context of an automated solution, such as a computer system. RSI use cases are typically developed at the domain level.

It is important to note that the primary value of the use case is its associated *textual* documentation, which describes the detail of each use case. A graphical notation, such as the one in Figure 2-1, helps to provide a high-level view of the major functions of the business or the domain and their relationships but does not serve as a replacement for the detailed documentation.

2.2 Goal-Oriented Use Case Analysis

Alistair Cockburn has done extensive work on use case analysis (1997, 2000). He recognized that use cases had "improved the situation that requirements documents [are] often an arbitrary collection of paragraphs, having a poor fit with both business re-engineering and implementation" (1997). He noted, however, that he had personally encountered 18 definitions of use cases, which had been provided by different, but expert teachers and consultants (1997). To remedy this, Cockburn went on to define a goal-oriented approach to use case analysis, describing a use case in terms of a goal-oriented sequence of business or work steps. The following use case extract was outlined in Cockburn's paper.[4]

Use Case: Get Paid for Car Accident (insurance system)

Actor—Claimant
Actor goal—to get paid for a car accident

1. Claimant submits claim with substantiating data

2. Insurance company verifies claimant owns a valid policy

3. Insurance company assigns agent to examine case

4. Agent verifies all details are within policy guidelines

5. Insurance company pays claimant

---

[4]Available at http://members.aol.com/acockburn/papers/usecases.htm.

Extensions:

    1a. Submitted data is incomplete

    1a1. Insurance company requests missing information

    1a2. Claimant supplies missing information

Note that in this description, some steps, such as step 1, are unlikely to be automated. Cockburn describes how each step in the description can be viewed as a "mini–use case" in its own right and with its own goals. Thus, use cases are decomposed into sub–use cases. Cockburn describes the classification of use cases into summary goals, user goals, and subfunctions.

Cockburn also clarified the definition of a *scenario;* the sequence of steps presented in the main portion of the use case is referred to as the *main success scenario* (2000, pp. 253–254). When a particular use case occurrence, or instance, is discussed, it is described with specific people and places and is referred to as a *concrete scenario.* For example: "Nigel Bandy filing a claim for the car accident on 3 September 1998 at Chiswick Roundabout in London" is a concrete scenario for the previous use case. A scenario is also referred to as a "flow of events."

The RSI approach to use case analysis builds on Cockburn's work. The RSI approach, however, differs in its classification of use case types and targets the decomposition of use cases into interface and service subtypes.

2.3 RSI Approach

The objectives of the RSI approach[5] to use case analysis follow. Note that these objectives relate directly to the questions posed at the beginning of this chapter.

- Provide a *guideline framework* for analyzing and considering what levels of granularity/abstraction of use cases can be used in a use case analysis process, under what circumstances the various levels of granularity/abstraction should be used, how they should be documented, and to whom descriptions should be targeted.
- Provide a clear place for *user interface design* in the use case analysis process while also maintaining a clear separation between interface—such as dialog box, button—and core domain—such as bank, account, customer—concerns.
- Provide a clearly defined, scalable *process* that links the varying use case levels so that initial descriptions of requirements can be traced through to low-level use cases.

---

[5]The RSI approach was developed by Mark Collins-Cope, Ratio Group Ltd. For more detailed papers on RSI, see http://www.ratio.co.uk/techlibrary.html. Mark can be reached by e-mail at markcc@ratio.co.uk.

- Encourage use case descriptions to be *cross-referenced against a domain model* when targeted at system developers.
- *Structure* the deliverables of the use case analysis process to assist in the ensuing development and testing processes.

Classification Levels of Granularity and Abstraction

The RSI approach provides three classifications for use case granularity, represented by the UML stereotypes *requirement, interface,* and *service.*[6]

Requirement Use Case

A requirement use case defines a business or work process, such as "sale of goods," or "open a new account," for which some automated system support may be required. Requirement use cases may be documented as described by Cockburn 1997, which provides details of the following elements:

- Actor(s): human users or other systems that will interact with the system during the execution of the use case
- Objective: the objective of the use case
- Level: the relationship of the use case to a specific user task, including *summary, user goal,* or *subfunction*
- Preconditions: other use cases that must have been performed, or conditions that must be true, prior to the execution of the use case
- Sequence of steps: goal-oriented decomposition of the use case into a sequence of steps, called the *main success scenario*
- Extensions: any deviations and exceptions from the main success scenario. Cockburn's extension number convention is particularly useful in these descriptions. Note that extensions can also be referred to as exceptions or as subflows.

Requirement use cases provide the starting point from which decisions about the scope and phasing of the functionality can be made. The individual steps, or subgoals, within the description are candidates for potential automation.

The objective of developing the requirements use case model is to clearly document the business drivers for a system in as concise a manner as possible. Requirement use cases may be decomposed by using the «includes» relationship to remove duplication of text across multiple use case descriptions.

---

[6]UML stereotypes are used to further refine UML elements. In this case, the UML use case element is refined into requirement, interface, and service use cases.

Interface Use Case

Interface use cases describe functionality that manages the interface between the actors of a system and the underlying services it offers. Interface use cases "translate" the information provided by an actor into a form acceptable to a set of underlying service use cases. To do this, interface use cases factor out the elements of functionality that are more related to the interface than to the underlying system. Interface use cases may be documented as follows:

- Objectives of the interface
- Detailed description of any interface formats used, which might include graphical user interface design, such as dialogs, report layouts, file formats, and so on
- Step-by-step description of the functional aspects of the interface, such as user interface dynamics—for example, "When the Select Customer button is clicked, the Accounts list box is refreshed"—file processing, and how report contents are generated

A useful addition to the latter two documentation items is a user interface prototype. The development of a prototype is more beneficial than the simple use of paper documentation, as it enables users to provide direct feedback on the interface presented to them.

The objective of developing the interface use case model is to clearly document—or to demonstrate, in the case of an interface prototype—in as concise a manner as possible the interfaces used by a system, providing traceability to antecedent requirement use case descriptions. Interfaces may be decomposed by using the «includes» stereotype, in order to portray the use of one interface use case and user interface element by another.

Service Use Case

Service use cases define the underlying functions offered by the functional core of a system, in a manner independent of any particular interface concerns. The service use case model documents the system functionality that provides the business logic to perform work on behalf of the interface use cases described in the previous section.

Service use cases are defined to be *atomic;* that is, they are *guaranteed* to run to completion without further actor interaction. This characteristic clearly differentiates them from requirement use cases, within which multiple actor interactions with the implied system almost always occur.

The target audience for service use cases is primarily system architects, designers, and developers, rather than end users. Hence, a more formal and concise format for the documentation is considered appropriate. Service use cases are specified as follows.

- A list of input parameters, such as customer, account, or date, detailing the information, if any, passed to the use case from its calling environment. Inputs are instances of types in the service use case model's associated domain model. A domain model illustrates the major types of objects, such as books, accounts, and users, and their relationships in the context of the system (Jacobson, Booch, and Rumbaugh 1999).

- A list of output parameters, such as a set of overdrawn customers or all new accounts, detailing the information, if any, passed from the use case to its calling environment on termination. Outputs can be classes from the domain model or other information, such as the result of an operation.

- Preconditions of the use case, describing what conditions must be true of the system before the use case can be initiated. Precondition descriptions cross-reference the domain model and may, when circumstances dictate, be formally specified by using the UML Object Constraint Language (OCL) (Warmer and Kleppe 1998).

- Postconditions of the use case, describing any changes that will be made to the internal state of the system once the use case has been completed. Like preconditions, postcondition descriptions cross-reference the domain model and may also be formally specified in OCL.

It may sometimes be appropriate to indicate that one service may be built up from another that exists *independently in its own right,* using the «includes» stereotype and relationship. However, service use cases should not in general be decomposed further, as this would intrude into the realm of the software design process. Two flavors of service use cases emerge: update services, which change system state, and query services, which retrieve information but do not change system state.

Another useful subclassification of services is the *essential* service set and the *consolidated* service set, consisting of the essential set plus any others. The essential service set is made up of those service use cases that are *directly* mandated by the requirement use cases, regardless of any interface design decisions. This distinction is important in analyzing the impact in changes to requirements using the traceability model (Figure 2-2). Also, the essential service use case set provides a clear definition of the atomic functions the system will implement. Essential services are generally updates.

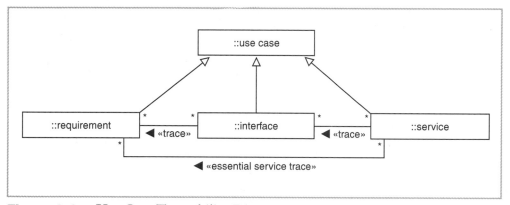

Figure 2-2   Use Case Traceability Diagram

Interrelationships between the Models

Figure 2-2 summarizes the relationships between the categorizations of use cases at a high level, using UML notation. The Unified Modeling Language (UML) provides a notation for modeling classes (and objects), and their relationships to each other. In Figure 2.2, the arrows from the requirement, interface, and service classes to the use case class indicate that they are all types of use cases.

Requirement use cases provide the starting point for use case analysis. They are refined into service and interface use cases, as indicated by the "generalization" relationships, necessary to implement those parts of the requirement for which a decision has been made to automate. The interrelationships between requirement and interface/service use cases may be shown by using «trace» dependencies on a use case traceability diagram. Note the many-to-many relationships, as indicated by an * on the diagram, between service, interface, and requirement use cases.

Interface use cases invoke service use cases to gain access to the functional core of the system, as depicted in Figure 2-3. The update/query subdivision of services is applied as follows.

- Interface use cases use query service use cases to retrieve information necessary for the construction of user interface dynamics. For example, in a banking system, double clicking on a particular customer in a Customers list box may cause an associated Accounts list box to be refreshed with the chosen customer's accounts. To retrieve this information, a query use case would be used—Select Accounts by Customer, in this case.
- Interface use cases use update service use cases to change the internal system state, to "do" something. The parameters of the update service use

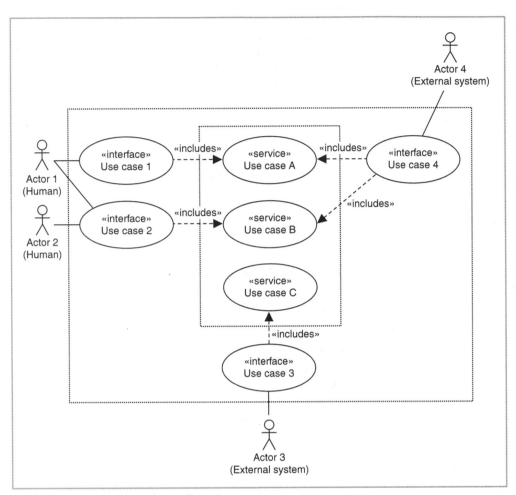

Figure 2-3   Service/Interface Separation

cases will typically have been returned by a previous invocation of a query service use case. The interrelationships between interface and service use cases may be shown by using a «trace» on the traceability model.

As depicted in Figure 2-3, the separation of service and interface use cases partitions functionality into the elements that are concerned primarily with manipulating the peculiarities of an interface and the elements that are fundamental to the system in question. This separation encourages the reuse of service use cases, from a variety of interface use cases, and enables a clear factoring out of interface concerns in the specification process, particularly as RSI encourages a semiformal or formal approach to service use case specification.

Often, the service/interface separation is clearcut, most often when the actor is a human user. Sometimes, however, it is not entirely clear where the dividing line between them should be. When this occurs, it is necessary to consider what aspects of functionality would change if the nature or the details of the interface changed. The aspects that remain constant constitute part of the service use case set; those that vary constitute part of the interface use case set.

2.4 RSI Model Development

The overall process of developing an RSI model, depicted in Figure 2-4 consists of four stages, two of which—stages 2a. and 2b.—are often undertaken in parallel.

1. Developing the requirements use case model: conceptualization

2a. Developing the interface use case model: specification

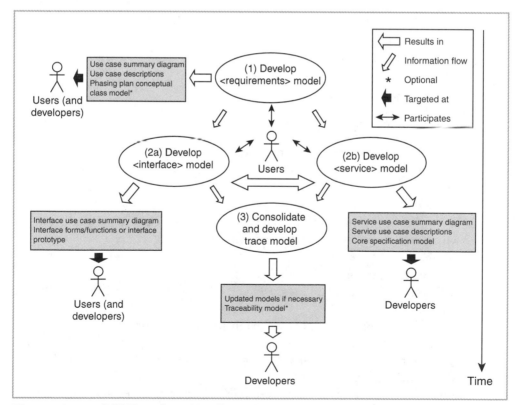

Figure 2-4   RSI Development Process

2b. Developing the service use case model: specification

3. Consolidating the models and producing the traceability model: specification

Requirement Use Case Model Development

The requirement use case model, the first part of the model to be developed, provides the starting point from which all other models can be traced. The process description here assumes some form of ad hoc project start-up document, often in the form of a business case for the required system. On small projects, it may be possible to develop a requirement model from scratch, based on discussions with users. On larger projects, some form of antecedent document will almost certainly be necessary.

Inputs to the requirement model include

- Ad hoc requirements or project start-up document

Outputs include

- Requirement use case summary diagram(s)
- Requirement use case textual descriptions
- Requirement use case scope and phasing plan
- Domain model (optional)

Subprocesses include

- Reviewing ad hoc requirements document with users
  —Identifying any business processes implied by the requirements document
  —Adding these to the list of potential requirement use cases
- Considering some or all potential requirement use cases in conjunction with users, along with prerequirements scoping if there are a very large number
  —Identifying the main flows
  —Developing extension flows, asking, "What could go wrong?" and "What might vary?"
  —Developing extension flows to extension flows in the same manner, until no further extensions are found
  —If a domain model is being developed, considering the impact of the preceding on it
- Finalizing and reviewing all deliverables, iterating as necessary

The requirement use case model does not contain a large amount of detail, as it is the basis on which the project will be scoped and phased. Including more detail would lead to a significant amount of wasted effort documenting steps that may never get automated. Experience using requirement use cases suggests that the exception flow analysis is particularly useful in ensuring that a complete model of the system is generated. It has also been demonstrated that accurate time estimates can be made at the end of this phase.

As mentioned, the requirements use case approach presented in this chapter is based on elements presented by Alistair Cockburn (2000). In particular, the concept of *goal levels* is important to requirement use cases, as they can be at high or low levels relative to the actor. The levels of scope are defined as follows (Cockburn 2000, pp. 62–66):

- *User goal:* the basic functional requirement level. Although a subjective process, classifying user goals can generally be thought of as a single, complete task that provides value to the actor. For example, Purchase an Item is a solid user goal that an actor would be likely to perform with the system. Another example would be View a Previous Order.
- *Summary goal:* Several user goals that may span large periods of time or several system areas. Examples of summary goals are Use the System or Manage Finances. Summary-level goals are useful for showing a higher-level picture of a portion of the system and help show how various user goals are connected.
- *Subfunction:* A smaller piece of a user goal. Subfunctions in themselves do not provide direct value to the user; they exist to support a user-level goal that does provide value. A good example of a subfunction requirement is Log in to System; the user does not interact with the system strictly for the purpose of logging in but rather to accomplish a higher-level goal. Subfunctions are generally shown only if they clarify the diagram or to simplify user goal descriptions if the subfunction is required by multiple user goals.

Technology Bookstore Case Study Example: Requirement Use Case Model

The Technology Bookstore (TBS) is a Web-enabled e-business venture that sells technology-related products, such as books, videos, and software. The business case for the Technology Bookstore Web system identified the need for the user to view item information in the catalog, purchase items from the catalog, and view information about previous orders, including status. For a full description of TBS, please refer to Appendix C.

The *business model* of the Technology Bookstore is fairly well understood, so the requirements analysis was performed exclusively at the *system* level. If the business had not been understood, perhaps because it was very large and complex, a model of the business processes, without mention of automation, would have been an important exercise prior to the system use case modeling effort.

The requirement use case summary diagram for the Technology Bookstore is depicted in Figure 2-5, using UML notation. Because the TBS system is rather small, it can be comfortably represented on a single diagram. Larger systems, however, will require multiple diagrams, usually subdivided by business area. Note the following about Figure 2-5.

- The dashed arrows indicate that the source use case *includes* the target use case in its entirety at a certain point in its scenario.

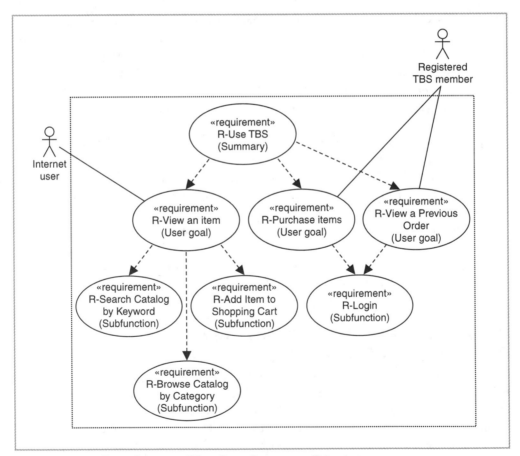

Figure 2-5   Requirement Use Case Summary Diagram

- Requirement use cases are prefixed with R to help in traceability among the three types of use cases. The service and interface use cases are prefixed with S and I, respectively.
- The goal level of the use case is indicated in parentheses, just below the use case name.

As shown in the figure, the TBS system has three main user goals: View an Item, Purchase Items, and View a Previous Order. The summary-level Use TBS use case ties the user goals together into a complete user interaction, which may span days or weeks, for example, place an order and then return the following week to check its status. Some of the user-level goals were also decomposed into sub-functions where necessary. For example, it was decided to show the subfunction Add Item to Shopping Cart, as it is an important system concept. The subfunction Login was also shown; it too is an important concept and is used by multiple user goals.

Use case models, such as the one in Figure 2-5, are not created as a whole in the first sitting but instead tend to *evolve* over time. It is useful to consider the system at progressively lower *levels of abstraction* while also attempting to define the requirements use cases. For example, the first iteration of the use case model could simply be R-Use TBS. Detailing that single, and high-level, summary use case will help shape the work that follows, which will be the definition of several user goal use cases. In the sessions that follow, the user goals can be augmented and refined, and subfunctions can be added where necessary. Evolving a use case model at these various levels of abstraction helps to guide the thought process of the use case modeler to produce a more consistent and logical use case model.

Following is the text description of the TBS requirement use case R-View Previous Order. Appendix C provides the complete set of «requirement» use cases for TBS. Note the following about the requirement use case descriptions.

- The convention of <u>underlining</u> a particular phrase in the text indicates inclusion of a subsidiary use case, meaning that its steps are inserted into the current use case at the underlined phrase.
- Preconditions refer to other use cases that must have been executed prior to the execution of the current use case.
- The Extensions section indicates alternative flows to the main success scenario, including errors.
- The Nonfunctional Requirements section lists any deviations or additions to the systemwide nonfunctional requirements specification. See Section 2.5 for more information.

«requirement» R-View a Previous Order

Actor: Internet User
Objective: To review the details of a previous order, including its
                  status
Level: User goal
Preconditions: Purchase Items

Main Success Scenario

1. User selects to view a previous order.
2. System prompts user to <u>log in</u> if user is not already logged in.
3. System displays a list of the user's previous orders.
4. User selects an order to view.
5. System displays the order information, including the status
    (processing, shipped, and so on) of the order.

Extensions: None

Nonfunctional Requirements Additions or Deviations: Communication of
    data to and from the user will occur over a secured connection, such
    as SSL.

The domain model for TBS, reflected in Figure 2-6 using UML notation, was developed in parallel with the use case specifications. Note that the nouns in the use case descriptions are good candidates for objects in the domain model.

Interface Use Case Model Development

The interface use case model documents the user interface of the proposed system. This model can also be used to document external system interfaces; however, they are not the focus of the discussion here. Unlike the other models that form part of the RSI deliverable set, the interface use case model is inherently dependent on technical domain decisions, such as the graphical user interface (GUI) chosen for development.

Inputs are as follows:

- Requirement use case summary diagram(s)
- Requirement use case textual descriptions
- Domain model (optional)
- Service use case definition (developed in parallel)

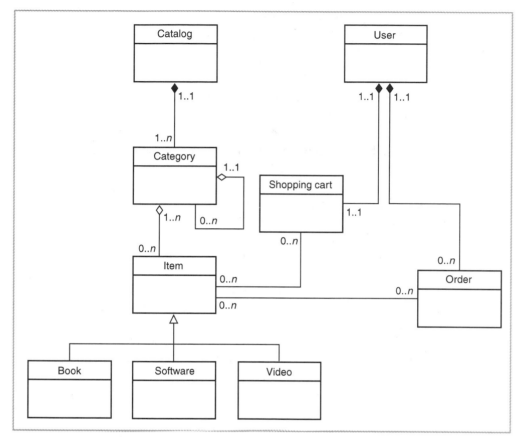

Figure 2-6   TBS Domain Model

Outputs are

- Interface use case summary diagram(s)
- Interface use case textual/diagrammatic descriptions and/or interface prototype
- Updated domain model

Subprocesses include

- Considering the requirement use case model with users, taking into account typical volumes of candidate objects
- Developing and refining the proposed interface—either on paper or as a prototype—with users
- Checking completeness by ensuring that all automated requirement steps can be traced from at least one interface
- Finalizing and reviewing all deliverables, iterating as necessary

Parts of the service model—in fact, the update services, which are being developed in parallel—may help in user interface design, as follows.

- Service descriptions may assist in that
  —Inputs typically indicate information that must be collected from the user.
  —Outputs indicate information that must be displayed to the user.
  —Preconditions indicate conditions that the interface must adhere to before invoking an underlying service and may suggest validation rules for the interface or, preferably, ways of presenting information to the user to ensure that they are always met, that is, that don't allow the user to make a mistake.
  —Postconditions may indicate information that may need to be fed back to the user.
- Domain models may assist in that
  —Associations suggest navigation routes by which objects can be identified and selected on the user interface.
  —Association multiplicities suggest appropriate user interface constructs: fixed multiplicities, such as 1 to 2 or 1 to 4, hint at the use of such constructs as radio buttons and check boxes; variable multiplicities, such as 1 to *, hint at the use of list boxes and drop-down lists.
  —The *relative* volumes of its types indicate whether it will be appropriate to navigate directly between them on the interface.

Technology Bookstore Example: Interface Use Case Model

Figure 2-7, the interface use case summary diagram, shows the navigation model for the TBS Web site. Figure 2-7 uses UML notation to depict the relationships between the «interface» use cases. The interface use case flow is reflected from the user's perspective, using the «link» stereotype between the use cases to indicate that the user selects an item, such as an icon, button, or a link, to move from one interface to the next. As indicated by the Registered TBS Member actor, only registered users can interact with the interfaces—and any interfaces that they link to—that require site membership.

Note that there is not a one-to-one relationship between «interface» use cases and «requirement» use cases. Some requirement use cases require multiple interface use cases to accomplish their goal; for example, R-View a Previous Order needs both I-View Order List and I-View Previous Order. Other interface use cases, such as I-TBS Menu, are not directly related to a requirement but are necessary to support general navigation of the system. These relationships are expressed on the *traceability* diagram, described later in Traceability Model.

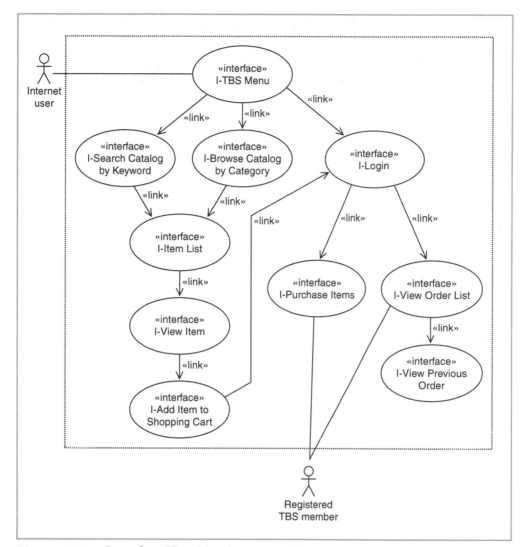

Figure 2-7   Interface Use Case Summary Diagram

The Web pages providing order list and status information for the Technology Bookstore Web site are depicted in Figure 2-8. The other Technology Bookstore Web pages, such as login, book list display, and the book purchase, are not described further here.

The I-View Order List use case follows. It includes sections for data elements from the domain model, service use cases that are invoked by this interface, and controls on the interface and their behavior.

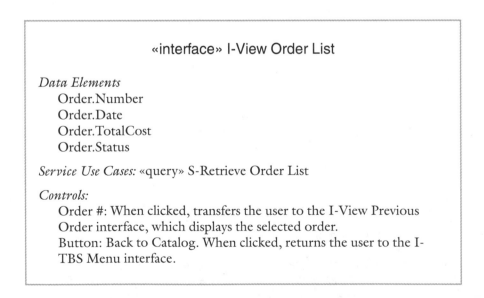

Figure 2-8   Web Page for Technology Bookstore Order List

«interface» I-View Order List

Data Elements
    Order.Number
    Order.Date
    Order.TotalCost
    Order.Status

Service Use Cases: «query» S-Retrieve Order List

Controls:
    Order #: When clicked, transfers the user to the I-View Previous
    Order interface, which displays the selected order.
    Button: Back to Catalog. When clicked, returns the user to the I-
    TBS Menu interface.

The View Previous Order page is depicted in Figure 2-9. A detailed description of the I-View Previous Order use case follows. It includes sections for data elements from the domain model, service use cases that are invoked by this interface, and controls on the interface and their behavior. Note that the Order.Items database

Figure 2-9 Web Page for Technology Bookstore View Previous Order

---

«interface» I-View Previous Order

Data Elements:
    Order.Number
    Order.Date
    Order.BillingAddress
    Order.ShippingAddress
    Order.PaymentInformation
      CardType
      PartialCardNumber
    Order.Items (table)
      SKU
      Description
      Price
      Quantity
    Order.Status

Service Use-Cases: «query» S-Retrieve Order

Controls: Button: Back to Order List. When clicked, returns the user to the I-Retrieve Order List interface.

---

table contains the data elements stock-keeping unit (SKU), description, price, and quantity. The stock-keeping unit represents a unique numeric identifier for a product.

Service Use Case Model Development

The service use case model is developed incrementally. Inputs to the service use case model include

- Requirement use case summary diagram
- Requirement use case textual descriptions
- Domain model (optional)
- Interfaces use case model (developed in parallel with service use cases)

Outputs include

- Service use case summary diagram
- Service use case textual descriptions
- Refined domain model (optional)

Subprocesses include

- Considering the requirement use case model with users
  —Identifying any service use cases directly implied by the requirement use case model
  —Adding them to the list of potential service use cases
- Considering the emerging interface use case model
  —Identifying any queries implied by it that are not in the essential service use case set
  —Adding them to the list of potential service use cases
- Considering the candidate service use case list
  —Undertaking a preliminary analysis of service use case inputs, outputs, pre- and postconditions, and forming a candidate object list
  —Updating the domain model as necessary
  —Refining the model and adding any invariants
- When the domain model is stable, documenting the service use cases against it
- Finalizing and reviewing all deliverables, iterating as necessary.

The interface use case model—under development in parallel—is required to develop the majority of the query parts of the service use case model. Much of a user interface entails functionality to allow the user to locate objects on which to subsequently apply updates. This functionality will be provided by queries; hence the dependency to the interface use case model.

The impact of the interface use case model on the service use case model can be summarized as follows. A user interface will have associated with it a number of actions, or dynamics, some of which will require support from the functional core of the system.

- Those that simply populate other parts of the user interface as an aid to helping the user locate another underlying object are candidates for of queries.
- The type of user interface control used—list box, radio button, and so on—will be indicative of the multiplicities of such associations.
- Those that change system state are candidates for updates.

Technology Bookstore Example: Service Use Case Model

The service use case model summary diagram is depicted in Figure 2-10. Following are the service use case specifications for the S-Retrieve Order List and S-Retrieve

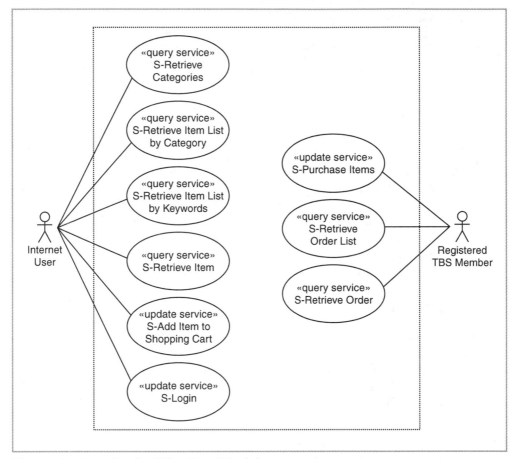

Figure 2-10 Service Use Case Model

Order use cases. A number of semiformal conventions, based loosely on OCL, are used in the specification to help remove ambiguity.

- Names that correspond to types in the specification model are capitalized; for example, User.
- Use of an instance of a type in the specification model is indicated by prefixing an "a" or "an" onto the type name. Additional qualification, such as aFirstCustomer, may be required if more than one instance needs to be identified.
- Use of attributes is shown by using a period (.) between the type name and the attribute name of the model. Thus, anOrder.status indicates the status attribute of anOrder.

- Navigation via associations is shown by the same convention. Thus the set of books, videos, and so on, that have been added to the current user's shopping cart is indicated by aRegisteredTBSMember..currentOrder.

«query service» S-Retrieve Order list

Actor: Registered TBS Member
Objective: To retrieve a list of previous orders

Inputs: aUser

Outputs: anOrderSet

Preconditions: S-Login has been executed.

Postconditions: None

«query service» S-Retrieve Order

Actor: Registered TBS Member
Objective: To retrieve a previous order

Inputs:
    aUser
    anOrderNumber (10 chars, [0-9])

Outputs:
    anOrder

Preconditions:
    S-Login has been executed.
    anOrderNumber is in aUser.Orders

Postconditions: None

Note that in the S-Retrieve Order use case, the input anOrderNumber has been constrained by length (ten characters) and allowable characters (the digits 0 through 9). This will facilitate length and allowable character constraint checking by the component that implements this use case. In larger systems, this type of information is often stored in a centralized *data dictionary* shared among all use cases, and used during testing for constraint verification.

Traceability Model

An RSI trace model shows the traceability relationships among the various classifications of use cases as UML dependency relationships, using the UML «trace» stereotype. Traceability models are useful in establishing the impact of change to requirements on a system. When a given requirement is varied, a traceability model enables the potential impact of this change to be traced through to the interface and service use case models.

Inputs to the traceability model include

- All previous models

Outputs include

- Updated models as required, that is, if problems are discovered
- RSI trace model

Subprocesses include

- Developing a trace model that shows the dependencies from
  —The essential services use case set to the requirements service use case set
  —All service use cases to interface use cases
  —Interface use cases to requirements use case steps
- Ensuring that
  —Each service use case to automated requirement use case step dependency has a corresponding pair of service use case to interface use case and interface use case to automated requirement use case step dependencies
  —Each service use case can be traced to at least one interface use case and that each essential service use case can be traced back to at least one automated requirement use case step
  —Each interface use case can be traced to at least one automated requirement use case step and that each automated requirement use case step can be traced to at least one interface use case step
- Iterating, updating models if any trace deficiencies are found, until the model is complete

Because trace models can get large, it is practical to divide them by «requirement» use case. Figures 2-11 and 2-12 show sample traceability diagrams.

Analysis with RSI Use Cases

Once the RSI use case models have been completed, the process of mapping the «service» and «interface» use cases onto analysis classes can begin. Note that this is not the same as design; analysis activities bring the requirements specifications into

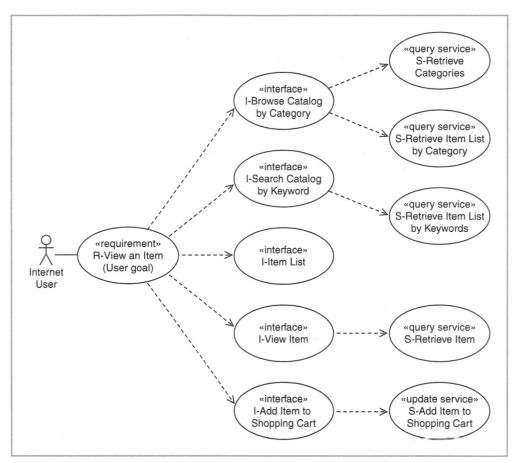

Figure 2-11   Traceability Model for R-View an Item

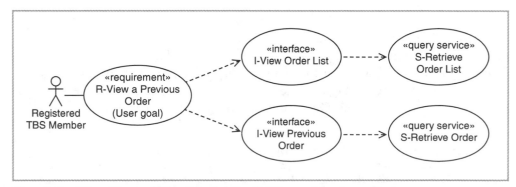

Figure 2-12   Traceability Model for R-View a Previous Order

the realm of the system, whereas design is more concerned with preparing the system for implementation with code. Although a full discussion of analysis and design is beyond the scope of this book, this section provides a starting point for crossing the boundary between requirements specification and analysis using RSI use cases.

Analysis modeling is performed using three types of classes (Jacobson, Booch, and Rumbaugh 1999, pp. 182–185).

- *Boundary classes:* Actors interact with the system through boundary classes, which can be user interfaces, APIs, queue messages, and so on.
- *Entity classes:* These analysis classes model real-world or system-relevant information. They are usually directly related to classes in the domain model.
- *Control classes:* Business logic and other functionality is placed into a control class. Control classes make use of entity classes to do their work and usually do it on behalf of boundary classes or other control classes.

Together, these three classes allow system functionality to be defined in a more precise way. They are brought together in what is known as a *use case realization,* which specifies how the use case is implemented, using the three analysis class types. Typically, use case realizations are diagrammed by using collaboration and/or sequence diagrams.[7]

RSI use cases and the associated domain model can be divided into analysis classes, using the following concepts.

- The «requirement» use cases map to *messages to* boundary classes.
- The «interface» use cases can be directly related to boundary classes in the analysis model.
- The domain model classes map to entity classes, including any additions necessary for the analysis activity.
- The «service» use cases map to *messages to* control classes or entities.

Collaboration diagrams are an excellent way to describe the steps necessary between analysis classes to accomplish the goal of the use case, as they focus on objects in the problem domain and their responsibilities (Jacobson, Booch, and Rumbaugh 1999, p. 186). The collaboration diagram for the R-View a Previous order use case, depicted in Figure 2-13, outlines the sequence of steps used to perform the R-View Previous Order use case, using analysis classes. Each step is

---

[7]UML collaboration diagrams and sequence diagrams show the relationship between classes (actors, boundary, and control classes in this case) and the ordered messages that flow between these classes. Collaboration diagrams focus the reader on the relationships while sequence diagrams focus on the order of messages.

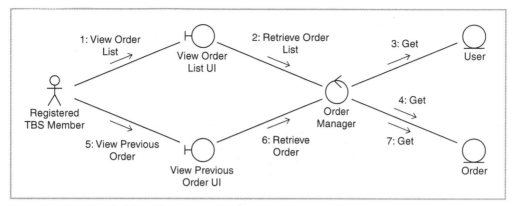

Figure 2-13 R-View Previous Order Use Case

numbered in order and connected to the receiving class. Here, we can see that the I-View Order List and the I-View Previous Order «interface» use cases are represented by their corresponding user interface (UI) boundary classes. Also, the User and Order classes from the domain model are represented as entity classes.

The Order Manager control class is necessary because it encapsulates logic to perform the S-Retrieve Order List and the S-Retrieve Order «service» use cases. For S-Retrieve Order List, the Order Manager control class must constrain the Orders retrieved by ensuring that they are associated with the specified User object, as documented in the precondition for S-Retrieve Order.

RSI Approach Summary

RSI structures use cases into three categories that reflect various levels of granularity—size of activity described in the use case—and abstraction—level of detail—described in the use case. The RSI approach provides a guideline framework that helps to define

- The level of use case granularity and abstraction that best support the use case analysis process
- Circumstances for which the various levels of granularity/abstraction should be used
- How the various levels of granularity/abstraction should be documented
- To whom descriptions should be targeted

This framework definition is accomplished by structuring use cases into three categories, which subdivide use cases by their granularity and the level of descriptive detail they contain:

- Requirement use cases
  —Describe business or work processes at a low degree of detail
  —Are developed as part of the business or domain analysis process
  —Are targeted primarily toward end users
  —Form the basis of project scope and phasing
- Interface use cases
  —Describe the interfaces presented by a system at a high degree of detail, often in the form of a user interface prototype
  —Are developed by user interface designers
  —Are targeted primarily toward end users
  —Provide a clear placeholder in the use case analysis process for user interface design
- Service use cases
  —Describe the functionality offered by the functional core of a system
  —Are developed by system designers and targeted toward system developers
  —Provide a starting point for the design process, based on the service use cases and the domain model

The essential elements of the service use case model also provide a clearly defined list of the bounded atomic system functions that are necessary to implement requirements, something clearly missing in many use case descriptions. All three levels of use cases described in the RSI approach may be appropriate on a project at different stages in the analysis process, which for larger projects, RSI divides into four stages:

1. Developing the requirement use case model—conceptualization—during which ad hoc requirements are mapped onto requirement use cases documenting business or work processes

2a. Developing the interface use case model—specification—during which requirement use cases may be decomposed and refined into interface use cases documenting system interface formats and associated functionality, providing a clear placeholder for *user interface design* in the use case analysis process while also maintaining a clear separation between interface—dialog box, button—and core domain—bank, account, customer—concerns

2b. Developing the service use case model—specification—during which requirement and interface use cases are refined into service use cases, which we encourage to be cross-referenced against a domain model

3. Consolidating the models and producing the traceability model

The RSI approach *structures* the deliverables of the use case analysis process to assist in the ensuing development process. Interface use cases clearly define the interface of the system to the outside world and provide a starting point for boundary class definition. Service use cases provide a starting point for the allocation of behavior to components, which are implemented either as methods on classes or as control classes in their own right.[8]

A use case is not complete, however, unless it has been verified by all respective parties—developers, test engineers, customer representatives, and other stakeholders—and unless a test procedure has verified that the use case is testable. The effort to derive test procedures from RSI-derived use cases is described in Section 2-7.

2.5 Nonfunctional Requirements

The RSI approach is a useful method for specifying the functionality of the system. However, another aspect of the system must also be considered: nonfunctional requirements, such as security, performance and scalability, usability, and compatibility. These types of requirements do not embody the system with any specific functions but instead constrain or further define how the system will perform any given function. Documenting nonfunctional requirements is usually done in two steps.

1. A systemwide specification is created that defines the nonfunctional requirements that apply to all use cases in the system. "The user interface of the Web system must be compatible with Netscape Navigator 4.x or higher and Microsoft Internet Explorer 4.x or higher browsers" is an example.

2. Each «requirement» use case description will contain a section titled Non-functional Requirements, which will document any specific nonfunctional needs of that particular use case that deviate from the system-wide specification.

Appendix C documents the systemwide nonfunctional requirements specification for the TBS case study.

2.6 Technology Selection

At some point in the process of designing the system, technology choices, such as platforms, languages, middleware, and Web presentation technologies—CSS, XML, and so on—must be made. These choices need to be made as early as possible in the

---

[8]Further information on RSI can be found in Collins-Cope 1998, 1999, 2000a,b. This work is dedicated to the memory of Michael John Cope.

process in order to mitigate technology-related risks. Early selection will also help ensure that the technologies can be used to build the Web system's required functionality constrained by its nonfunctional requirements. In addition, the test effort will be selecting testing tools and defining black-box and gray-box testing strategies for the Web project. In doing so, they will need to ensure that the site's technologies and architecture are supported by the tools.

These choices are often made during the development of an *architecture baseline,* or prototype (Jacobson, Booch, and Rumbaugh 1999, pp. 66–69). The architecture baseline generally consists of a small, early system version that implements certain *architecturally significant* use cases. These use cases should be ones considered critical to the goals of the system, namely, major functionality concepts. This set should include use cases that carry a certain amount of technological risk to implement, owing to their complexity or reliance on recently developed technologies.

Once the architecturally significant use cases have been identified, they are implemented into a small system—the architectural baseline. The baseline is evaluated to determine that it properly delivers the functional and nonfunctional requirements of the architecturally significant use cases. When the result is deemed satisfactory, the selected technologies used to build the baseline can be considered appropriate for implementing the full set of system use cases. This construction of an architectural baseline is usually performed early in the project life cycle, prior to the beginning of a true construction phase, in order to address high-risk areas up front.

The development of the architectural baseline can be done in parallel with the definition of other requirements use cases. The baseline will probably be developed in an iterative[9] fashion—only a small number of iterations are recommended—as the use cases are developed iteratively as well. As a result, important use cases are defined, a satisfactory baseline is constructed, more use cases are defined, the baseline is augmented, and so on. Ideally, a complete set of architecturally significant use cases has been generated after two or three iterations, and then the remainder of the use cases are additions to that set. An important goal here is to avoid, late in the process, arriving at a particular use case that invalidates one of the technology choices, which can result in a costly rearchitecture of the system.

During the development of the architectural baseline, decisions on technology are made, constrained by the functional and nonfunctional requirements and other factors, such as legacy systems. Once this architectural baseline has been deemed acceptable, the majority of the technology choices for the project have already been made and can be communicated to the test team for consideration when defining a testing strategy and selecting a set of testing tools for the Web project.

---

[9]In an iterative development process, activities such as analysis, design, and implementation are repeated many times throughout the development cycle. This is in contrast to the classic "waterfall" model, where each of these activities are performed once (or a very few times) over the life of the project.

2.7 Test Procedures from RSI Use Cases

Test engineers need to take part in use case development in order to gain an understanding of the use case requirement and hence the interaction of the system with the outside world. *Use case walkthroughs* during the requirements phase are an appropriate mechanism with which to involve the test team early in the development life cycle. Use case walkthroughs involving all stakeholders allow for discovery of new issues. Any required use case changes can be implemented before the design and coding phases, thus potentially reducing cost. With this approach, succeeding phases are less likely to create new faults on existing ones. Many statistics show that the earlier in the life cycle a defect is discovered, the cheaper it will be to fix it.

It is important that use case modeling guidelines and organization be defined at the onset of the Web project. Similarly, use case guidelines—the RSI approach to use cases—and use case templates need to be defined. With this documentation in hand, stakeholders will be equipped to verify the correctness of each use case. *Correctness* is judged based on the documented standard. In addition to correctness, the use cases will need to be verified for consistency, completeness, and testability.

Completeness ensures that no required elements are missing, whereas *consistency* verifies that there are no internal or external contradictions among the elements within the work products or between work products. *Testability* will verify that the use case requirement can be tested. As already mentioned, a use case should not be considered complete and approved unless a test procedure has been created for it.

The analysis performed to derive a test procedure from a use case has, in many instances, uncovered issues or holes that have been overlooked during use case development. Creating test procedures from use cases sometimes parallels a cut-and-paste operation, as the use cases and the test procedures are often so closely related. However, deriving a test procedure always entails analytical work. RSI-derived use cases become the baseline for creating test procedures. The resulting *test procedure* will specify how to test the use case or a specific scenario of a use case. The test procedure is designed to ensure that its execution will verify that the objectives of the use case have been met.

The RSI use case traceability model can be used as the overall high-level design for deriving test procedures, as the defined requirements use cases provide the starting point for the *test procedure analysis* process. Whereas the RSI approach breaks requirements, interface, and services into their own respective, separate use cases, steps in a test procedure will generally combine a set of RSI use cases into one test procedure to allow for sequence and flow.

The test procedure steps derived from requirements use cases in general specify *black-box* test steps, or testing performed on system externals: application behavior against use case requirements. Additionally, the test procedure steps derived from interface and service use cases specify a combination of *black-box* and *gray-box* test steps, meaning that in addition to testing system externals, gray-box testing includes tests that address the internal interaction between components of the system.

As a general guideline, the RSI approach breaks down the use case into test procedure steps, using the following process.

- Following the test procedure template outline defined in Figure 2-15, the requirements and interface use case steps will generally populate the *user actions* and/or the *expected result* columns of the test procedure.
- The services use case steps will be verified by using the *trace log information*, discussed later in satisfying the service use cases.
- The translation of RSI use case steps into test procedure steps is not a simple cut-and-paste exercise, as many would like it to be. Rather, detailed analysis and test design are required to translate the RSI use cases into test procedures, as discussed next.

Satisfying the Requirements Use Case[10]

Requirement use cases provide the starting point for a test procedure. They can be translated into the "user action" and/or "expected results" steps, described in the test procedure template in Figure 2-15. After reviewing these use cases to perform additional analysis, test procedure steps must be included to

- Determine the expected result of the interaction between the actors and the system.
- Determine that the preconditions specified by the use case are satisfied: the inputs and expected outputs.
- Determine the order, or sequence, in which specific transactions must be tested either to accommodate database issues or as a result of control or workflow (scenarios).
- Identify any patterns of similar actions or events that are used by several or many transactions. The «includes» relationships depicted in the use case are indicators of such patterns. As noted previously, requirement use cases are decomposed, using the «includes» relationship, in order to remove duplication of text across multiple use case descriptions. You can take advantage of the «includes» relationship to create modular test procedures. You can

---

[10]In order to derive the most efficient test procedures, it is necessary to understand the various testing techniques. For more information, see Beizer (1990).

review the use case traceability model in order to outline the sequence of
test procedure execution.

- Include a set of test steps for any extensions dealing with deviations and
exceptions in the normal sequence of events.
- Include a set of test steps to account for unexpected input and/or output.
- Review critical and high-risk use cases in order to place greater emphasis
for tests addressing this functionality, adding test procedures for higher-risk
areas, and to outline the associated test procedures early in the development
schedule.
- Determine the overall test technique to be used to verify the use case.

For sample requirements test case steps associated with the R-View a Previous Order
use case described previously, refer to the User Action (Inputs) column in Figure 2-14.

Satisfying the Interface Use Case

Interface use cases describe functionality that manages the interface between the
actors of a system and the underlying services it offers. As mentioned, interface use
cases can often be translated into the "expected result" steps described in the test
procedure template in Figure 2-15 after a "user action" (a requirements use case
step) has been executed. In other cases, *interface* use case elements can become
the "user action" in Figure 2-14.

Interface use cases translate the information provided by an actor into a form
acceptable to a set of underlying service use cases. The *expected result* in the test
procedure is used to verify that the use case requirements have been met. It will also
be necessary to review these use cases to perform additional analysis and to include
test procedure steps in order to

- Determine that the objectives of the use case have been met.
- Include data required to verify each use case action. *Note:* Data constraints
are listed in the data dictionary; therefore, it is recommended that they not
be repeated in a test procedure, so as to avoid duplication and additional
maintenance. Instead, the test procedure should simply include steps that
refer to the data dictionary.
- Determine that the detailed test procedure executes the steps to cause the
system to produce interfaces as expected. This might include verification of
graphical user interface design, report layouts, file formats, and so on. In
Figure 2-14, the specific interface elements are listed in the Expected
Results column. Note that the interface design information does not need
to be repeated in the test procedure; simply refer to the «interface» use
case in the test procedure documentation.

- Determine the step-by-step test procedure steps of the functional aspects of the interface, such as user interface dynamics—for example, when the Select Customer button is clicked, the Accounts list box is refreshed—file processing, and how report contents are made up. (In Figure 2-14, these types of interface elements can be listed in the User Action (Inputs) and the respective Expected Results columns).

For sample interface test case steps associated with the R-View a Previous Order use case described previously refer to the User Actions (Inputs) and Expected Results columns in Figure 2-14.

Satisfying the Services Use Case

Service use cases define the underlying functions offered by the functional core of a system in a manner independent of any particular interface concerns. The services use case steps are verified and translated by using the trace log information. These test steps are considered gray-box testing, which examines the activity of the back-end components during a test case. Three types of problems may be encountered during gray-box testing.

- A component may encounter a failure, causing the operation to be aborted. The user interface will typically indicate that an error has occurred.
- The test may execute in full but with incorrect results. Somewhere in the system, a component processed data incorrectly, causing the error in the results.
- A component fails during execution, but does not notify the user interface that an error has occurred (a "false positive").

In both of these situations, gray-box testing can assist in isolating the components responsible for the errors. One of the more effective ways to monitor the behavior of back-end components is through the use of a logging (trace log) system. During execution, all components will write log entries detailing what methods, or functions, they are executing and the major objects they are dealing with. The log entries can be written to a text file, database, or other kind of repository.

Enough information must be put into the log to make it useful with gray-box testing techniques but not so much as to make it unhelpful. Following is a list of the recommended log items.

- Class name and method name, or simply the function name if not a member of any class, important for determining a path of execution through several components.

- Timestamp, to the millisecond, of the entry. An accurate timestamp on all entries will allow the events to be lined up if they occur in parallel or on different machines.
- Persistent entity database IDs or keys. Each service use case typically operates on entities from the system's domain model. In the case of persistent entities, logging the database IDs or keys of these items will facilitate the mapping of component execution to database records, which is useful for examining the data source for the results of an operation or determining whether data stored in the database is responsible for a runtime error.
- Results or status codes. If components return a status code, this should be written to the log as well.
- Errors of any kind. A failure encountered anywhere in a component should be recorded in the log, along with the reason for the error.

With these items written to the log file by every method of every component in the system, the execution of a test case can be traced through the system and lined up with the data in the database it is operating on. In case of a serious failure, the responsible component will be indicated by the log file records. In case of a computational error, the log file will contain all the components that participated in the test case, along with the IDs or keys of all entities used. Together with the entity data from the database, this should be enough information to isolate the error in source code.

For sample services test case steps associated with the R-View a Previous Order use case described previously, refer to the Trace Log Information column in Figure 2-14. Figure 2-14 depicts a sample test procedure for the functional test requirements for the View Previous Order use case only.

Mapping Test Data Requirements

During the performance of detailed test design, test data requirements need to be mapped against the defined test procedures (Dustin, Rashka, and Paul 1999, pp. 277–280). The analysis and generation of interface use cases will generate much of the data requirements. While generating test procedures, the data requirements field is filled in and yields the information required to populate the test database. For example, for Check Order Status, the test database has to be populated so an order status can be viewed. Other data required can be gathered from the detailed design documentation that feeds the data dictionary, along with the interface and service use cases. In addition to providing data element names, definitions, and structures, the data dictionary may provide data structures, data models, edits, cardinality, formats, usage rules, ranges, data types and domains, and other constraints. A test database will need to be created based on the defined data

Figure 2-14 Sample Test Procedure

Test Procedure ID: T-VP0001

Date Executed: MM/DD/YYYY

Test Procedure Author: Jackie D.

Test Name: T-View a Previous Order

Test Engineer Initials: JD

Test Objective: This test procedure verifies the View a Previous Order functionality. The user will be able to review the details of a previous order, including its status.

Related Use Case(s)/Requirement Number: Use TBS, Login, Purchase Items

Precondition/Assumption/Dependency: Purchase Items

Verification Method: Automated test

Functional Testing Steps

Automated/Manual: Underline selection

Step #	User Action (Inputs)	Expected Results	Trace Log Information	Actual Results	Test Data Required	Pass/ Fail	Use Case Step or Requirement Number
1.	User selects to view a previous order.	1. If user is not already logged in, system prompts user for login (execute I-Login test procedure)[1]. 2. System displays a list of the user's previous orders.	aUser		See data dictionary for data constraints		
2.	User views the order list.	See I-View Order List interface and verify that the display is as defined.[2] (See Figure 2-9 and its accompanying use case documentation). Also verify that the following data elements are present: Order.Number Order.Date Order.TotalCost Order.Status	anOrderset				

1. When creating RSI-derived test procedures we recommend that the modularity be kept intact; that is, a separate test procedure should be developed for each R-use case, but the test procedure should reference the R-use case within the test procedure.

2. Instead of cutting and pasting the printout of what the interface should look like, simply refer to the interface use case screen print document and verify that the application's screen looks as required.

48

Step #	User Action (Inputs)	Expected Results	Trace Log Information	Actual Results	Test Data Required	Pass/Fail	Use Case Step or Requirement Number
3.	User clicks on button Back to Catalog.	User is returned to the TBS Menu interface.					

4.	Repeat steps 1 and 2. User clicks on order #10010.	See I-View Previous Order screen and verify that the display is as defined. Also verify that the following data elements are present:
		Order.Number
		Order.Date
		Order.BillingAddress
		Order.ShippingAddress
		Order.PaymentInformation
		    CardType
		    PartialCardNumber
		Order.Items (table)
		    SKU
		    Description
		    Price
		    Quantity
		Order.Status
			anOrder				

5.	User clicks on button Back to Catalog.	User is returned to the TBS Menu interface.					
6.	Repeat step 1 with a user who has not purchased any items.	An error message should be displayed; see error message guide for details.					

requirements. Once test data requirements are outlined, it is necessary to plan how to obtain, generate, or develop the test data.

Use case sequence diagrams, described previously, can be used to incorporate the flow of data into the selection of test procedures. Using this technique will help identify the selection of test path segments that satisfy some characteristic of data flows for all possible types of data objects.

Most test techniques require that test data be defined and developed to support resulting test procedures. The identification of test data requirements is an important step in the definition of test design. When defining test data requirements associated with the various test procedures test data should be defined to allow such activities as executing every program statement at least once, ensuring that each condition is tested, and verifying the expected results to include as many variations and combinations as possible and feasible. Test data is also required to ensure that each boundary condition is exercised. As part of the process for identifying test data requirements, it is beneficial to develop a matrix listing the various test procedures in one column and a list of test data requirements in another column.

As mentioned, in addition to defining the requirements for test data, it is also necessary to identify the means to develop or obtain the necessary test data. When reviewing system-level data concerns, it is beneficial to be aware of possible sources to obtain or derive sample data, and to determine how the test data will be generated and who will be responsible for doing so. Such source documents may also clarify issues and questions about the kind of test data required. Source documentation that may be helpful for deriving test data, includes the following items:

- Design documents: structure charts, decision tables, action diagrams
- Detailed function and system specifications
- Data flow diagrams
- Data dictionary: data elements, data type, ranges, and so on
- Design documents: class diagrams, sequence diagrams, collaborations, and so on
- RSI-derived use cases, that is, interface use cases

In support of black-box testing, test data is required to help ensure that each system-level requirement is tested and verified. A review of test data requirements should address several data concerns, including the following:[11]

- Depth: database volume, or size
- Breadth: variation of data values and data value categories

---

[11] Adapted from Elfriede Dustin, Jeff Rashka, and John Paul, *Automated Software Testing: Introduction, Management, and Performance*, Reading, MA: Addison-Wesley, 1999.

- Scope: the accuracy and completeness of the data
- Test-execution data integrity: the ability to maintain data integrity
- Conditions: the ability to store particular data conditions

The depth—volume, or size—of the database records needed to support tests must be considered.[12] The test team needs to determine whether 10 records in a database or a particular table are sufficient or whether 10,000 records are necessary. Early life-cycle tests, such as unit or build verification tests, should use small, hand-crafted databases, which offer maximum control and minimal disturbances. As the test effort progresses through the various phases and types of tests, the size of the database should increase to one that is appropriate for the particular tests. For example, performance and volume tests are not meaningful in the procedure where the production environment database contains 1,000,000 records and the tests are performed against a database containing only 100 records.

The breadth—variation of the data values, such as 10,000 different accounts and a number of types of accounts—is also an important consideration.[13] A well-designed test will incorporate variations of test data, and tests for which all the data is similar will produce limited results. For example, tests may need to consider the fact that some accounts may have negative balances, as well as those that have balances in the low range ($100s), moderate range ($1,000s), high range ($100,000s), and very high range ($10,000,000s). Tests must also reflect data representing an average range. In addition, bank customer accounts might be classified in several ways, such as savings, checking, loans, student, joint, and business.

The scope of test data is pertinent to the accuracy, relevance, and completeness of the data.[14] For example, when testing the queries used to identify the various kinds of bank accounts that have a balance due of more than $100, numerous accounts meeting this criterion must exist, and the tests also need to reflect additional data, such as reason codes, contact histories, and account owner demographic data. The inclusion of the complete set of test data enables the test procedure to fully validate and exercise the system and support evaluation of results. It is also necessary to verify that the inclusion of a record returned as a result of this query is valid for the specific purpose rather than from a missing or inappropriate value.

---

[12]Adapted from Elfriede Dustin, Jeff Rashka, and John Paul, *Automated Software Testing: Introduction, Management, and Performance,* Reading, Mass.: Addison-Wesley, 1999, p. 279.

[13]Ibid.

[14]Ibid.

Another consideration involves the need to maintain data integrity while performing tests.[15] Throughout test operations it will be necessary to segregate data, modify selected data, and return the database to its initial state. In addition, test executions must be safe to perform in parallel, meaning one test won't adversely affect the other tests and, in the case of using an automated testing tool, that the scripts won't fail because the test database is not in the expected state.

Data integrity also entails data used in support of tests but that cannot be accessed through the user interface. An example might be a data value that is updated from another server. These types of values and elements should be identified and a method or resource identified that supports read-only data. Following test execution it is often necessary to reset the test data set to an initial—baseline—state, therefore, a procedure must be in place to allow the test data to be reloaded into the database.

Test data reflecting specific conditions must be managed and stored.[16] For example, health information systems commonly perform a year-end closeout. Storing data in the year-end condition enables the test of a year-end closeout to occur without having to enter the data for the entire year. When testing a health information system application for which the year-end closeout function has not yet been implemented as part of an operational system, test data will need to be created that reflects the entire year.

Generic Test Procedure Template

The standards for manual test procedures should include an example of how much detail a test procedure should contain. The level of detail may be as simple as outlining the steps to be taken: Step 1, click on the File menu selection; step 2, select Open; step 3, select directory.

Depending on the size of the application being tested, writing extensive test procedures may be too time consuming, in which case the test procedure would contain only a high-level test procedure description. Also keep in mind that if a test procedure is written using very low-level detail, maintenance can become very difficult. Therefore, it is important to write modular, reusable test procedures.

Test procedure standards can include guidelines on how the expected result is supposed to be documented. The standard should address several questions. Will tests require screen prints? Will tests require sign-off by a second person who observes the execution of the test?

---

[15] Ibid., p. 280.

[16] Ibid.

Figure 2-15 Test Procedure Template

Test Procedure ID: Follow naming convention: TF ID is based on requirements use cases but starts with T- instead of R-. **Test Name:** High-level description of what is being tested.

Date Executed:

Test Procedure Author: **Test Engineer Initials:**

Test Objective: Briefly describe the purpose, or intent, of the procedure.

Related Use Case(s)/Requirement Number: Identify/list any use case name and number(s) being tested under this test objective.

Precondition/Assumption/Dependency: List any conditions, assumptions, and dependencies that need to be satisfied before these test procedure steps can be executed. This can be done in a bulleted list. Often the same preconditions as in the use case apply here.

Verification Method: Specify the method of verification.

Functional Testing Steps

Automated/Manual: Underline selection

Step #	User Action (Inputs)	Expected Results	Trace Log Information	Actual Results	Test Data Required	Pass/ Fail	Use Case Step or Requirement Number

Security Testing Steps (See Appendix C for testing steps on the View Previous Order functionality.)

Automated/Manual: Underline selection

Step #	User Action (Inputs)	Expected Results	Trace Log Information	Actual Results	Test Data Required	Pass/ Fail	Use Case Step or Requirement Number

continued

53

Figure 2-15 Test Procedure Template *continued*

Performance and Scalability Testing Steps (See Appendix C for testing steps on the View Previous Order functionality.)

Automated/Manual: Underline selection

Step #	User Action (Inputs)	Expected Results	Trace Log Information	Actual Results	Test Data Required	Pass/ Fail	Use Case Step or Requirement Number

Compatibility Testing Steps (See Appendix C for testing steps on the View Previous Order functionality.)

Automated/Manual: Underline selection

Step #	User Action (Inputs)	Expected Results	Trace Log Information	Actual Results	Test Data Required	Pass/ Fail	Use Case Step or Requirement Number

Usability Testing Steps (See Appendix C for testing steps on the View Previous Order functionality.)

Automated/Manual: Underline selection

Step #	User Action (Inputs)	Expected Results	Trace Log Information	Actual Results	Test Data Required	Pass/ Fail	Use Case Step or Requirement Number

54

The primary elements of the standard test procedure, shown in Figure 2-15, are as follows. For additional information on functional testing and a checklist, see Appendix A.

- Test procedure ID: Use a naming convention when filling in the test procedure ID.
- Test name: Provide a longer description of the test procedure.
- Date executed: State when the test procedure was executed.
- Test engineer initials: Provide the initials of the test engineer executing the test procedure.
- Test procedure author: Identify the developer of the test procedure.
- Test objective: Outline the objective of the test procedure.
- Related use case/requirement number: Identify the requirement identification number that the test procedure is validating.
- Precondition/assumption/dependency: Provide the criteria, or prerequisite information, needed before the test procedure can be run, such as specific data setup requirements. This field is completed when the test procedure is dependent on a test procedure that needs to be performed before the first test procedure can be performed. This field is also completed to support instances when two test procedures would conflict when performed at the same time. Note that the precondition for a use case often becomes the precondition for a test procedure.
- Verification method: This field may state certification, automated or manual test, inspection, and analysis.
- User action: Here, the goals and expectations of a test procedure are clearly defined. This can be accomplished by documenting the steps needed to create a test, much as you might write pseudocode in software development. Completing this field allows for clarification and documentation of the test steps required to verify the use case.
- Expected results: Define the expected results associated with executing the particular test procedure.
- Trace log information: Monitor the behavior of back-end components. During execution, Web system components will write log entries detailing the functions they are executing and the major objects for which they are interacting. These log entries can be captured within the test procedure.
- Actual result: This field may have a default value, such as "Same as Expected Result," that is changed to describe the actual result if the test procedure fails.
- Test data required: List the set of test data required to support execution of the test procedure.

- Status (pass/fail): This field may indicate testable/passed, testable/failed, not testable, partially not testable/passed, or partially not testable/failed. A test requirement could not be testable, for example, because the functionality has not been implemented yet or has been implemented only partially. The status field is updated after test execution. Using the status field, a progress report can be created, based on the test procedures executed and passed versus those test procedures that executed and failed.

Note that the test procedure in Figure 2-15 is divided into five sections—one for functional testing steps, and the remainder for the nonfunctional areas of security, performance and scalability, compatibility, and usability.

2.8 Chapter Summary

- The primary factor the customer values is the quality of the functionality provided by a Web system. Engineering functionality into a system begins with the proper definition of system requirements. Use cases are a widely used method for requirements capture.
- The Requirements-Service-Interface (RSI) approach to use case analysis provides a framework for analyzing and understanding potential use case deliverables and their interrelationships.
- Use case graphical notation helps provide a high-level view of the major functions of the business, or domain, and their relationships. The primary value of the use case resides in its associated *textual* documentation.
- The RSI approach provides three classifications for use case granularity, represented by the UML stereotypes *requirement, interface,* and *service.*
- The interrelationships between requirement and interface/service use cases may be shown by using «trace» dependencies on a use case traceability diagram, or model.
- The overall process of developing an RSI model consists of four stages: developing the requirements use case model, developing the interface use case model, developing the service use case model, and preparing the traceability model.
- Requirement use cases provide the starting point for the use case analysis process, forming the basis on which the project will be scoped and phased.
- Traceability models are useful in establishing the impact of change to requirements on a system. If a given requirement is then varied, a traceability model enables the potential impact of this change to be traced through to the interface and service use case models.

⚠ Test engineers need to take part in use case development in order to gain an understanding of the use case requirement. *Use case walkthroughs* during the requirements phase are an appropriate mechanism with which to involve the test team early in the development life cycle.

⚠ Use cases (such as RSI-derived use cases) become the baseline for creating test procedures. The resulting *test procedure* will specify how to test the use case or a specific scenario of a use case.

⚠ The test procedure steps derived from requirement use cases in general specify *black-box* testing steps. Test procedure steps derived from interface and services use cases specify a combination of *black-box* and *gray-box* test steps; in addition to testing system externals (black box), gray-box testing includes tests that address the internal interaction between components of the system.

⚠ Whereas the RSI approach breaks requirements, interface, and services requirements into their own respective separate use cases, the test procedure steps will generally combine a set of RSI use cases into one test procedure in order to allow for sequence and flow.

2.9 References

Beizer, Boris. 1990. *Software Testing Techniques.* 2d ed. New York: Van Nostrand Reinhold.

Cockburn, Alistair. 1997. "Structuring Use Cases with Goals." *Journal of Object Oriented Programming.* (Sept./Oct. and Oct./Nov.) Also available at http://members.aol.com/acockburn/papers/usecases.htm.

Cockburn, Alistair. 2000. *Writing Effective Use Cases (The Crystal Collection for Software Professionals).* Reading, Mass.: Addison-Wesley.

Collins-Cope, M. "The Requirements/Service/Interface (RSI) Approach to Use Case Analysis," Tools 29, Nancy, France. June 7–10, 1999. Also available at www.ratio.co.uk/rsi.html.

Dustin, Elfriede, Jeff Rashka, and John Paul. 1999. *Automated Software Testing Introduction, Management, and Performance.* Reading, Mass.: Addison-Wesley.

Jacobson, Ivar, Magnus Christerson, Patrick Jonsson, and Gunnar Övergaard, 1992. *Object-Oriented Software Engineering: A Use Case Driven Approach.* Addison-Wesley.

Jacobson, Ivar, Grady Booch, and James Rumbaugh. 1999. *United Software Development Process.* Reading, Mass.: Addison-Wesley.

Myers, G. J. 1979. *The Art of Software Testing.* New York: Wiley.

Warmer, Jos, and Anneke Kleppe. 1998. *The Object Constraint Language: Precise Modeling with UML.* Reading, Mass.: Addison-Wesley.

chapter 3

Security

System security vulnerability and the corresponding impact of a security lapse on the organization and its customers are significant.

Ensuring the security of a Web system is a difficult task. Given the open nature and original intent of the Internet as a data-sharing medium among research scientists worldwide, many aspects of the Internet work against the security interests of a Web site. A user anywhere in the world can connect to a Web site in a fairly anonymous fashion. Although many Internet services and operating systems include auditing mechanisms for tracking users, a knowledgeable attacker will know how to trick or avoid these mechanisms, and tracking down an Internet intruder is a very complicated and laborsome task.

Because they handle sensitive and personal information, e-commerce Web systems have particular security concerns. Electronic payment is generally a necessary function of an e-commerce Web system, and this type of transaction requires the system to gather a customer's payment information, which usually includes a credit card number and some personal data. Most e-commerce systems retain this information in order to support the processing of future transactions or to enhance a user's future browsing experience. In addition, merchants usually retain customer credit information for the duration of a dispute period, for the purpose of linking the payment information to the transaction. It is critical that this data be safeguarded against retrieval by unauthorized users.

This chapter covers the following aspects of Web system security:

- *Overview:* The threats and aspects of the Internet that make all sites inherently insecure.
- *Web and application servers:* A detailed examination of Web components on these servers to ensure that they do not provide ways for an attacker to enter the system.
- *Database server:* The safeguarding of site data and user confidential information to protect it from being accessed by unauthorized users.
- *Client computers and browsers:* User components can host a variety of site-specific code and data storage, such as ActiveX controls and cookies, and can also, unfortunately, provide an opportunity for exploits and loss of user privacy.
- *Secure communications:* Transmission of critical user data, such as payment and other private information, via a secure protocol, such as SSL, to protect user information from network eavesdroppers.
- *Network:* The use of firewalls and other mechanisms to hide and to restrict access to the Web system's servers, thereby preventing intruders from probing for entry points into the site's network.
- *Security evaluation:* Step-by-step strategies for testing the security of the site. These strategies can be used as the basis for security test case development.

This chapter is concerned primarily with the security of software and components developed by an organization, as well as some large-scale site design considerations. Therefore, coverage of file permissions, operating system and Web server configurations, and other such issues is limited. However, many books and Internet resources on those subjects are available, and many are specific to the operating system and software in use by the site.

The material in this chapter references two types of utilities that are useful in the evaluation of Web site security:

- A *port-scanning tool* allows the user to scan a host or range of hosts to determine whether they are exposing services (server processes) on some or all ports. Because some of these services contain known security problems, a port scanner allows an outside user to determine whether a potential entry point on a server may be used to gain access to the system. Several port-scanning tools are available as shareware or as freeware; it is best to use a few different port scanners, as they each offer different feature sets.
- A network monitor, or *sniffer,* is a tool that supports the detailed examination of packets being transmitted across a network.

3.1 Overview

This section describes the Internet security issues that Web sites must be aware of, owing to the nature of the Internet. In addition, a brief discussion of operating system and service security is presented, as well as the need to consider security risks and outsourcing.

Internet Security Issues

Many things working against the security of a Web system are unavoidable facts of the Internet. Therefore, a few fundamental principles must be understood to successfully approach the task of securing the Web system.

The Internet and the machines that connect to it are inherently insecure. The Internet was not built on a secure foundation. For much of the Internet's history, data traveled between hosts in an unencrypted, plaintext form. This data could readily be intercepted and read by a third party, potentially compromising passwords or important content. For electronic commerce, transmitting information in plaintext format was clearly not acceptable, given the transmission of private, financial, and other sensitive data. With the advent of security protocols, such as the Secure Sockets Layer (SSL), this problem of insecure data transmission has been largely remedied since data can now travel over the Internet in an encrypted form. Nonetheless, other Internet security concerns remain.

The modern Internet was built primarily on the use of servers running the UNIX operating system. Although some security controls were necessary to enable the Internet's use as a multiuser system, it was not long before holes were discovered that allowed unscrupulous users to penetrate system security. Although the security of UNIX systems has been vastly improved over the years, and other secure operating systems, such as Windows NT/2000, have been developed, the host security problem still exists. In fact, as more users and computers continue to be connected to the Internet and as additional vulnerabilities are discovered and exploited, the host security problem may never be completely resolved.

Web sites are continuously being scanned by attackers probing for potential entry points. On the Internet, no Web systems are exempt from examination by would-be intruders. One must assume that no host is safe and that all security mechanisms must be in place and active at all times to prevent intrusion. Any door left open has a high degree of probability of being exploited by an attacker. Even small security holes can lead to an attacker ultimately gaining administrative access to the system.

All server software and operating systems are inherently insecure. It has been said that the only secure computer is one that is physically inaccessible and not connected to any network. New security flaws are discovered nearly every day, even within the latest, most secured operating systems and software. Therefore, it must be assumed that a Web system's services and software are not without security flaws and are at risk of being compromised at any time.

Even the most thorough security preparations may miss a security flaw. Although this sounds quite disheartening, the basic principle that applies to Web system deployment is that the system cannot rely on any single security mechanism. For example, simply having a firewall to block unwanted traffic is not enough to ensure the security of a Web system and its data. It must be assumed that a knowledgeable attacker will find a way to bypass the firewall and to gain access to a computer residing on an internal network. In view of such grim odds, it is clear that each aspect of the system must be considered from a security point of view and that any applicable, and practical, security measures must be applied. The odds of an attacker's defeating one mechanism are high; the odds of an attacker's defeating multiple different mechanisms, however, are much lower.

Operating System and Service Security

As outlined in Chapter 1, most Web systems are built with an *n*-tier architectural pattern, whereby several types of servers work together to provide the functionality offered by the Web site. The most common types of servers in this scenario are the *Web server,* the *application server,* and the *database server.* Although these three server types perform vastly different functions, they still perform as servers in the general sense and must be secured at the operating system and service levels, meaning such aspects as file system permissions, user accounts, Web server functions, file transfer, and printing services.

Although the minute details of configuring the operating system and service security are beyond the scope of this book and are not discussed in depth, an overview is provided here, together with a listing of a few Internet resources for further information. Note that securing a server of any kind requires a multitude of configuration changes. A server can be attacked in many ways, so it is imperative that the server be thoroughly secured prior to being placed in a production environment with a connection to the Internet. Securing a server entails two steps. First, it is necessary to secure the base operating system. Second, services running on the server need to be secured.

The action to secure the operating system focuses on properly configuring the installation of the operating system in order to keep unauthorized users from being able to connect to the particular computer and accessing configuration or data files located on its file system. The following list highlights some of the major areas of security concern for the operating system configuration:

- Unnecessary user accounts
- File and directory permissions, especially critical configuration files
- Networked disk volumes, such as Network File Service (NFS) or Windows shared directories
- Log files
- Registry on Windows NT/2000 machines
- Unnecessary background processes
- Password policy

Services and other software running on the server are the most likely points of entry for an attacker. Many services, such as File Transfer Protocol (FTP) and Web servers, are provided with the operating system. In addition, a Web site may require other commercial software to be installed to provide additional or enhanced services. All must be properly configured to prevent unwanted intrusion. Although each service will have its own particular configuration issues, the following list illustrates some of the major areas of service security concern:

- Service user—the user the service is running as
- Configuration files—permissions
- Additional service settings that may allow access to other parts of the server

Many books deal with the intricacies of securing a server for use on the Internet. In addition, many Web sites provide detailed instructions for securing servers, including

- Microsoft Security: http://www.microsoft.com/security
- W3C Web security FAQ: http://www.w3.org/Security/Faq/

The discussion of security in this chapter assumes that the server has been secured from the base operating system and service perspectives. The focus of this chapter is on security concerns pertinent to the architecture, design, and implementation of a Web site's components and content, typically developed in-house by the organization.

Security Risk and Outsourcing

Each Web site needs to gauge the potential severity of a security problem, given the nature of the content and cost to the business should a security-related incident occur. For example, banks and e-commerce sites should regard security as a very high risk to their customers and to the image of the organizations, in addition to having possible legal ramifications. Other sites may have considerably fewer security-related risks, especially if the content is nonconfidential and a security-related incident would not result in much loss of business.

Given the proliferation of hacking and security tampering occurring on the Web, all sites should consider security to some extent. Following the practices outlined in this chapter when developing system components and designing the network configuration will greatly help ensure a secure site. However, some sites with high security-related risks, such as banks and other e-commerce sites, should also consider outsourcing the security evaluation of the site to a third-party security organization. Doing so will ensure that the latest and most thorough evaluation procedures are used to greatly reduce the possibility of a security breach.

3.2 Web and Application Servers

Web servers and application servers, the front line of a Web system, have specific security requirements. Web and application server security involves the proper operation of user authentication and access control, as well as a detailed examination of the Web system components used to drive dynamic and interactive content.

Authentication

The security mechanism that verifies a user's identity is referred to as *authentication*. Users can prove their identity in several ways, most commonly through a user ID and password. Many Web systems provide a combination of public and private areas. The content in the public areas is accessible to the general public, whereas content in private areas requires users to authenticate themselves prior to being granted access. This section describes the two most common authentication methods used on public Internet severs: *HTTP basic authentication* and *custom authentication forms*.

HTTP Basic Authentication

This type of authentication is the *standard* method of access control provided by most major browsers. Basic authentication is supported at the HTTP level by most Web servers and requires little or no development effort to implement. Unfortunately, because HTTP basic authentication does not provide protection of the user ID and password during transmission from the user's computer to the site's Web server, that information may be intercepted by a third party. Such protection usually requires the establishment of a secure HTTP connection, typically through the use of SSL.

HTTP basic authentication is readily identifiable by its use of the access control dialog box. The standard Microsoft Internet Explorer Basic Authentication dialog is depicted in Figure 3-1. Basic authentication is also compatible with proxy servers and firewalls, so it is preferable to some of the other, platform-specific authentication techniques. When the Web system uses the Microsoft Internet Information Server (IIS) on a Windows NT/2000 platform, user accounts and permissions are integrated with the operating system's user database, allowing management of Web user accounts through the familiar, operating system–provided tools. Most UNIX-based Web servers use a separate user ID and password file, although some are capable of using a Lightweight Directory Access Protocol (LDAP) directory server for authentication.

Figure 3-2 documents an exchange of packets, or messages, between a browser and a Web server engaging in HTTP basic authentication captured through the use of the Windows 2000 network monitor. Each frame number lists one packet sent from the source host to the destination host during the retrieval of a secured, or private, page. In this example, LOCAL is the client machine running the browser, and HOMER is the Web server machine.

Frame 1 represents the initial request by the client computer for the secured page. In this example, LOCAL, the client computer, is performing a simple retrieval

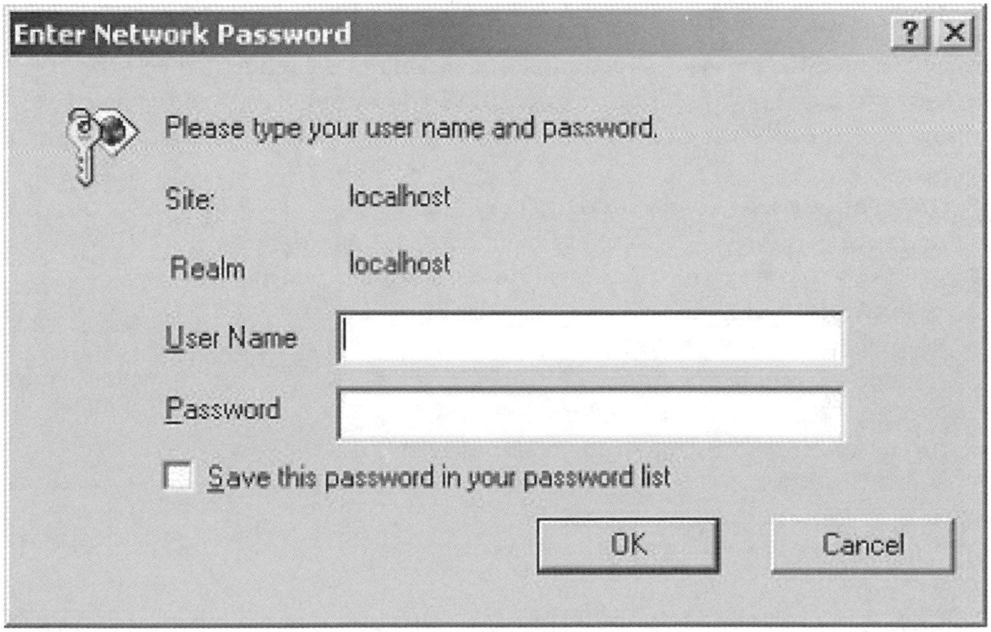

Figure 3-1   Basic Authentication Dialog Box

Frame Number	Source Host	Destination Host	Protocol	Description
1	LOCAL	HOMER	HTTP	GET Request (from client using port 1857)
2	HOMER	LOCAL	HTTP	Response (to client using port 1857)
3	HOMER	LOCAL	HTTP	Response (to client using port 1857)
4	HOMER	LOCAL	HTTP	Response (to client using port 1857)
5	LOCAL	HOMER	HTTP	GET Request (from client using port 1858)
6	HOMER	LOCAL	HTTP	Response (to client using port 1858)

Figure 3-2   Basic Authentication Network Capture

using the HTTP GET method—the most common way that Web browsers retrieve pages from Web servers. When it receives the request, HOMER, the Web server computer, examines the data in the request. HOMER examines the request, checks for authorization, and responds once it has completed its examination of the data. Following is the message data sent from LOCAL to HOMER in the GET request:

```
GET /secured/secure.html HTTP/1.1
Accept: image/gif, image/x-xbitmap, image/jpeg,
   image/pjpeg, application/vnd.ms-powerpoint,
   application/vnd.ms-excel, application/msword
Referer: http://Homer/
Accept-Language: en-us
Accept-Encoding: gzip, deflate
User-Agent: Mozilla/4.0 (compatible; MSIE 5.01;
   Windows NT 5.0)
Host: Homer
Connection: Keep-Alive
```

HOMER is configured to protect the page—that is, it is not accessible by anonymous users—so it therefore requires that authentication data be provided by the client computer. HTTP basic authentication enables the client computer to deliver the authentication within the HTTP request, using the authorization field in the request message. In this case, that field is not present in the initial message sent by the LOCAL, as reflected in frame 1, so HOMER returns an error to LOCAL, indicating that the page cannot be delivered without this information. Frames 2–4 represent HOMER's response to LOCAL, conveying error 401.2— Unauthorized. The message is spread across three packets, as the maximum transmittable unit (MTU) of the network in this example is 1,500 bytes. HOMER's response includes a nicely formatted error page, so it is quite long (more than 4,000 bytes).

After receiving these three packets, LOCAL knows that it must prompt the user for the user ID and password in order to give HOMER the information it needs and so displays a login dialog box similar to that of Figure 3-1. Once the user enters the user ID and password and clicks OK, the browser will *lightly* encode them, using a base64 encoding algorithm.[1] The browser then resends the request for the page to the Web server, HOMER, including the encoded user ID and password. Note the term *encoded,* which is not the same as *encrypted*. Frame 5 reflects the action of LOCAL in resending the request to the Web server, this time with the encoded user ID and password. The message data sent in frame 5 is as follows:

```
GET /secured/secure.html HTTP 1.1
    .
    .
    .
Authorization: BASIC aG10aGVyZTplbmNvZGVk
```

HOMER receives this request and validates the user ID and password that the user entered, by decoding the authorization string and attempting to perform a logon with the supplied credentials. In our example, the logon succeeds, and HOMER sends back the requested page, in frame 6. An important thing to note here is that the next time a page is requested from the "secured" directory on HOMER, the browser will automatically include the encoded user ID and password string within the request. This condition remains true until the browser is closed, at which point the encoded user ID and password string is discarded.

As illustrated in frame 5's message data, the authorization field is the encoded user ID and password. This field is in plaintext and, as we have seen, can be captured by a third party using a network monitor or any one of a number of other tools.

---

[1]Enfield, Paul, "Implementing a Secure Site with ASP, Microsoft Developer Network," October 24, 1997, at msdn.microsoft.com/library/backgrnd/html/msdn_implement.htm.

Once this plaintext is captured, the third party can either decode the user ID and password and attempt to use this information to log on to the system or replay the authorization string to retrieve pages from the server.

This potential situation highlights the primary security issue with HTTP basic authentication: plaintext transmission of user IDs and passwords across the Internet. To protect this information, the only real option is to use SSL or an equivalent secure protocol. Using basic authentication over an unsecured connection is extremely hazardous and allows a third party to possibly intercept the request and decode the user ID and password. Note that it is not sufficient to use SSL only during the initial logon when using HTTP Basic Authentication, since the Authorization string is retransmitted with each request. Therefore, it is necessary to encrypt the entire session with SSL in order to protect the user's credentials.

An SSL-encrypted session would render the captured packets unreadable by a third party. For example, if the same sequence of frames were exchanged over an SSL connection, frame 5 would look something like the following string of text:

```
϶◆EγK Z∇©≈≥⊂Zh&|¾ė Eo©H@ qĂ R"Px∃Y⊂}y'Q{‖.N∉Z:0%_?_
{V̄òâ&]RüP]yl/ô?@ė 9j{z2eě $∂̃N
```

If a third party captures that string of text, considerable time would be needed to decrypt the character string into something meaningful.

Custom Authentication Form

Some Web systems incorporate the use of a login interface by creating a customized form that is used to obtain a user ID and password from the user. Custom authentication forms are more attractive than the HTTP basic authentication dialog box, providing a professional look and a better end user experience (Figure 3-3). In this figure, the User ID field is a standard <INPUT TYPE="text"> HTML element, whereas the Password field is defined as <INPUT TYPE="password">, which instructs the browser to hide the password characters from the user as the user types in the password. To initiate the login process, the user clicks the Login button.

This approach does have quite a few security implications, however. Because authentication is not supported at the HTTP level with this approach, a standard HTML form on a Web page must be used to create the login page. From the browser and the server perspective, these authentication forms are handled just like any other form on a Web page. As with HTTP basic authentication, the password is not encrypted, so this method is typically combined with a secure HTTP connection in order to protect the password during transmission.

A server-side component, such as Active Server Pages (ASP) script, Component Object Model (COM) object, or Web server extension, needs to be created

Figure 3-3   Custom Authentication Form

to perform the authentication, which verifies the user ID and password through an external mechanism, such as the Web server or the operating system's API. In addition, Web server components must verify that the user has logged in prior to allowing access to any page in a secured area. Without this check, a user could simply bypass the logon form and directly request a page. In contrast, HTTP basic authentication performs this check automatically. Because of these additional requirements, custom authentication forms are more expensive to implement from a development perspective.

Figure 3-4 shows the message dialog captured by the network monitor, reflecting the communication between the client browser and the Web server following the user's clicking the Login button.

Frame Number	Source Host	Destination Host	Protocol	Description
1	LOCAL	HOMER	HTTP	POST Request (from client using port 4538)
2	HOMER	LOCAL	HTTP	Response (to client using port 4538)
3	HOMER	LOCAL	HTTP	Response (to client using port 4538)

Figure 3-4   Network Monitor Capture

Frame 1 represents the POST request being transmitted from LOCAL, the client computer, to HOMER, the Web server. Within the packet being sent, LOCAL provides the form values that the user provided for the user ID and password fields. The data of the packet transmitted in frame 1 is as follows:

```
POST /login.asp HTTP/1.1
Accept: image/gif, image/x-xbitmap, image/jpeg,
   image/pjpeg, application/vnd.ms-powerpoint,
   application/vnd.ms-excel, application/msword
Referer: http://Homer/
Accept-Language: en-us
Accept-Encoding: gzip, deflate
User-Agent: Mozilla/4.0 (compatible; MSIE 5.01;
   Windows NT 5.0)
Host: Homer
Content-Length: 44
Connection: Keep-Alive
userid=James&password=secretword
```

The last line in the packet contains the form field values. The user ID entered on the form is present as the text James, as well as the value for the password, in readable form, as the text secretword. This example clearly demonstrates the need for invoking secure HTTP (SSL). Recall that when this type of communication exchange occurs between a client computer and a Web server over a secure connection, the text of such a packet appears as a long string of strange characters.

It is not always possible to tell whether the login is being performed over a secure connection simply by looking for the lock icon on the status bar. A Web page can be received on the user's computer over a non-SSL connection that includes an HTML *form*. The *form* given to the user contains some fields for the user to enter and also provides a way for the user to *submit* the contents of the form back to the Web server. The form also contains an *action,* which specifies the URL that the browser should use to submit the form contents. The form action can specify a SSL connection, which in this case would *submit* the form data over an encrypted connection. Thus, the credentials will still be transmitted in a secure manner, even though the browser is not displaying a secure icon during user entry of the credentials.

Following acceptance of the form information by the Web server, it may then choose to redirect the user back to a non-SSL connection. This is usually done to avoid the server and network performance overhead involved with unnecessary encrypted communication. The use of SSL is expensive for the server in terms of bandwidth and central processing unit (CPU) usage, so it is beneficial to encrypt only the transmission of user credentials—the user ID and password. Specifying an encrypted connection for getting the credentials from the client to the server is all that is necessary in this case. Note, however, that encrypting just the credentials is not always the case. Web systems operated by most banks, brokerages, and similar businesses commonly use encryption on a full-time basis, as most of the data being passed back and forth is sensitive. As previously mentioned, sites making use of HTTP Basic Authentication should encrypt the entire session with SSL to protect the user's credentials.

Authorization

For a Web system, *authorization* means giving a user permission to access a resource, such as a Web page, on the Web server. Web sites generally contain a combination of public and private content, requiring the user to log in to view the private content. Once the user has successfully logged in to a secure area, the system allows the user to view pages and to invoke back-end scripts to perform various tasks. Once the user completes the login procedure, the security approach taken by the system will vary, depending on its access control requirements.

In general, the system can invoke two categories of access control:

- *Web server access:* Physical access to HTML pages, ASP scripts, and so on, on the Web server. The web server will restrict access to pages and scripts to authorized users.
- *Database access:* Access to read or write data stored in the site's database. This access may vary, depending on the data the user is attempting to read or change, and may not be constant for the user across the entire database.

In the Technology Bookstore case study, described in Appendix C, users are either *anonymous* or *authorized.* Anonymous users are Internet users browsing the item catalog. They are accessing public data that does not require any security checks. Authorized users are customers who wish to make a purchase or access customer service functionality. These users possess a user ID and password and can log on to the site and access the customer service pages to view a previous order or to make a purchase. All authorized users are considered equal; no users are designated as being more privileged than others.

It is good user interface (UI) practice to disable or hide functions that the user is not allowed to perform. This makes for a more pleasant user experience, as users are not shown "access denied" messages, the cause of which may not be immediately obvious. It is not prudent in a Web application, however, to rely on the absence of a UI button or control as a means of enforcing security. Users lacking a Delete button may nonetheless attempt to access the `delete` script by trying to identify the appropriate URL. One way to restrict access to the script on the server is to use the server's access control mechanism to restrict certain users from accessing it at all. Users who do not have the appropriate permissions to access the script will receive a message indicating that they are not authorized to view the page. Unfortunately, this is not always an appropriate solution, as those users may need to access the script based on the data they are working with at the time.

The TBS case study, for example, allows users to view their previous orders. Although it is acceptable for all authorized users to have access to execute the `ViewPreviousOrder` script, they cannot use it to view all the data accessible to these scripts. For example, a user is presented with the order list page, which contains hyperlinks for several orders the customer has placed. The user could modify the order numbers and attempt to view orders placed by someone else. To prevent this type of security violation, the script must verify that the data the user is attempting to access does in fact belong to that user. In the case of `ViewPreviousOrder`, that can be accomplished by associating the user's ID with the order records in the site's database.

Content Attacks

Most Web sites rely on dynamic pages—ASP, PHP, or JSP—CGI scripts or executables, and other forms of dynamic content delivery to provide a useful and interesting experience for the user. Unfortunately, these technologies are often the source of security holes.

These technologies are often used by Web sites to provide a mechanism for the user to send data to the Web server by submitting a form or clicking a link with variables in the URL. A component on the Web server will take these inputs and execute some useful business logic, such as retrieving a product page from a catalog or supplying bank account information for display back on the user's Web browser.

Depending on the technologies being used, a malicious user can manipulate these user-supplied inputs to cause the component to perform a function that it was not intended to perform. For example, an attacker could embed special characters in a form field—for example, "customer name" or "address"—in addition to a system command. When the form is submitted, the component, if susceptible to this kind of attack, will be tricked into executing the system command, as it was expecting a string containing the customer's name or address, not a special sequence of characters and a system command, to be placed into the field. In this way, an attacker could gain unauthorized access to the system by using a Web server component to invoke commands on the server.

System Command Execution

Many programming languages enable a developer to execute a *system command* from code. Perl, for example, provides several functions for this purpose, including `system()`, `exec()`, and back-tick (`` ` ``) quotes. The C/C++ language also supports this type of activity through the `popen()` and `system()` commands.

Program code containing these types of instructions is a convenient way to implement scripts that need to perform functions that are already provided by the operating system or by other scripts. As a simple example, a Perl script could use the `system()` function to place the current time, according to the Web server, into a page that is being sent to the client browser. More complicated scripts could use `system()` to invoke mail programs, complex UNIX commands, or other scripts and programs.

The security implications associated with the use of these types of commands within system code can be quite serious when a script uses a portion of the form variables to invoke a system call, particularly on a UNIX-based Web server. The exact reasons for the vulnerabilities are quite specific to the script language being used; here, we consider an example that applies to Perl scripts. The basic problem from a security perspective is the fact that the execution of a system command may often lead to the creation of a *subshell*—a child process containing a command processing environment—to carry out the system call. Consider the following line of Perl code:

```
system("echo $mail_message_text >> tmpfile");
```

At first glance, this code appears to be harmless, demonstrating a quick way to create a temporary file on the server disk containing the contents of a form field. When Perl sees this command, it will create a *child process* on the server and, on UNIX systems, will pass the command to the shell interpreter in the child process for processing. Because this command contains the text of a user form field, the shell interpreter in the child process must examine the contents of the field prior to processing the command. This is the source of the security problem.

On a UNIX system, the shell will look for certain characters, called *meta-characters,* in the string that it is processing, in order for the user to specify any additional shell operations. One such character is the *semicolon.* Placing this character in a shell string will cause the shell to break up the command into two commands, one on each side of the semicolon. So, in our previous example, the user could enter something like the following into the form field:

```
; cp /etc/passwd /home/ftp/pub; echo gotcha!
```

During execution of the system command, the Perl interpreter will pass the following string to the child process's shell interpreter for processing:

```
echo ; cp /etc/passwd /home/ftp/pub; echo gotcha! >>
   tmpfile
```

The shell interpreter will break the shell string into three separate commands, as follows, based on the location of the semicolon characters:

```
echo
cp /etc/passwd /home/ftp/pub
echo gotcha! >> tmpfile
```

The first echo won't do much; it will simply print a blank line for no reason. The next command does the real damage, copying the system password file to the public directory of the FTP server, where the attacker can then retrieve it in order to be able to perform dictionary or brute-force password cracking against it. The last command simply writes the text gotcha! to a temporary file. Granted, this exact sequence of events can be foiled by the most basic of security measures— shadow password files, running the Web server or CGIs as a nonroot user, properly securing the FTP public directory against writes—but with a little creativity, an attacker can probably find an opening with which to make full use of this kind of exploit.

It is important to avoid user input in file access–related system commands in Web system components. However, if it is absolutely necessary, it is critical to check the user input for shell metacharacters before passing the input to a system call. Alternatively, it may be easier to filter for *allowable* characters instead of dangerous characters, as the characters you wish to allow will probably vary by situation (Garfinkel and Spafford 1997). The reason is that it is time consuming and difficult to track user input through all possible paths. In addition, it is good practice to check all inputs first, prior to performing any other component logic. Doing so protects against future changes and unforeseen use of user-supplied input from opening up future security holes.

The following characters should be considered dangerous and filtered out of all inputs, preferably by rejecting inputs that contain any of them:

```
&;`'\"|*?~<>^()[]{}$ \n \r
```

In addition, most form field values should not allow the user to specify file path operations, so the following character sequence should be checked as well:

```
/..
```

When using system commands in program scripts, it is worthwhile to bypass the creation of a subshell in the child process, when supported by the language. For example, the Perl `system` command supports this capability by allowing arguments to be passed as individual parameters to the system call, as follows:

```
system(echo, "string1", "string2");
```

It is also important to remember that system or third-party-supplied executables may contain flaws that may be exploitable by potential attackers. An attacker who learns that the script is invoking a potentially unsafe system executable may be able to exploit the flaws in that executable through user input (Kamthan 1999). Finally, it should be readily apparent that storing arguments to system commands or entire system command lines in hidden form fields (`<INPUT TYPE="hidden">`) should be avoided entirely, for the same reasons that the use of form input in system commands should be avoided.

Server-Side File Access

Server-side components often need to access files on the Web server in order to perform a task or to assist in creating a Web page for the user. This kind of file access can be initiated from just about any kind of Web system component, including ASP, Perl- or C/C++-based CGI executables, and so on. For example, a script that provides a simple Web voting or poll interface may store the votes in a text file on the server and embed the name of this file in the Web page sent to the user, most likely as a hidden form field in the voting form. This form field is sent to the server when the user votes, and the script accepts the user input and then updates the file with the new vote. This type of interaction is illustrated in Figure 3-5.

Figure 3-6 shows how an attacker could simply save the page source to a local disk and modify the name of the file to point elsewhere on the server, perhaps to an important system configuration file or the password file, and then reload the page and submit the form. Depending on how the script is implemented, this action

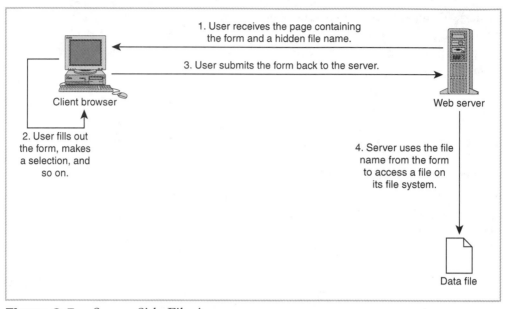

Figure 3-5   Server-Side File Access

could damage the file's contents or possibly even display the file's contents to the attacker. Such file name vulnerabilities are a very serious security concern.

A slight variation of this kind of security problem pertains to the use of a hidden form field as a *component* of a file name. In the voting example, instead of placing the entire file name and path into the hidden form field, the name of the topic is stored in the hidden form field. This topic name is then concatenated onto the prefix of the file name, such as `votes_`, in order to be able to locate the correct file for this topic. In this case, the attacker could attempt to place a series of `../` character sequences onto the end of the topic name and attempt to navigate to another part of the file system on the server. This second type of exploit would be caught through the implementation of a proper user input filter, however, as discussed in the previous section. Because of the danger that this type of file access can impose, the best approach is to avoid storing file names and paths in hidden form fields or browser cookies. When storage of file names and paths is necessary, storing a file name suffix in the variable and filtering the input for file path characters as described is a much safer approach.

Buffer Overflows

One common security hole exploited on Web systems is the *buffer overflow*, used mostly against compiled executables, particularly operating system tools and

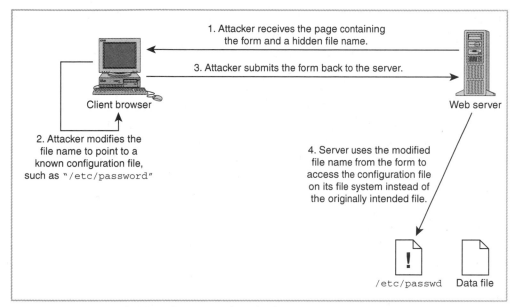

Figure 3-6 Exploiting Server-Side File Access

utilities. A buffer overflow occurs when the length of a program or a function input exceeds the space allocated to store it. C/C++ programs are particularly vulnerable to this kind of attack, as developers often declare variables that reside on the program's *stack*. For example, consider the following C/C++ code:

```
void createFullName(char* firstName, char* lastName)
{
    char fullName[1024];

    strcpy(fullName, firstName);
    strcat(fullName, " ");
    strcat(fullName, lastName);
}
```

This C++ code simply takes the supplied first and last names and puts them together, separated by a space. Of particular importance is the fullName variable. The way it is declared causes it to reside on the stack. The problem is that this variable can easily exceed 1,024 characters whenever firstName or lastName or both values are too long.

In most cases, this situation will simply cause a program crash as the stack is corrupted by the strcpy or strcat function calls. However, if these arguments are carefully crafted, they can in fact be used to send malicious code to the program, embedded in the first- and last-name arguments. If the arguments manage to overflow the `fullName` stack variable, they can cause the execution of this code by manipulating the `return address`, which also resides on the stack.

The `return address` is a hidden piece of data that resides on the stack with the rest of the variables passed to a function. Depending on the specific language, compiled programs place this data on the stack prior to calling the function. That way, the program knows where to go when the function is finished.

By overflowing one of the variables on the stack, a malicious input can overwrite the return address, as it exists on the stack as well. In the example of `createFullName`, by overflowing the `firstName` or `lastName` inputs with precisely the correct number of characters, the return address can be overwritten and made to point back to a specific place in the data that was supplied in the `firstName` or `lastName` inputs. With a little creativity, this data can be executable program code, with malicious intent. Because the return address is simply a pointer to code, the return address is pulled off the stack when the function completes and is used as the place to start executing the next sequence of instructions.[2] Unfortunately, the next sequence of instructions is code written by the attacker and will be blindly executed by the server.

Once the malicious program argument has been submitted and the input buffer has been successfully overflowed, the attacker effectively has his or her own code executing on the site's Web server machine. Depending on the buffer size, a lot of bad things can happen. The code could read the contents of the password file, e-mail the file, make changes to configuration files, start up a TELNET session, or even connect to another Web server and download a larger, more damaging program, such as a Trojan horse.

Preventing buffer overflows consists mainly of checking the length of user-supplied input variables. In the previous example, limiting the size of the `firstName` and the `lastName` inputs to 511 bytes would protect against overflows (511*2 = 1,022, plus one for the space and one for the terminating "null" totals 1,024). In addition, using the `strncpy` and the `strncat` functions instead of `strcpy` and `strcat` is also advised, as the former two functions limit the number of characters copied into the buffer. Keep in mind that it is not realistic to restrict the input on the Web page or form, as a malicious user could simply alter the page on his or her local disk and remove the length restrictions on the form fields or simply access the

---

[2]Note that this only applies to hardware platforms on which the stack is executable, such as Intel x86 platforms. Some platforms, such as Sun SPARC, allow stack execution to be disabled, which can be used to defeat buffer overflow attacks. Unfortunately, Intel x86 platforms currently do not support the disabling of stack execution.

URL of the form action directly, without using the form itself. The only sure way to prevent buffer overflows is to examine and to reject excessively long inputs in all Web system components.

Again, the most common source of buffer overflows is C/C++ code, particularly when string manipulation is involved. Scripting languages, such as Perl, and Java code are less of a risk, as they use dynamic memory management to allocate space for variables. This does not mean that input lengths should be ignored when using scripting languages or Java. It is still possible that these variables could be passed to other programs that are susceptible to buffer overflows.

Sometimes, variables are simply "passed through" a program. For example, a Perl script could be created that takes a form input, such as a customer name, and simply hands it off to another program, possibly one written in C++ or one that came with the operating system that was probably also written in C or C++. The second program in the chain may be susceptible to buffer overflows, so the attacker could still cause damage. It just wouldn't affect the Perl script, as it is passing it through. Therefore, it's important to always check input lengths regardless of language, function, and so on.

3.3 Database Server

The storage of data and user-specific information by the Web system requires that safeguards be in place to protect this information. Database servers, although typically not directly visible to a client computer, must be secured as if the Web server has been compromised. Securing the site's database is not limited to the database host itself; any Web system components or other data retrieval mechanisms that operate on the data residing in the database must be properly designed and implemented to protect against database content attacks.

As discussed earlier in the chapter, all servers on the site's network must be properly secured from the operating system and commercial software perspectives. Any server can possibly be used to gain an administrative foothold on the network. This, of course, applies to the database server as well. User accounts, file systems, and server software running on the database server must be properly configured to prevent unauthorized access by an intruder. This section assumes that the computer on which the database is running—either standalone or colocated with the Web server—has been properly secured from the perspective of user accounts, file systems, and server software.

This section focuses on the following aspects of securing the site's database:

- *Database overview.* Some of the more common ways that databases are implemented for Web systems are described.

- *Security of content stored in the database.* Properly securing sensitive data stored in an Internet-accessible database is possibly the most important security concern for a Web system. As suggested throughout this chapter, one must assume that the servers supporting a Web system will be compromised. Depending on the knowledge level of the attacker, this compromise very possibly could include unauthorized access to data in the site's database. Another consideration is the temporary storage of private user data during processing, either before or after it is stored in the database, in plaintext files on a server's file system (Sullivan 2000).
- *Database access from the Web server.* Web system components typically provide access to data stored in the Web site's database. With this access mechanism comes additional security concerns over the handling of database schema and connection information (Rahmel 1997).

Database Overview

In general, a database that supports a Web application can have three configurations:

- A file-based database usually residing on the Web server machine. The Web system components use an API, such as Active Data Objects (ADO), to access the file directly. The file must be secured like any other in the file system, to prevent it from being downloaded, accessed, or manipulated by an intruder. Examples of this kind of database are Microsoft Access on Windows platforms and mySQL on UNIX platforms.
- A mainstream relational database management system (RDBMS) such as Microsoft SQL Server or Oracle colocated with the Web server, meaning that it is on the same machine.
- A mainstream RDBMS running on its own server and accessed over a network by the Web server machine. The addition of a second firewall between the Web server machine and the database machine make this the most secure configuration and is the most common one for large Web applications.

One of these general configurations will be selected and implemented for a Web system, based on defined system requirements and the available development budget. Although these three approaches are quite different from a deployment standpoint, they have several similar aspects that must be considered for proper security administration of the database and access to the data it contains.

Many Web systems will be set up to access the database as a single, privileged user, as it is generally easier to configure. It is easier to set up all the Web system components to connect to the database as the same user—with the same ID and password—rather than have several different users and maintain the ID and password in many different scripts.

Additionally, accessing the database as a single user can offer better performance on Microsoft Windows NT/2000 systems, because of connection pooling, which allows the operating system to keep database connections open even though they are not currently in use, by placing them into a "pool" of open, ready-to-use connections. As a result, the next time the program requires a connection, one is instantly provided from the pool, without the normal start-up overhead. This is worthwhile, as creating and opening the connection to the database can be expensive in terms of performance.

Security in this case is enforced at the Web server component level rather than at the database level. For example, a component will first make sure that the user who connected to the Web server has the appropriate level of access to perform a particular operation. After it is determined that the user is authorized to perform the action, the component will then access the database as a highly privileged user. If the component didn't perform this check, lower-level users could execute database operations outside their level of access. A single database user is also a bit more secure from the database perspective, as fewer users are defined in the database itself, which can be a potential source for intrusions.

Database Content

Data Privacy

Maintaining the confidentiality of Web system data must be a top priority, particularly for e-commerce systems. When customers make a purchase from an e-commerce site, they are placing a significant amount of trust in the Web system to safeguard their personal data and to ensure that this personal information will not be further distributed to external parties that could cause them harm, financially or otherwise. To this end, when dealing with sensitive user information, such as names, addresses, telephone numbers, and credit card numbers, the Web system's primary concern should be the privacy of the end user.

However, merchants are usually obligated to retain certain information after a payment transaction has been processed, for a period of time known as the dispute period. Because a customer may dispute a credit card charge for various reasons, including fraud, the merchant must be able to audit the transaction back to the payment information used during the transaction. Keep in mind that this type of payment transaction history is quite different from the storage of personal user data used to increase the user's experience of the Web site. Payment transaction history data is used for internal purposes by the merchant and should not be readily accessible by any means to an end user. In fact, it is recommended that transaction history information be stored in encrypted form in a separate, write-only database.

A Web site can facilitate the secure storage of payment transaction history data by creating a separate database, possibly on a separate server, for this purpose. The following steps demonstrate the configuration of a transaction history database on Microsoft SQL Server.

1. Create a new database on the desired machine.

2. Create a database user account that will be used by the components that need to store payment transaction history information, such as `PaymentHistoryUser`.

3. Create a table (or tables if necessary) that will store the necessary pieces of information for the transaction history.

4. Remove all permissions on this table from all database users and roles; in other words, do not allow select, insert, update, delete, or any other operations on this table to any users of the database, including `PaymentHistoryUser`.

5. Create a stored procedure to insert the customer and payment information into the transaction history table. This stored procedure will be able to access the table even though the `PaymentHistoryUser` cannot directly access the table itself.

6. Grant execute access on the stored procedure to the `PaymentHistoryUser` account.

7. In the components that need to store transaction history information, invoke the stored procedure to insert the data into the table.

8. As an added security measure, encrypt all information, as discussed in the next section, prior to passing it to the stored procedure.

The architecture depicted in Figure 3-7 ensures that the database containing the sensitive payment transaction history data will remain isolated from the rest of the Web site's data and will be less susceptible to attack, owing to the write-only nature of the database.

Data Encryption

The safest way to avoid problems with unauthorized access to site data is to encrypt the data while it is stored in the database. When it must be accessed for processing, the data is read from the database and then decrypted in memory. Web system components can make use of certain operating system functions to encrypt important data prior to performing insertions or updates to the database.

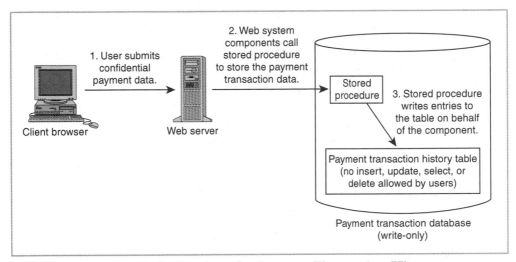

Figure 3-7   Write-Only Database for Payment Transaction History

Encryption of the data ensures that whenever an attacker finds a way to access the system database or, in the case of a file-based database, simply downloads it, the data will be unreadable.

For example, consider a customer service facility that allows customers to view their account information, including full names, addresses, and phone numbers. This sensitive information is encrypted and stored in a database table. When the system invokes a component to view user information, the component reads the encrypted data from the database, decrypts the data in memory, and forwards the data to the client computer over a secured HTTP (SSL) connection. In this way, the data cannot be viewed by hacking into the database—owing to the encryption on the stored data—or intercepted by a third party during transmission—owing to the secured connection.[3]

Encrypting/decrypting information on the fly can be performed with certain APIs available on most operating systems and through the use of some scripting languages:

- CryptAPI, available from Microsoft: a set of Win32-style API calls
- The `crypt` function available on most UNIX systems
- `::Crypt` modules for Perl scripts

---

[3]Note that, in this scenario, the data will exist in an unencrypted state for some period of time in the component's memory space. Although the risk here is usually low, if maximum security is required, a more complex architecture will need to be developed.

These APIs require the use of an encryption key, which is used as the basis for encrypting the data. Deciding where to store the key, however, is a somewhat complicated issue. If an intruder manages to get the encryption key, the data in the database will then be compromised. For some Web systems, storing the key in a compiled, binary component is enough, relying on the fact that the key is somewhat hidden since it is not easily viewable. However, the reality is that a knowledgeable intruder will probably be able to extract the key from a binary component, thus rendering this approach useless. Unfortunately, there is no absolute solution to this problem, only somewhat stronger alternatives:

- Store the key in a file and rely on operating system security to protect the contents of the file, meaning, only give read permission on this file to the user identity that the Web system server components execute under. If the server is properly secured, this file should not be accessible by other users—including intruders—with access to the server's file system.
- Create a binary component that programmatically creates the encryption key, rather than storing it as a string in source code. This will make it impossible for the encryption key to be discovered by simply dumping the strings from the binary component.

Temporary and Log Files

Encrypting the data stored in the database is a critical step in securing private user data. However, Web system components accessing this data may inadvertently place the unencrypted form of this data into a temporary file or a log file on the Web server's disk. This can happen either before the data is encrypted and stored in the database or after the data is retrieved from the database and decrypted. The latter case may not occur until long after the user has departed, such as in after-hours batch processing or reports. Because the temporary and log files are often stored in obscure directories, they can remain unnoticed from a security perspective. If the directories containing temporary and log files are not tightly controlled and maintained, an unauthorized user may gain access to them. Log file entries should not include sensitive data. Because some third-party applications may also log data, it is important to inspect all third-party software logging functionality to ensure that sensitive data is not logged.

In most cases, it is better to avoid the use of temporary files in a Web system. From a security perspective, it is not sufficient to assume that Web system components will remove temporary files after they are finished using them. A Web system component may crash, either inadvertently or maliciously when manipulated by an attacker, leaving the temporary file "orphaned" on the server's file system. Another possibility is that the temporary file may be accessed by an attacker at the same time that it is being used by the Web system component: a *race condition*. Because of these problems, avoid the use of temporary files from Web system components. When the use of a temporary file cannot be avoided, make sure that sensitive data placed in a temporary file is encrypted. If the encryption of the data in the temporary file is not possible, consider an alternative approach to processing the data that does not involve the use of temporary files.

Access to Database Objects

As described earlier, many Web systems make use of a *single log-on* technique for accessing data stored in the database. The reasons for using a single log-on technique are *ease of administration*—no need to add accounts for each user—*better performance*—connections can be reused—and *simplicity*—less work to determine which credentials to use. Web systems that use a single log-on technique typically enforce access control at the "boundaries" of the system, meaning that the Web system components verify that the user has permission to access the specified content.

Although the system's components are performing access checks prior to accessing the database, it should not be assumed that the data in the database can be left wide open, accessible to any database user. Access to tables, views, and other database objects should be granted only to the privileged Web access account(s) and should not be viewable to other database users, when they exist.

Database Access

Web system components access the database through an API such as ODBC (Open Database Connectivity), JDBC (Java Database Connectivity), or ADO. In order to interact with the database through such APIs, the back-end components must be able to connect to the database as users and to construct queries against tables and other objects in the database. Two security concerns arise from this situation.

Database User ID and Password

Web system components need to be able to connect to the database and typically have a predetermined user ID and password *hard coded* in their source code or possibly even in a configuration file. This is largely because of the widespread use of the single database user approach, as outlined earlier. It is important to secure the user ID and password information so that it cannot be retrieved by an intruder and then used to access the database.

Note that the discussion presented applies only to architectures that store a text user ID and password for connecting to the database from the Web system components. Some architectures, such as one that makes use of Microsoft's IIS and

SQL Server, can use an *integrated security* technique, whereby the database connection information is not stored in the component but instead is taken from the identity of the Web server process or the user connecting to the Web server.

In nonintegrated security Web architectures, the user ID and password data can be stored for later use in several ways. The login data may be placed directly into the script or component source code and used when needed.

Alternatively, components may store the password outside of the executable files or scripts, within a configuration file or within the registry on Windows NT/2000 machines. Because components need the database user ID and password in order to establish connection with the database, the storage of this information for ready access by a component is a necessity. Care must be taken, however, to store the data for back-end components and, through encryption, still make it difficult for an intruder to access the login data, if an intruder is able to gain access to the system.

One approach is to store the user ID and password outside the component source code through the use of a configuration file, and rely on operating system security on the file to keep the information safe. If the configuration file is compromised, however, the user ID and password information are easily viewable.

Another approach is to store the user ID and a password in component source code, in a configuration file, in the registry, in an encrypted form. For a further discussion on encryption techniques, refer to the "Data Encryption" section earlier in this chapter.

Database Schema Information

In order to access data from the system database, Web system components will need to possess knowledge of the database schema: database, table and column names, data types, and so on. Schema information is used to build queries against the database, such as retrieving and updating records.

At times, it may seem beneficial for the Web system to store database schema information or even entire queries within hidden form fields on a Web page or in cookies, which are sent back to the server automatically when the user submits a form or accesses a different Web page. This practice, however, may expose the system's database to intrusion, allowing an attacker to learn the structure of the database and possibly to modify the database query to be able to operate against a different part of the database. Therefore, all database schema–related information must remain private to Web system components and should not be sent to the client browser.

A related issue is the storage of schema information or queries within HTML comments. Sometimes, this type of storage is used to support debugging and tracing, but doing so in a production environment needlessly exposes the system's database schema to unauthorized users.

3.4 Client Computer

Today's browsers provide many capabilities that enrich the user experience. Client-side scripting, ActiveX controls, Java applets, and plug-ins provide a level of interactivity that most users now expect to see when they connect to a Web site. In addition, the use of cookies provides a convenient way to maintain a user session by storing some pieces of information on the user's computer. All these technologies come together to enable the creation of the kind of complex user interface and Web system design that most prominent Web sites will want to incorporate.

In recent years, a number of security flaws have been uncovered with many client-side technologies. Even though client-side scripts and Java applets are supposed to offer a high degree of security, flaws in many Web browsers can be exploited by malicious scripts or applets to work around the security of the browser and to access private files on the unsuspecting user's hard disk. As these flaws are identified, Web browser vendors have generally been quick to fix the problem and to distribute a patch.

Although browser vendors must resolve most of the client-side security problems in their browser products, some technologies, such as ActiveX controls and cookies, can be inadvertently used by a site to open up potential security problems on a visiting Web user's computer. This section focuses on ensuring that computers and private data of Web users visiting a site are not made vulnerable to intrusion by attackers through the use of ActiveX controls and cookies distributed by the site.

ActiveX Controls

As one of the more powerful forms of client-side content, ActiveX controls carry significant security implications. Unlike Java applets, ActiveX controls have no safety net. With the use of ActiveX controls, any operating system API call, disk file, or network connection can be used by the control. ActiveX controls can be written in many languages, such as C++, Visual Basic, and Visual J++, and they operate just like any other application installed on the user's computer. The user trusts the content of the control to its author with regard to the potential for the control to do damage.

Microsoft has designed its Authenticode technology to be able to sign controls with the author's identity and to verify that the control has not been modified. Although this does offer some level of security, it does not prevent controls from being tricked into behaving in ways other than those originally intended. In addition, the use of ActiveX controls by a browser are not restricted to any particular site. For example, a control developed for Web site A may be used by Web site B. Web site B can stipulate that users to its site will obtain an ActiveX control from site A, together with defined parameters that are provided from site B. Therefore, when a Web site uses an ActiveX control, any other site that the user may visit can attempt to create this control on the user's machine and to interact with it. Note that depending on the security level set by the user, the browser may or may not prompt or alert the user that the site is attempting to use an ActiveX control, although it probably will display the certificate if the control is being used for the first time. Even with prompts and alerts, the user will probably not be entirely aware of what is happening.

This type of flexibility opens up the possibility that the well-intentioned Web site could provide the means for malicious operators of other sites to exploit a user's machine. Figure 3-8 shows how this could occur.

A browser can use an ActiveX control in two primary ways.

- *OBJECT tag.* This is the most common way that ActiveX controls are embedded into a Web page. This tag contains several pieces of information about the control, including the location where the browser can go to retrieve the ActiveX control. In addition, the OBJECT tag can contain one or more PARAM tags, which are used to provide the Web page with the parameter values necessary to initialize the control.
- *Scripts.* Client-side scripts can also manipulate the control, calling functions, referred to as *methods,* to perform tasks and accessing properties to set and to retrieve data inside the control.

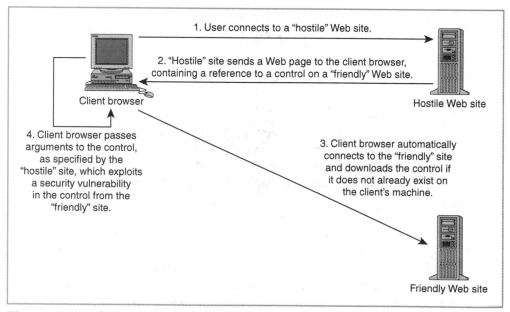

Figure 3-8   ActiveX Control Manipulation

Both of these access methods allow information to be passed to or retrieved from the control. For example, a customer service control could be initialized with the user's name and customer number through the OBJECT tag and then queried for those properties later through JScript on the Web page. The ActiveX control can do whatever it likes with this data, such as storing it in memory, placing the value within the registry, or even saving the data to a disk file. Because any site can make use of the control, any site can call methods and access properties of the control. This also opens up the possibility that another site, operated by an attacker, will manipulate the properties of the control through its inputs.

As documented in the section Content Attacks, inputs to a program can be used to take control of a target machine through the creation of a buffer overflow condition. ActiveX controls, if written in a susceptible language, can also be the target of buffer overflow attacks. In addition, when the control's inputs provide for the specification of a file name or a registry key, this information could be used by a malicious Web site operator to access files or areas of the system registry through client-side HTML and scripting. Consider the following vulnerabilities and privacy violations for any of the site's ActiveX controls.

- *Buffer overflows:* The length of any user input data should be restricted to avoid possible buffer overflow conditions, as buffer overflows can be used to execute malicious code on the client computer. See the section Buffer Overflows for more information.
- *File access:* Controls should not be written to accept file names as parameter values within OBJECT tags or function parameters. The file name parameter could be abused by a malicious Web site operator and changed to point to a system or other private file on the user's computer.
- *Storing private information:* Using an ActiveX control in order to store private user information on the client's computer may seem harmless but can potentially expose user information to an intruder, especially when the control provides a means to retrieve that data. As any site can access the control and call its methods, other sites may be able to retrieve the data without the user's knowledge. In addition, if the data is stored in an unencrypted form, intruders who manage to gain access to the client's computer through other means may locate the information by browsing disk files or the registry.

Cookies

Web systems can store small pieces of data on the client computer through *cookies.* Cookies, supported by most mainstream browsers, are stored in one or more files on the client computer's hard disk. After a Web system forwards the cookie for placement on the user's computer, the cookie value is automatically forwarded back to the Web server in an HTTP message header each time the client computer requests a page from the particular Web site. A typical example of cookie usage is the *shopping cart,* whereby the item IDs and quantities are stored in a cookie on the user's machine.

Cookies are stored in plaintext files on the user's computer. This means that anyone who has access, authorized or not, to the files on the user's computer can read their contents. This is a problem when a Web server is saving data on the user's computer as a *cookie* and it contains sensitive information, such as the user's credit card information. An intruder who manages to gain access to a user's file system through a browser flaw, insecure ActiveX or Java control, or a Trojan horse, may be able to access cookie information without the knowledge of the user.

If it is necessary for the Web system to store sensitive information in a cookie on the user's local machine, the data placed in the cookie should be encrypted, using the techniques described in the section Data Encryption. Any Web system components that wish to store sensitive data in a cookie will encrypt it prior to issuing the `set cookie` command. Later, when it needs to use the cookie information, a component must first decrypt the data.

3.5 Secure Communications

One of the major advancements supporting the proliferation of e-commerce pertains to the creation of secure communication protocols, such as the Secure Sockets Layer (SSL). These protocols have given Web users greater confidence that their transactions across the Internet will not be intercepted by a third party eavesdropping on the connection between the user and the Web system.

SSL enables two parties to communicate in an encrypted form over a network. Establishing a secure communications session between a browser client and a Web server entails several steps.

1. A well-known certificate authority must grant the Web server a valid certificate. The certificate stores information about the host, including its public key (Powell, Braginski, 1998, p. 332). A *public key* consists of a large number that can be used to encrypt a message that can then be decrypted only with the corresponding *private key.* The reverse is also possible; a message encrypted with the private key can be decrypted only by using the public key. On the Internet, private keys are closely guarded by their owners, whereas public keys are available to anyone. A private key owner is any individual user or a Web server having an assigned certificate.

This type of encryption is usually referred to as *asymmetric encryption,* as two keys are used in the encryption/decryption process.

2. The client computer must be configured with the public key of the certificate authority (CA) that issued the server's certificate. This is necessary to verify that the certificate from the host is valid and belongs to the host in question. Several independent commercial companies, such as Verisign, are certificate authorities. The client uses the public key of the CA to verify the authenticity of the server's certificate.

3. The client computer challenges the host to encrypt a random piece of data with the private key—known only by the host—and the client must be able to successfully decrypt it with the public key. If the client is not able to do so, the session is aborted, as the client is not able to successfully authenticate the server.

4. If it has successfully authenticated the server, the client computer must generate a session key that will be used for all communications for the remainder of the session. The session key is encrypted with the server's public key so it cannot be read by anyone else and is sent to the server. (Prowell, Braginski, 1998, p. 329.) The session key is used because it is faster than public/private key cryptography. Session key encryption is also called *symmetric encryption,* as only one key is used for the encryption/decryption process.

Once these steps have been followed, the client computer and the Web server communicate by using the session key for the remainder of their conversation. This complicated exchange of certificates and keys is necessary in order to verify the identity of the Web server and to transfer the session key from the client to the server. Then the two parties can communicate using symmetric encryption, without a third party being able to decrypt the conversation; the third party does not know and cannot acquire the session key.

Most e-commerce Web systems allow users to browse products on the Web site without the use of an encrypted channel, as the information being exchanged is intended to be available to the general public. When it comes time for the user to make a purchase, however, the client computer connects to a special port on the Web server, known as the secure HTTP, or SSL, port. As soon as this connection is made, the client and the server engage in the initial *handshake,* outlined in the preceding steps, in order to verify the server's identity and to exchange the session key. At this point, the user can enter sensitive information, such as a credit card number, and be confident that the information cannot be read by a third party.

3.6 Network Security

Most Web systems use routers and firewalls, hereafter referred to as simply firewalls, in order to restrict access to the computers that support the Web system. Firewalls are capable of preventing incoming connections and packets from reaching certain hosts or parts of hosts located on the Web system's local network. Typically, a Web system restricts outside access to all ports except for port 80, which is the main HTTP port. When using secure HTTP, the site also allows connections to a secure port, usually 443.

The main reason for implementing a firewall is to prevent unwanted connections to services or computers residing on the Web site's local network. Some computers run services, such as FTP, for which access is not acceptable for the general public through the Internet. Such services are often the source of break-ins or other exploits that can ultimately compromise the security of the site. It is also desirable to prevent users from being able to see certain computers, such as database servers, from outside the firewall. Certain types of servers should be accessible only by the site's Web servers, not by external users.

Port scanning is the process of attempting to connect to many or all Transmission Control Protocol/Internet Protocol (TCP/IP) or User Datagram Protocol/Internet Protocol (UDP/IP) ports on a wide range of servers on the Internet. An attacker runs the scanner over a period of time and reviews the resulting list of open ports found on each computer. Often, the response from the computer indicates the service type running on that port and possibly also the version. Thus, port scanning gives the attacker a catalog of potential entry points. If the Web site is relatively well known, the attacker may simply try several common service ports, such as HTTP (web server), FTP (file transfer server), DNS (name lookup service), LPD (printing service), SMTP (electronic mail), or NNTP (Internet news), in an attempt to locate a vulnerable service. This manual method of attack requires only the knowledge of which ports to examine, and this is generally common knowledge for network intruders. Many utilities are available for port scanning a target host, and these utilities can be used by site administrators to determine whether the site's firewall or servers have vulnerabilities. Many of these tools are also used by potential attackers against the Web site.

As port scanning finds network services on the machine, they should be located in the process list of the server and removed from the server's configuration files. For some services, the port scanner will not know the type of service that is listening on the port, making it difficult to locate the responsible process. On a UNIX system, it is possible to associate a port with a process by using the `lsof` command. For example, on some UNIX systems, the following command lists the process(es) associated with port 21:

```
lsof -P | grep :21
```

In some cases, the port scanner may detect a service listening on the server, but the service cannot be located in the process list or by using the `lsof` command. If this occurs, it may be necessary to manually connect to the service from another machine prior to examining the process list or using the `lsof` command, as some services are started on demand. This can be accomplished on most platforms by using the `telnet` command and supplying an alternative port number.

3.7 Verifying Site Security

This section discusses strategies for verifying the security of a Web system, providing step-by-step procedures for testing the areas discussed previously.

Authentication

Security verification of the Web system's authentication mechanism concentrates on the packet-level security of the login data: user ID and password. This evaluation is accomplished by using a packet sniffer tool, such as the Windows NT/2000 Network Monitor. The strategy presented here will help determine whether the user ID and password information is being transmitted in a secure fashion to the server across the Internet.

1. Acquire the ports used to access the site by both HTTP and HTTPS (SSL) connections. Typically, port 80 is used for HTTP, and port 443 is used for HTTPS. This example will use these two ports.

2. Connect to the site and navigate to the basic authentication dialog or the custom authentication form.

3. Start the network monitoring tool. At this point, it may be useful to filter out some of the network traffic to minimize the amount of captured messages. With the Windows NT/2000 Network Monitor, this is accomplished by selecting Filter . . . from the Capture menu, then double-clicking the SAP/ETYPE list entry. Click the Disable All button, select the IP – ETYPE protocol entry from the list, and click Enable.

4. Switch back to the browser and enter the user ID and password of a valid test user in the basic authentication dialog box or the custom authentication form. Do not submit the data yet; simply enter the data into the fields.

5. Switch to the network monitor tool and start capturing network packets. With the NT/2000 Network Monitor, this is accomplished by selecting Start from the Capture menu or by pressing F10.

6. Switch back to the browser and click the OK button on the login dialog, or submit the custom form and wait for the next page to load.

7. Stop the capture in the network monitoring tool once the next page is received.

8. View the captured data by selecting Display Captured Data from the Capture menu or by pressing F12.

First, locate the initial entry from the client to the server, which is the entry that should contain the user ID and password. This entry should resemble the following:

```
Source:       Name or address of the machine running the
              browser
Destination:  Name or address of the Web server host
Protocol:     HTTP, HTTPS or TCP
Dest. Port:   80 (HTTP) or 443 (HTTPS)
```

If this entry is HTTP on port 80, the data in the packet should contain either the Authorization entry for Basic Authentication or the POST command with the form variables containing the user ID and password for the custom authentication form. If the data in the packet contains this information in plaintext, readable form, a security flaw exists.

If this entry is HTTPS or TCP on port 443, the packet data should be encrypted and therefore unreadable. Either of these packets should be followed by responses from the server to the client over HTTP, HTTPS, or TCP.

Authorization

Two separate kinds of tests are required to evaluate the correctness of the Web server authorization process. One test focuses on page/script accessibility and the other on data accessibility.

Page/Script Accessibility

For this test, first obtain a list of the pages and server-side components, including paths and required parameters, that are available to the Web system's various user roles. This list will vary, depending on the type of site that is being tested. If the engineering techniques presented in Chapter 2 were followed, this list will closely resemble the list of «interface» use cases. For TBS, a subset of the list of scripts looks like this.

Script	Parameters	Role
`/asp/BrowseByCategory.asp`	`None`	`All (including anonymous users - no login required)`
`/asp/ViewPreviousOrder.asp`	`id=<order ID>`	`TBS Registered Users`

In addition, obtain a valid user account for each role. Once these two items have been obtained, test for page/script accessibility by attempting to access each script in the list by directly accessing the script. Do not log in to the site. For example, to test the I-Browse Catalog by Keyword functionality of the TBS case study, the following URL would be entered into the *address* box of the browser:

`http://Homer/asp/BrowseByCategory.asp`

This script is available to all users, so it should execute properly. If the script requires a parameter, you may need to obtain some additional information for the parameter. For example, the View Previous Order functionality requires an `OrderID`, so a valid ID would need to be obtained from the database. The URL for `ViewPreviousOrder.asp` would look like this:

`http://Homer/asp/ViewPreviousOrder.asp?id=938193`.

This script should fail to execute, as we have not logged in yet. If it does execute, a security flaw exists.

Data Accessibility

Even though the user is limited to the appropriate scripts, it may be necessary to restrict the data the user can view. For example, in the TBS case study, the user should not be able to view orders for other customers. For this part of the test process, you will need to obtain multiple valid users who have the same level of access but are allowed to view different data. You will also need the list of scripts and their parameters from the preceding part of the test strategy. You can safely remove from the list any scripts that do not retrieve data associated with a specific user, such as `BrowseByCategory.asp`, which retrieves the same data regardless of the user.

1. Log in with one of the user accounts and access one of the listed scripts. Make note of the data provided to the script used for retrieving the user's information. For example, the `ViewPreviousOrder.asp` script will require an `OrderID` to use as a basis for retrieving the order status.

2. Log in with one of the other user accounts, one that has the same level of access as in step 1, and attempt to access the script with the data used by

the first user (`OrderID`). This should generate an error message denying access. If it is possible to log in with a different user account and to view the data belonging to the user from step 1, a security flaw may exist, as the system is displaying a user's private data to another user.

Content Attacks

To properly test most of the system security scenarios presented here, the Web system component must return a predictable error page if a problem is discovered with an input field. For example, if it detects that an input is too long or contains special characters, a component should display or redirect the browser to a predictable error page, such as "input error detected." This will be the indicator for the test to determine whether the script has effectively managed the input error. If the script does not detect a problem with an input field but still encounters an error, the Web server's standard internal error page should be returned. This will allow input-field error checking to be differentiated from other kinds of component errors.

Some of the strategies presented here may require manual editing of HTML pages. In other words, the page is saved to the local disk from the browser and then edited with a text editor and re-sent to the Web server.

System Command Execution

Testing for vulnerabilities in components that use system commands is somewhat dependent on the languages being used and the operating system on which the server is running. It is recommended, however, the Web system restrict all user input to support only acceptable characters, regardless of the back-end technology and operating system being used. This area of testing requires the Web server component to actively check for metacharacters in all its inputs. "Actively checking" means that the component examines all input data fed to it when the component is invoked. When it detects one of these characters, the component must return a predetermined error page, which will be the basis of the success or failure of the test.

The text on the error page can also assist in automated testing, as the testing script will know that the test has passed when it sees the expected error page. For example, consider an error page stating "Error: Invalid characters detected." An automated testing tool could be scripted to look for this page as the basis for a successful test, as the component properly detected the bad characters and returned the error page.

To further assist in the testing process, the component should check all its inputs up front—meaning as early as possible—if possible. This will reduce the number of test cases, as some components may require a combination of good and bad inputs to produce the test case if the *good* inputs are needed to get to the point of checking for the *bad* inputs.

Obtain a list of Web server components, derived from the «interface» use cases, and their inputs. Each input should have a list of acceptable input characters associated with it. The list will look something like the following:

Component	Parameters	Valid input characters
/asp/BrowseByCategory.asp	None	N/A
/asp/ViewPreviousOrder.asp	id=<order ID>	[0-9]

This list should also include hidden form fields.

1. Verify that the components will return a predetermined error page when an invalid input character is detected. The predetermined error page can be captured by an automated testing tool, if desired; the successful capture of the error page represents the success indicator for the test.

2. For each input to the component, supply a single input character from the set of escape sequences or metacharacters that may cause unexpected behavior. On a UNIX system, the standard list of shell metacharacters is as follows (Kamthan 1999):

    ```
    &;`'\"|*?~<>^()[]{}$ \n and \r
    ```

3. Most form field values should not allow the user to specify file path operations, so also check the following character sequence:

    ```
    /..
    ```

4. Test each field individually; that is, do not attempt to populate all the fields with a bad character and send them in at the same time. Test one at a time so you can isolate any fields that may not be properly filtered.

Note that option and hidden inputs cannot be directly modified through the form page. This problem can be solved in several ways.

- Save the page to disk and directly edit the value property of the input field.
- If using an automated testing tool, directly modify the script to read the value from a file.
- Supply the desired input values on the URL line. Note that all values must be entered in the URL for this method to function properly. Also verify that this is possible in the target Web system.

Server-Side File Access

Using the list of Web server components obtained in the previous section, examine the list of inputs for fully formed file names, including paths, or file name fragments. You may need to talk with the component's developer in order to determine the exact usage of some of the inputs.

Component inputs that can consist of fully formed file names present a possible security problem. The recommended action here is to have the component modified in order to eliminate this type of usage. However, if the server configuration is secured so as to protect against a user's accessing a dangerous file, this security mechanism can be tested by supplying an alternative file name in place of the one in the form before it is submitted. This type of test can be performed by using an automated tool or by saving the page to disk and manually editing the field value. Some coordination with system administrators may be necessary to find appropriate file names with which to test.

If the input is a file name fragment, it should be tested as outlined in the previous section. Particular attention needs to be paid to the `../` sequence of characters.

Buffer Overflows

Much like testing component inputs for dangerous metacharacters, testing buffer overflows requires that the component actively check the lengths of all inputs. Component inputs are either HTML form fields or name/value pairs. A name/value pair is a field name and a value, separated by = on the URL line and is formatted as a *name/value* pair. A sample set of input might look something like `name=Norma, orderID=12345`.

When an input string that exceeds the maximum length is detected, the component should return a predetermined error page. The successful display of the error page represents a successful test result. The security test procedure is concerned with verifying that an overflow condition cannot be created, by supplying long inputs to the component. The error message produced is simply a way to confirm that the component has properly detected the invalid input and then aborted the activity.

1. The list of Web system components should be augmented with the maximum length of each input that the component will accept. If the engineering techniques described in Chapter 2 are used, these lengths should be documented in the «interface» use case descriptions. If the input length exceeds this value, the component must return the predetermined error page. If the error page is not returned, a security flaw exists.

2. For each input to the component, supply an input string that exceeds the maximum size by one character. This should return the predetermined error page. Also try the test with an input string that is exactly equal to the

maximum size of the field and watch the behavior of the component with this input. Boundary conditions often cause problems when dealing with buffers and string operations. Any printable character is acceptable as input, as long as it is within the valid set of characters that the component is willing to process. A long string of A characters will usually suffice.

Typically this type of test must be performed either by saving the HTML page to disk and manually editing the value attribute of an input field or by using an automated testing tool to send in the data. As with metacharacter testing, make sure that each field is tested one at a time so any problematic fields can be isolated.

Database Security

Most of the database test strategies are difficult to carry out in an automated fashion, as the access methods and data involved are quite variable. Therefore, testing in this section assumes that the proper vendor-supplied database tools to connect to and to query the database are available.

Data Encryption

This test strategy is aimed at verifying that data in the database is being stored in an encrypted form. Test steps include submitting sensitive data and then executing a query for the data in the database. These types of activities require a working knowledge of the database access tools pertinent to the particular database being used. Knowledge of the system's database schema is also necessary.

1. Enter values for each form field that requests sensitive information, such as first/last names, telephone numbers, addresses, and credit card numbers. Note the exact values entered and submit the form. It may be necessary to navigate through several forms to ensure that the information has been stored in the Web system's database. For example, it may be necessary to navigate through all the forms necessary to complete a payment transaction.

2. Once the form has completed processing, open the database query tool and query the appropriate table and columns for the fields entered in the previous step. If the data is successfully queried, it is stored in an unencrypted form and should be regarded as a possible security risk.

Temporary and Log Files

The following strategy investigates the use of temporary and log files by Web system components. The goal is to locate components that expose private data by storing it on the server's file system in an unencrypted form.

1. Obtain a high-privilege user account on the server, such as one of the Web servers or another back-end server, that processes sensitive data. This account must have a very high privilege, such as the root account on a UNIX system or the administrator account on a Windows NT/2000 system.

2. Also obtain a list of the Web system pages that invoke the processing of sensitive user data, including the submission of payment information or the management of account data. Note that access to some of these operations may not be possible through the Web server, such as after-hours batch processing.

3. For each operation in the list, from the previous step, enter a set of sensitive data and invoke the operation.

4. For each piece of sensitive information entered in the previous script, search the server's file system for all files containing this data. On UNIX, this can be accomplished by using the `find` command, as follows:

    ```
    find / -type f | xargs grep "private data"
    ```

    On Windows NT/2000, select Search from the Start menu, choose For Files or Folders, and enter the private data in the Containing Text box.

5. If the data travels through multiple servers, such as the Web server and then a credit card processing server, make sure to search each server's file system. Any files discovered containing this data should be considered a security hazard, as they exist after the processes have completed executing.

This test strategy will not detect temporary files used in a transient fashion by server processes.

Access to Database Objects

This test requires the availability of the appropriate database tools and knowledge of the system's database schema. Sample data must also be prepared and stored in a test database.

1. Obtain a low-privileged, temporary user account for access to the database that contains the Web system data.

2. Next, try to query database tables commonly accessed by the system. Make sure to test all operations, including select, update, insert, and delete. Any successful queries against the database by this user indicate that the objects in question are not properly secured.

3. After the tests are completed, remove the temporary user account from the database.

Database User ID and Password

This strategy attempts to locate plaintext user ID and password information in Web server components. Used to connect to the site's database, this information may be hard coded into Web system components—either in script source or in binary components—or stored in a configuration file or the registry.

1. Obtain a high-privileged user account on the server containing the system components that access the database. The user account must have very high privileges, such as the root account on a UNIX system or the administrator account on a Windows NT/2000 system.

2. Obtain the user ID and password information used to access the database server. Note that several database accounts may be used by Web system components, as some systems may be designed to have their components connect to the database server as one of several users, to support different access levels. Therefore, it is important to obtain the complete list of accounts. Note that databases can typically maintain their own user account lists. So technically, a database account is the same as a user account, but it's not the same as a user account managed by the operating system. For example, a user named Joe might be in the database yet not have any corresponding user account managed by the operating system.

3. For each database account, search the server's file system for all files containing the user ID and password. On UNIX, this can be accomplished by using the `find` command:

    ```
    find / -type f | xargs grep -E "userID | password"
    ```

    On Windows NT/2000, select Search from the Start menu, choose For Files or Folders, and enter the user ID in the Containing Text box. If any files are located, examine them for the presence of the password as well.

4. Any files discovered containing this data should be considered a security hazard, as they contain plaintext database user ID and password information. The information in these files should be properly encrypted to protect against unauthorized access.

If the Web server is running on a Windows NT/2000 platform, also search the system registry for each database account user ID and password, using the `regedit` utility.

Database Schema

This test requires knowledge of the database schema, preferably in documentation form with all table and column names.

1. Obtain a list of the interface pages that result in access to data in the site's database, such as `ViewPreviousOrder.asp` in the TBS case study.

2. Access each of these pages and save each page to disk as an HTML file in a local directory on the client computer.

3. Perform a Find in Files function (Windows) or a `grep` function (UNIX) and search for the database schema elements in the text of the HTML files. If any are found, each instance should be examined as a potential security issue.

Client Computer

This section examines the validation of security vulnerabilities in client-side ActiveX controls and cookies.

ActiveX Control Buffer Overflows

When it detects an input-length error, the component being tested must be coded to return a specific error. An ActiveX control must return a unique error code, or `hresult`, indicating that it has properly handled the input-length error. This code can be determined by wrapping the calls to the control in a `try/catch` block for JScript or setting the On Error handler for VBScript. The error code can be determined by examining the error object's error number property.

The following steps demonstrate how to perform ActiveX control input-length testing.

1. Obtain a list of the accepted inputs to the ActiveX control and the associated maximum length of each input. The control will have three ways of receiving input parameters: (a) `PARAM` attributes of the `OBJECT` tag, used to initialize the control with values when it is created on the page; (b) Properties that can be set through client-side script languages, such as JScript; (c) method calls from client-side scripts that take inputs. If the field length exceeds the length value for any of these inputs, the control must return the predetermined `hresult` code. If the code is not returned, a security flaw exists in the control

2. Test the inputs that are passed by the `PARAM` attributes of the `OBJECT` tag. Test one `PARAM` at a time and watch for the appropriate error to be returned by the control. For example:

```
<OBJECT ID="mycontrol"
   WIDTH="255" HEIGHT="50"
   CLASSID="CLSID:0918329-B8D0-101A-91F3-1183EA001DA3"
   CODEBASE="http://Homer/mycontrol.cab#Version=1,0,0,001">

   <PARAM NAME="UserName" VALUE="Julie">

</OBJECT>
```

To test the `UserName` parameter, replace `Julie` with a string that exceeds the maximum length specified by the control's developer. Also try the test with an input string that is exactly equal to the maximum size of the input. This should be accepted by the control, but watch the behavior of the control with this input, as boundary conditions often cause problems when dealing with buffers and string operations. Use any printable character, making sure that it is within the valid set of characters that the control is willing to process. A long string of `A` characters will usually suffice.

3. For each property or method of the control, supply an input string that exceeds the maximum size by one character. The control should return the appropriate error code, as demonstrated by the call to `e.number`. For example, assume that the control created in step 2 has a property, `customerID`, and a method, `AddToCart`, that accepts and stores a string input:

```
<SCRIPT LANGUAGE="JScript">
function testTheControl()
{
  try
  {
      mycontrol.customerID = "115A";
      mycontrol.AddToCart("Television");
  }
  catch(e)
  {
      // display the error code
      window.alert(e.number);
  }
}
</SCRIPT>
```

ActiveX Control File Access

ActiveX controls must be tested to determine whether they accept and use file names as inputs. Controls that do accept such input could result in malicious manipulation to access other files on the user's local disk.

1. Using the list of input parameters for the control obtained in the previous section, look for any inputs that are fully formed file names, including paths, or file name fragments. This may require some discussions with the control's developer to determine the exact usage of some of the inputs.

2. If the input is a fully formed file name or a fragment, a possible security problem exists. The recommended action here is to revise the control to eliminate this type of usage.

ActiveX Control Storage of Private Information

ActiveX controls are essentially full-featured programs, so they can store information in files on the user's local disk. If this information is private or confidential, the control may be a security risk. This test attempts to determine whether the control is storing any data on the local disk of a client machine.

1. Using the list of input parameters for the control obtained in the previous section, exercise each of the control's PARAM elements, properties, and methods, using the same value. This value should be relatively obscure, such as ABC123DEF456. Some discussion with the control's developer may be necessary to properly use the control's methods.

2. Once each input has been exercised, search the client machine for occurrences of this string in both the file system and the system registry. Searching the file system on a Windows machine can be accomplished by selecting Search from the Start menu, choosing For Files or Folders, and entering the string data in the Containing Text box. The registry can be searched by using the regedit tool provided with the Windows operating system. Any occurrences of the unique string in either place should be examined for potential privacy problems. In some cases, this problem could be solved by the ActiveX control making use of the Crypto API to encrypt the information prior to storing it on disk or in the registry.

Cookies

Cookies present another opportunity for the storage of sensitive user data on the local disk, which may be compromised if an intruder gains access to the user's machine. This test examines cookies set by the Web site to determine whether any confidential information is stored.

1. Obtain a list of the Web pages that accept private user information, such as names, addresses, telephone numbers, and credit card information.

2. For each page on the list, enter some test information into the fields. Make sure to note the data entered or to print out each page following entry of the data.

3. Examine the site's cookie file by opening it as a text file. With the Microsoft Internet Explorer browser, cookies are stored in the user's Temporary Internet Files folder, with a name similar to the following:

```
Cookie:<username>@<sitename>
```

The site name will be the host name portion of the URL. For example, in http://Homer/shoppingcart.htm, the site name would be Homer. If any of the data entered in the page is present in the cookie file, a security flaw exists. As with client-side file use, the recommended action is not to store data this way; however, the data can be encrypted to prevent cleartext access.

Secure Communications

The test strategy in this section verifies that any private information transmitted between the user's browser and the Web site is encrypted to prevent third parties from intercepting the data while it is in transit. This section requires the use of a *sniffer* program, such as the Windows NT/2000 Network Monitor.

1. Obtain a list of the server pages that accept private user information, such as names, addresses, telephone numbers, and credit card information. These pages should be the ones protected by a secure channel.

2. On a client machine, set the browser to warn when switching between secure and insecure communications. This will provide feedback when the secure channel is being entered and exited by the client browser.

3. Start the network monitoring tool. It may be useful to filter out some of the network traffic to keep the capture small. With the NT/2000 Network Monitor, this is accomplished by selecting Filter... from the Capture menu and then double-clicking the SAP/ETYPE list entry. Click the Disable All button; then select the IP – ETYPE protocol from the list and click Enable.

4. Navigate to the page that requests private user information. You may or may not receive a warning from the browser about a switch to a secure channel. The reason is that it is possible to receive the form from the server over an unencrypted channel and then enter the secure channel when the

form is sent back to the server. If you do receive a warning from the browser, select OK to proceed.

5. Enter values for each form field that requests sensitive information, such as first/last names, telephone numbers, addresses, credit card numbers, and so on. Note the exact values entered. Do not submit the data yet; simply enter the data into the fields.

6. Switch to the network monitor tool and start capturing network packets.

7. Switch back to the browser and submit the form and wait for the response from the server. If you have not received the warning about switching to a secure channel yet, you should receive it now. If not, the channel very likely is not secure.

8. Stop the capture and view the data. You should see several entries with the source and destination matching the client's name or IP address and server's name or IP address. The protocol should be HTTPS or TCP. Double-click and examine each entry with the `Src Other Addr` having the name or IP address of the client computer you are using. The data in these packets should be unreadable; carefully examine them for the data you entered in the form. If the packet is readable, it is not encrypted, and the site's HTML and script files should be examined, since this may constitute a security flaw.

Network

Web systems use firewalls and routers to restrict access to servers from outside the site's network. This section verifies that only the necessary ports on externally visible servers can be accessed from outside the site's network.

1. Obtain a list of all the IP addresses, including externally visible routers and firewalls, in use by the servers that make up the site. Also include in this list the services, such as FTP and HTTP, running on each machine and whether the hosts and/or services should be visible to outside clients. The list may look something like this:

IP Address	Type	Visible Ports	Other ports (not visible from outside)
192.168.10.1	firewall	None	None
192.168.10.2	web server	80 (HTTP), 443 (HTTPS)	21 (FTP)
192.168.10.3	db server	1433 (SQL Server)	21 (FTP)

2. From a client machine outside the firewall, attempt to connect to each machine by IP address, specifying one of the ports in the list. This can be accomplished by using the TELNET utility and specifying a port number.

```
telnet 192.168.10.2 80
telnet 192.168.10.2 21
telnet 192.168.10.3 21
```

The first example should result in a connection—press Enter a few times after the connection succeeds to see some output from the HTTP server—whereas the second and third examples should be refused by the firewall, as this site does not want the FTP service to be used by outside clients.

External testing of a server machine can be performed most accurately by using port-scanning software against the machine. Some Web sites will do an automated port scan, free of charge. Scanning in this way will identify the services running on the machine, the ports they are listening on, and, possibly, the version. Typically, port scanners can be configured to test only the common ports, such as FTP and HTTP. Test each IP address in the list, using the port scanner. The scanner should find only the ports listed in the `Visible Ports` column. All other ports the scanner finds should be investigated, as they indicate possible security holes into the network.

3.8 TBS Case Study

This section demonstrates a few selected security verification examples from the I-View Previous Order use case in the TBS case study. Although not a complete test of this use case, these examples demonstrate how to execute some of the testing strategies in Section 3.7 on a concrete use case.

I-View Previous Order is implemented by several components in the TBS system:

- `ViewPreviousOrder.asp`: The ASP page containing server-side JScript code that is executed by the Web server when the user attempts to load the page.
- `TBS.ViewPreviousOrder` COM component: A C++ component that is called by the ASP page to retrieve the user's order. The component's `ViewPreviousOrder` method takes two arguments, `userID` and `orderID` and returns an XML string containing the order data.
- Database tables needed to gather the data about the user's order: `OrderInfo`, `OrderLineItem`, and `Item`.

The following information is also necessary to accurately perform the tests:

- `ViewPreviousOrder` URL: The full URL to gain access to the `ViewPreviousOrder` interface: http://TBSServer/TBS/ViewPreviousOrder.asp.
- Sample data: Sample user IDs and orders created for the tests:
  —User IDs: `testuser1` and `testuser2`
  —Order IDs: `10010` (belonging to `testuser1`) and `20020` (for `testuser2`)
- Required input restrictions: For the order ID input, a maximum of ten characters containing only the digits 0–9. The user ID argument is not passed in from the Web browser and as such is not a candidate for testing from the `I-ViewPreviousOrder` interface.

Authorization

Because the `I-ViewPreviousOrder` interface is accessible only by registered TBS members, the user is prompted by TBS to log on prior to the display of the interface. The first part of the authorization test will determine whether the user is able to access the interface without logging in, which would be considered a serious security problem.

To perform the test, enter the following into the browser's address box:

```
http://TBSServer/TBS/ViewPreviousOrder.asp?orderID=10010
```

In this URL, one of the test order numbers has been supplied, which is required by `ViewPreviousOrder.asp`. It is important to note that this step was performed without logging in to the system—a fresh browser process was used, specifically avoiding the TBS system until the URL was entered into the address box.

TBS responded to this connection attempt with the message shown in Figure 3-9. From this message, we can tell that TBS properly intercepted our attempt to access the `ViewPreviousOrder` interface without logging on and denied access to the order information. Internally, TBS was able to do this by examining an ASP session variable that is set during the logon. If the variable was not set, TBS knows that the user has not been authenticated. The following ASP JScript code demonstrates this technique:

```
// check login
if (Session("isAuthenticated") != true)
{
    Response.Redirect("NotAuthorized.html");
}
```

Figure 3-9   Not Authorized Error Page

This check is performed as the very first step in all private components, so no code executes if this check fails.

The next part of the authorization test is to verify that we cannot use the `ViewPreviousOrder` interface to access data that belongs to another user. To perform this test, we log on as the first sample user, `testuser1` and attempt to view the sample order, `20020`, which belongs to the second sample user. This is accomplished by entering the following URL after a successful logon:

```
http://TBSServer/TBS/ViewPreviousOrder.asp?orderID=20020
```

When supplied with this URL, TBS did not retrieve the order and instead responded with the Web page shown in Figure 3-10.

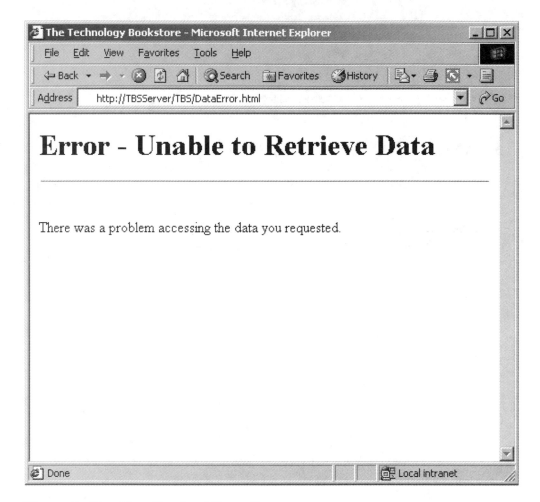

Figure 3-10   Data Retrieval Error Page

Internally, TBS stores the user ID in the record with the order ID. These two items are the primary key of the OrderInfo table, so they are used during database access to locate the order record. Because the user ID component of the key is not passed in from the browser but rather is stored in the Web server's session, the only component that can be manipulated is the order ID. The test URL entered attempted to access order number 20020, which belongs to testuser2. However, because the logon was performed with the testuser1 user ID, the ViewPreviousOrder component will attempt to use testuser1, 20020 as the key into the order table, which does not locate any records. Therefore, the error page is displayed.

Buffer Overflows

Any Web system component that accepts an input from the browser—or anywhere else, for that matter—must check the length of the input and restrict it to an appropriate length to prevent buffer overflow attacks. Buffer overflows are documented in detail in the section titled "Content Attacks," earlier in this chapter. To test the input length handling on the I-View Previous Order use case, a URL is entered into the browser's address box, using a length that exceeds the maximum input length. For the order ID input, the maximum length is 10 characters, so an input of 11 characters should be trapped as an error. As previously discussed, Web system components should return a predetermined input error page to indicate that they have successfully trapped an input error. This page should be different from other error pages so it can be used as a basis for the success or failure of input tests.

The following URL is used to test the input-length handling:

```
http://TBSServer/TBS/ViewPreviousOrder.asp?orderID=
12345678901
```

Note that a logon must occur prior to attempting to access this URL, as TBS will reject the attempt to access the script if the user is not authenticated. When this URL was used to access the TBS server, the error page illustrated in Figure 3-10 was displayed. This indicates a problem, as TBS tried to retrieve order number `12345678901` instead of rejecting that order ID with an input error as it should have, as the length exceeds ten characters. An investigation of the source code of the `TBS.ViewPreviousOrder` C++ COM component revealed that the component was not checking the length of the input. To correct this situation, the following code was added:

```
if (orderID.length() > 10)
{
    return E_INVALIDARG;
}
```

In addition, the ASP page was modified to look for this error and to redirect the client to the input error page.

3.9 Chapter Summary

⚠ Given today's computer system security vulnerabilities, organizations need to take action to ensure that security controls and procedures are implemented and that security testing is performed on the Web system before it goes live.

⚠ E-commerce Web systems have particular security concerns because they handle sensitive and personal information.

⚠ The port scanner and the network monitor are two types of utilities that are useful in the evaluation of Web site security. Port scanning is used on a host server or a range of hosts to determine whether they are exposing services on some or all ports. The network monitor, or sniffer, examines packets that are being transmitted across a network.

⚠ Securing a server involves two steps. First, it is necessary to secure the base operating system. Second, services running on the server need to be secured.

⚠ Web and application server security involves the proper operation of user authentication and access control, as well as a detailed examination of the Web system components that are used to drive dynamic and interactive content.

⚠ The effort to secure a Web site's database involves more than securing the database host itself. Web system components or other data retrieval mechanisms that operate on the data residing in the database must be properly designed and implemented to protect against database content attacks.

⚠ User accounts, file systems, and server software running on the database server must be properly configured to prevent unauthorized access by an intruder.

⚠ In recent years, a number of security flaws have been uncovered with many client-side technologies. Flaws in many Web browsers can be exploited by malicious scripts or applets to work around the security of the browser. As these flaws are identified, Web browser vendors have generally been quick to fix the problem and to distribute a patch.

⚠ Some technologies, such as ActiveX controls and cookies, can be used by a malicious intruder to open up potential security problems on a visiting Web user's computer. Section 3.4 provides guidance on ensuring that computers and the private data of Web users visiting a site are not made vulnerable to intrusion by attackers through the use of ActiveX controls and cookies.

⚠ Secure communication protocols, such as the Secure Sockets Layer (SSL), are available. SSL is an encryption protocol that enables two parties to communicate over a network in an encrypted form.

⚠ Several elements are involved in establishing a secure communications session between a browser client and a Web server, including Web server possession of a valid certificate, configuration of the client computer with the public key of the certificate authority, client authentication of the Web system server, and client generation of a session key.

⚠ Section 3.7 provides strategies for evaluating the security of a Web system through the conduct of step-by-step procedures addressing authentication, authorization, content attacks, database security, client computer security, communications, and the network.

3.10 References

Garfinkel, Simson, L., and Eugene H. Spafford. 1997. "Secure CGI/API Programming," *Web Server Online Magazine.* July. webserver.cpg.com/features/cover/2.6. See also, Simson L., Garfinkel, with Eugene H. Spafford. 1997. *Web Security & Commerce.* Cambridge, Mass.: O'Reilly & Associates.

Powell, Matt and Leonid Braginski. 1998. *Running Microsoft Internet Information Server.* Redmond, Washington: Microsoft Press, p. 332.

Kamthan, Pankaj. 1999. "CGI Security: Better Safe than Sorry." 19 September. Internet Related Technologies: http://tech.irt.org/articles/js184.

Rahmel, Dan. 1977. "Database Security." 1997. www.dbmsmag.com/9704i03.html.

Sullivan, Bob. 2000. "Credit Card Fraud—It Was Easy." 11 January. MSNBC: www.msnbc.com/news/356376.asp.

chapter 4

Performance and Scalability

Performance and scalability are top concerns cited by information technology (IT) managers as they prepare to deploy new Internet and intranet applications for their organizations.

The ability of a Web system to deliver content to an ever-changing number of simultaneous Web users is one of its most important features. Building and delivering a Web system that can service its customers in a timely fashion is critical to the survival of a business Web site. A Web system that *feels* slow may give the customer a negative impression of the business and may give that customer cause to seek out a competing system. Beyond the subjective feel of the system is the capability of the site to carry out the requests of the user in a timely fashion, with optimal use of system resources. With this in mind, the architecture shown in Figure 1-1 can be *scaled* in several places, namely, the Web server tier, the application server tier, and the database server tier. These tiers can be augmented with additional machines in order to handle the increased load that results from a higher number of concurrent users.

Web sites experience load in a *bursty* manner (Chiu 1999). Sites must be able to deal with bursts of user load at certain times during the day or week, holiday seasons, or perhaps in response to an aggressive advertising campaign. In short, the site must be able to tolerate peak usage without failure.

This chapter addresses the following topics:

- *Performance and scalability requirements,* which must be defined in the context of the site's expected usage
- *Evaluation strategy,* which entails gathering data on the site's performance and scalability behavior
- *Verification phases,* or the steps required for conducting essential performance and scalability testing
- *Interpreting the results,* the difficult task of analyzing the data produced from a set of performance tests
- *Performance and scalability improvement* arising from issues uncovered pertaining to the site's ability to function or scale with load
- *Scalability and cost analysis* to determine the suitability of the site in the face of varying load requirements and the costs of scaling

4.1 Overview

Web system performance and scalability are closely related. As such, they must be measured together in order to obtain an accurate picture of the Web system's capability to service users under various conditions. To properly grasp the importance of scalability, it is first necessary to understand the implications of performance on a Web system, and that requires understanding the terms that apply to Web system performance and scalability.

Performance

Web system performance can be described from two perspectives. To an end user, *response time* is the basic measure used to judge the quality of a Web site's performance. Administrators, on the other hand, are concerned not only with response time but also with the site's *resource utilization.*

Response times increase as the number of users increases, owing to higher levels of resource utilization on the system's servers and network. Response time can also be affected by factors not related to user load, such as database size and poor software implementation. Web system end users typically perceive response time to be the amount of time taken from the moment they click the mouse to the moment that a new Web page has been fully displayed on the screen. Based on this perceived time, users may judge system performance as too sluggish. Response time performance factors include the following:

- *Request submission:* The amount of time required for the client browser to make a connection to the Web site and transmit any user-supplied data. These response times can be affected by the speed of the user's Internet connection, the number of network *hops* between the user and the target site, any transient congestion or traffic present on those portions of the Internet, and, to some extent, the size of the user data included in the request. In addition, the bandwidth available on the Web system's local area network (LAN) and Internet connection play a role.
- *Processing time:* The time required for a request to be processed by one or more servers in order to carry out the function initiated by the user. Processing may involve the simple retrieval of a static HTML page, or it may require much more complex interaction among the Web, application, and database servers. In any case, the duration of processing time is under the control of the Web site and can be improved by adding more server resources or optimizing some of the site's components.
- *Response:* The time needed to transmit the page or data resulting from a processed request back to the user's browser. Again, this time is subject to traffic conditions on the site's network and the Internet, as well as the speed of the user's Internet connection, the processing power of the user's computer, and the size of the data being transmitted in the response.

Even though a particular Web system component may complete its work with an acceptable response time, it may do so with an unacceptable amount of server resource utilization. Both of these factors must be considered when evaluating the performance of a site.

Scalability

Web system scalability is the ability to add computing resources to a site in order to obtain acceptable or improved response time, stability, and throughput under a particular load. In this context, load refers to the number of users accessing the site at the same time.

As more users access the site, the site's servers will use more of their CPU, input/output (I/O), and memory resources to handle the load. Eventually, one or more of these resources will become *saturated*, meaning that the system cannot efficiently process all the requests and must force some to wait for processing. In most cases, the computer's CPU will be the first component to become saturated. The end result of a saturated server resource is an increase in response time. Scaling allows the site to cope with additional load by providing more resources to process requests.

The architecture depicted in Figure 1-1 provides for scaling in each of the three server-side tiers. These tiers can be scaled as follows (Microsoft 1999b).

- *Vertical scaling* is achieved by upgrading or replacing a server with more powerful components or an entirely new, larger server. Prior to the advent of distributed computing, vertical scaling was the only way to enable a system to handle more users with acceptable response times. Vertical scaling can usually be achieved with little or no software modification. Although minor server upgrades, such as a faster processor or more memory, are not very costly, the cost of large-scale system replacement can be astronomical.
- *Horizontal scaling* refers to the ability to add more servers to a Web system configuration. This usually requires the site's architecture to support such scaling, as software issues may arise when multiple machines are used. In addition, high horizontal scaling capability increases the *availability* of the site, as server failures will have less impact when the site has more servers. The architecture depicted in Figure 1-1 can be scaled horizontally in the Web, application, and database server tiers. This kind of scaling requires *load balancing,* which is discussed later in this chapter.
- *Functional scaling* involves the separation of groups of functions, such as catalog browsing and purchasing operations, onto different groups of servers, allowing for more accurate horizontal and vertical scaling techniques. These groups of functions typically involve different usage of server resources and are difficult to scale when they reside on the same machines.

  Functional scaling can also be done by server type. For example, HTTP, HTTPS (SSL), and FTP functions can be placed on different groups of servers. These functions put different types of demands on the servers, and as a result, scaling tends to be done differently. HTTPS (SSL) functions are more expensive yet less common than HTTP functions. SSL is CPU intensive, as the encryption/decryption of the data takes a lot of processing time. As a result, it may make sense to scale vertically instead of horizontally in this case. FTP servers tend to be disk I/O intensive, so either a better disk system (vertical) or more machines (horizontal) would work as a scaling scheme.

Network

As more clients request data from the network, the amount of available bandwidth on the network decreases. On Ethernet networks, servers attempting to communicate on the network will experience greater contention for network availability where network requests *collide* with one another more frequently, in which case network requests must be retried. Eventually, the delays associated with attempts to retry communications will significantly impact site performance.

Bottlenecks

When multiple servers are involved in processing a request, they will probably experience unequal loads. For example, many Web server requests involve the participation of an application server and a database server. One of these servers may be experiencing a heavy load, performing a task in an inefficient manner, or simply lacking processing capacity to perform the task quickly. This server will cause others in the chain of communication to wait for it to finish its work, resulting in an increase in overall processing time. This situation is known as the *bottleneck* for the operation.

In some cases, a processing bottleneck may not be a problem. If the operation is still performed with an adequate response time, the bottleneck situation may not need to be addressed. Typically, as the number of users increases, the bottleneck will, at some point, push the response time over an acceptable limit. In this case, it is necessary to correct the bottleneck condition through component optimizations or scaling in order to restore system response time to an acceptable level.

The term *bottleneck* is also used to describe the limiting resource on a server. For example, when a component running on a server is not doing its work quickly enough, perhaps the CPU is the limiting factor on the server, with low measures of disk input/output and memory utilization but high CPU utilization.

Linear Scaling

An important feature of horizontal scaling is the ability to scale *linearly,* meaning that the site can handle an additional number of users, which is directly related to the multiple number of servers added to the site. For example, a twofold increase in servers would result in a twofold increase in the maximum number of users. Linear scaling is possible only when the addition of servers to a tier does not cause a bottleneck somewhere else in the system. For instance, doubling the number of Web servers in the site may cause the application servers to become overloaded, unable to process requests within an acceptable time frame. A bottleneck in this case would increase the processing time and prevent the site from servicing all the users within an acceptable response time.

4.2 Performance and Scalability Requirements

Performance and scalability requirements are used to judge whether the site will perform properly under various conditions of load. These requirements are used as a basis for determining whether the site is capable of meeting the expectations of the system's customer base. Such requirements are also used to support *scalability and cost analysis* (see Section 4.7). The following are commonly used criteria for defining performance and scalability requirements:

- *Response time:* A major performance gauge for a Web site. Many factors contribute to a Web site's response time, and some are outside the Web site's control, such as the speed of an Internet connection for a user. Because many Internet users use modems, the response time may need to be adjusted for modem speed. For example, an acceptable response time goal for a 56K modem user might be 6 seconds, whereas the goal for a user accessing the Internet via a T1 line might be 2 seconds.

- *Required number of concurrent users:* The ability to support a large number of concurrent users with little or no degradation in response time. Quantifying the appropriate number of users is difficult, but such measures can be derived by examining similar sites, performing market research, or, possibly, looking at existing, non-Web products. When a Web site has already gone live, statistics can be obtained from the Web server logs to determine typical usage patterns.

- *Cost:* The number of servers and the administration time required (Menasce and Almeida 1998, p. 68). When such costs are too high, architectural changes or component optimization must be considered. This issue is discussed in more detail in Section 4.7.

- *Normal versus peak:* The effect of these figures on the three previous factors. For example, a site may experience a normal user load of 300 concurrent users, but that load will at times climb as high as 1,000 users. With that load, it may be acceptable for the Web system to experience a small degradation in response time.

- *Degradation under stress:* The specific degradation that occurs when system load capacity is exceeded. For example, how many users get partial, or broken, pages under this condition? Measures collected might indicate, for example, that 5 percent of system users get incomplete Web pages under a load of 1,000 concurrent users versus 10 percent when load is increased to 1,500 simultaneous users. Additionally, the Web site's stability should be evaluated to make sure that server processes do not crash or corrupt data while under various levels of stress.

- *Reliability:* A Web system's performance following long use versus that during its first 24 hours of use. This type of requirement statement defines the time period for which a Web site must perform at certain response time levels in order to be viewed as reliable for production use. For example, the duration may be defined as a week, during which time the performance numbers and stability measurements should be relatively constant. The definition of a reliability requirement should take into account such factors as regular maintenance intervals that will restart the site's machines.

4.3 Verifying Site Performance and Scalability

The goal of performance and scalability testing is to monitor and report on the site's behavior under various load conditions. This data will be used later to analyze the state of the Web site and to plan for growth based on expectations of additional load. This data will also allow costs associated with the projected growth to be calculated, based on the required capacities and performance of the site.

Formal performance and scalability tests are typically conducted at the end of a development iteration, after the functional tests and any corrections have been performed, as these problems may alter the results of the performance tests. It is best practice to conduct informal performance monitoring throughout the development effort, whereas the formal tests are used to validate whether performance-related requirements have been satisfied.

In order to ensure accurate test execution and results gathering, an automated testing tool should be used to execute the performance tests. It's almost impossible to conduct performance testing without the use of tools, which can simulate thousands of simultaneous users. Many tools are available for this purpose; some of them are described in Chapter 7 and Appendix B. Test tools can greatly assist in the creation of test scripts and the monitoring of end user response times. In addition, load-testing tools typically have a large number of options, including *think time* and *connection speed,* to more accurately simulate end user interaction with the system.

Test Types

Four major types of performance-related tests need to be considered:

- *Base performance* testing determines the response time and server resource usage of each system function (use case) individually under optimal system conditions. This type of test is performed with only one user, to uncover any immediate performance issues with components in the use case. If poor results are recorded for a use case during the base performance test, it is almost certain to display problems during load tests. When performance problems are identified during base performance testing, the component's developer will typically need to investigate the problem and correct any components prior to the execution of any load tests using those components.

- *Load* behavior is one of the most important areas of analysis. The goal of load testing is to simulate real-world usage to determine response time and server resource use, allowing the calculation of a maximum number of site users per machine. To simulate real users, scripts are created that tie together many common user actions into virtual *sessions*. Bottlenecks in the system will usually become apparent during this type of test. Load testing is also performed with single operations, or use cases, in order to help locate performance issues with specific components under load.

   Load testing is performed incrementally, with a fixed number of users added per increment. As users are added, the response time and server resource use values will increase. Obtaining these performance measures helps facilitate planning, as the maximum number of site users supported by the system may not be acceptable for future needs. Also, analysis may indicate that the site needs to be scaled in order to accommodate defined performance requirements.

- *Stress* testing too consists of simulating access to a Web site by multiple users. Stress testing, however, seeks to determine the behavior of the system once it reaches load limits, when the server can no longer cope with the load. When system load approaches its threshold, the system may reject users or return incomplete pages, or components and services may crash. Most Web sites strive for graceful degradation under load, through the action of simply rejecting users instead of bringing the entire site down. Stress testing can help determine when the system should initiate such corrective action.

- *Reliability* testing is used to verify that no hidden opportunities for failure exist. Memory leaks, disk file issues, or database transaction log size are problems that may surface only after the system has been running for long periods of time (Rational Software Corporation 1999).

The various types of performance-related tests are shown in Figure 4-1.

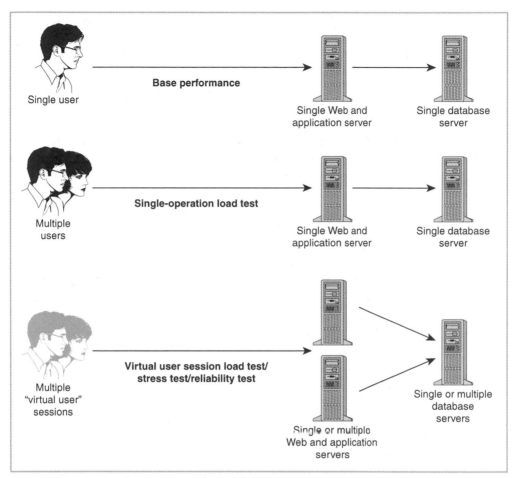

Figure 4-1 Performance and Scalability Test Types

Configurations

Performance-related tests are executed with various configuration elements:

- *Server hardware and number of servers.* In order to properly obtain performance and scalability measures for a Web site, load and stress tests should be run using various configurations of server hardware and with various numbers of servers at each tier. Consider, for example, using two Web servers, one application server, and one database server; single-processor and multiprocessor Web servers; and separate Web and application server machines versus a collocated Web/application server.

It is important to test the system using the *base configuration* in order to assist in determining scalability. A base configuration should generally include the minimum number of servers required for the site to function. For example, a site's base configuration may consist of one Web server; one application server, if used; and one database server. Measures of performance obtained under this configuration are useful in scalability analysis, as the measures collectively provide a *base unit of scalability* for the site.

- *Database size.* It is vital to execute each type of test using multiple database sizes, in order to determine how they impact system performance and whether any database schema or configuration changes are necessary. Schema design, database configuration options, and the use of indexes can have a significant performance impact when operating on a table with a large number of records. As a result, it is important to factor database size into the performance-related tests in order to make sure that the site performs acceptably with large data sets.

- *Location of test client machines.* Ideally, the site should be tested from both inside and outside the site's network and firewall to uncover any network-related issues. Sometimes, however, testing the site from outside the firewall may not be appropriate, depending on the throughput capabilities of the firewall, which may not be able to pass enough client connections through at one time to adequately load the servers.

- *SSL versus Non-SSL.* Because the use of SSL carries a high penalty in terms of server performance, it is often useful to execute both SSL and non-SSL tests so that the performance versus security trade-off measures can be quantified.

- *Image retrieval.* Depending on the test being performed, it may not be desirable to retrieve images from the Web server during performance testing. Image retrieval occupies the Web server's resources, taking time away from processing "active" pages that will exercise more important system components. Therefore, tests involving the use of images should be avoided when the Web server is known to be a bottleneck, as that condition will prevent higher loads from being experienced on the back-end tiers, including the application server and database server tiers.

Measurements

During the execution of performance-related tests, measurements are typically continually taken on all servers, clients, and the network. The gathering of these measures is key to the success of results and scalability analysis, as these activities rely on performance data to locate problems and to plan for the future. The following list describes several of the more important performance measurements that must be obtained during the execution of performance and scalability tests. This list is a general guide; additional measurements tailored to the specific Web site's implementation may need to be taken as well.

- *Client machines.* The systems used for simulating multiple user access to a Web site are typically measured by a load testing tool, which can be configured with such test parameters as the *number of users* and can then obtain measures of *response time* (min/max/average). The tool effectively tracks and reports response time for the various levels of users that have been simulated. In addition, measures of CPU use on the client machines should be monitored in order to make sure that they are not overloaded and that adequate load is being placed on the servers.
- *Server machines.* The site's Web, application, and database servers should be monitored by using a tool such as Performance Monitor, available on Windows NT/2000. Some load testing tools also include built-in monitors for this purpose. Performance measures of interest across all server platforms include CPU, percent total processor time; memory (Microsoft 2000a, p. 5), available kilobytes and page faults/second; disk, percent disk time; and network, total bytes/second (Microsoft 2000b, p. 2).
- *Web servers.* The following performance measures, in addition to those in the preceding bullet item, should be obtained for all Web server machines: files/second, maximum simultaneous connections experienced (Microsoft 2000b, p. 2), and error measures.
- *Database servers.* Performance measures for transactions/second and the cache hit ratio (Microsoft 2000b, p. 1) should be obtained for all database servers.
- *Network.* It is important to monitor the bandwidth utilization on the site's network, and any subnets within, in order to ensure that the network has not become a bottleneck for the Web site. Network monitoring can be performed by using one of several available software packages or a specialized piece of hardware, known as a LAN analyzer. On a *switched* Ethernet network, the bandwidth must be monitored on each separate server connection, as each connection is isolated from the others (Microsoft 2000a, p. 24).

4.4 Verification Phases

This section addresses the essential performance and scalability test phases: test planning, script creation, and test execution. This section also discusses common performance-related pitfalls to avoid during development and testing.

Prior to building scripts and executing tests, the Web system and the associated user base must be analyzed to determine the typical functions exercised during a user session. The types of tests to be executed and their configurations are identified during this first test phase. Next, scripts must be created for each function and tied together to simulate those sessions. Finally, the test scripts are executed against the system. The duration of tests will depend on the complexity of the Web site and the number of test scenarios.

Test Planning

The three major elements required for conducting performance and scalability test planning are *site operations* or *«interface» use-cases, virtual user sessions,* and *test scenarios*. First, a listing that documents the set of all operations that can be performed on the site is prepared. When the RSI use case approach is used to analyze the site's requirements, the «interface» use cases can be used to build the list of operations. For example, the I-Purchase Items and I-View Order List «interface» use cases are single operations that can be performed by the user. If RSI use cases were not used to analyze the site, this list of operations can typically be derived from the set of ASP, PHP, CGI, or other active documents implemented by the site.

As discussed in Chapter 1, it may not be practical to test all the site operations; they must be prioritized in terms of risk, usage patterns, and other criteria, and some will necessarily be eliminated, owing to time and cost constraints.

Second, virtual user sessions are defined and created that tie together a number of these functions in order to closely simulate a user on the system. Finally, test scenarios are defined and created. They provide details of each test type, such as the number of users, the various hardware and site configurations, and whether the test is performed with or without SSL.

The first step involves preparing a list that documents the set of all operations that can be performed on the site. This step may well be the least time consuming when the functional engineering guidelines presented in Chapter 2 have been followed. The set of all site operations or use cases is the same as the set of «interface» use cases. A subset of the site operations will be used during base performance and load testing to help isolate performance issues with components. Each operation in the list should note the dependent operations, such as the dependency of I-View Order List on I-Login, as depicted in Figure 2-7.

The list of system operations or «interface» use cases is also used to create virtual user sessions, the main vehicle for simulating the use of a Web system by large numbers of users. Sessions combine many single operations into a single script to navigate through the site. Following is a list of several sample user sessions from the Technology Bookstore case study described in Appendix C. Although the virtual user session needs of each Web system will vary with functionality, adequate coverage of system functionality must be obtained to ensure a successful load test.

- The *browsing-user* session simulates a user looking through the product catalog and viewing a few items. This simulation consists of several invocations of the I-Browse Catalog by Category, I-Search Catalog by Keyword, I-Item List, and I-View Item operations.
- The *purchasing-user* makes use of the I-Add Item to Shopping Cart, I-Login, and I-Purchase Items operations. The script is hard coded to always add the same item to the shopping cart, thus bypassing the catalog and view-item operations. This enables the functionality of this virtual user session to be isolated on the purchasing activity.
- A combination of the previous two sessions, the *browsing- and purchasing-user* session simulates a user browsing the catalog before deciding to make a purchase.
- The *customer support user* session uses the I-Login, I-View Order List, and I-View Previous Order operations.

The development of test scenarios, the final step in the planning phase, involves the various combinations of test types, site and hardware configurations, database sizes, number of virtual user sessions, and the numerous parameters for the execution of the tests. The combinations of these items should produce enough data from measurements to adequately analyze the site's behavior under load and the effect of various site configurations.

Several elements are applicable to each type of performance test. To create a test scenario for base performance, for example, criteria must be selected for each element applicable to that type. Enough scenarios must be created from the possible elements to allow for analysis of the site's behavior, which is discussed later in this chapter.

- *Base performance* tests, the first to be executed, measure the response time of a component accessed by a single user under optimal conditions. Because load conditions are not of concern, the test need not be run within a full-blown distributed configuration that might include multiple Web servers and application servers. Rather, the objective of the test is to examine how a particular component performs, so the hardware configuration used to support the test should be small enough to isolate the performance activity. The base configuration of the site, as described previously in this section, should be used for this type of test. Several factors should be considered when building a list of the base performance scenarios. Base performance tests should be executed first, in order to highlight any problems with response time under optimal conditions. Heavy load testing against a component that cannot perform properly with a single user will not be useful. Site operations, or «interface» use cases, database size in records—for example, 10K, 100K, 500K, and 1M—and functionality performed with and without the use of SSL are elements of the base performance tests.

- *Single-operation load testing* extends the base performance tests by adding more users. This type of test is conducted more to discover component development issues than to simulate site load. Single-operation load tests should incorporate site operations or «interface» use cases; incrementing from a low number to a target number of users, such as 10–200, and equal increments, such as 10, for each run of the load test; database size in records, such as 10K, 100K, 500K, and 1M; and functionality performed with and without the use of SSL.

  The *number of users* should be derived from the response time and load requirements analysis performed prior to the conduct of test planning (see Section 4.2). As with base performance tests, single-operation load tests should be performed on a hardware configuration small enough to isolate the performance activity, such as the site's base configuration. Any problems uncovered during this testing should be corrected prior to performing any subsequent tests.

- *Virtual user load-testing sessions* are used once the base performance and single operation load tests have been successfully performed and any problems have been corrected. The site can then be tested for real-world performance and scalability using the virtual user sessions to simulate real users against the system. When test scenarios for this kind of testing are designed, the following factors need to be considered:

  —Virtual user sessions: The percentage of use, such as 80 percent browsing sessions and 20 percent purchasing sessions

  —Number of users: Increment from a low number to the target number, such as 10–200, as well as equal increments for each load test run, such as increments of 10

  —Web server configurations: The number of processors, amount of physical memory, and total number of servers

  —Application server configurations: The number of processors, amount of physical memory, and total number of servers

  —Database server configurations: The number of processors, amount of physical memory, and total number of servers

  —Database size in records, such as 10K, 100K, 500K, and 1M

  —Test-run length, expressed in terms of hours or days

  —*Think time* of simulated users: Random spread of think time

—Connection speed of simulated users: simulate modem, DSL, or higher connection speeds

—Firewall separation: Client computers inside versus outside a site's firewall

—Image retrieval: Functionality with and without image retrieval

—SSL: Functionality performed with and without the use of SSL

- *Stress tests* are normally performed with a high number of users in an attempt to saturate many of the site's servers while monitoring response time behavior. This type of testing follows virtual user session load testing. Stress test scenarios should be created from the same set of factors as load tests, with the exception of the number of users, which should be set high enough to cause rejected connections or system failure.

- *Reliability* is quite similar to virtual user session load testing, with the exception of a fixed number of users and a smaller set of hardware configurations. The goal of reliability testing is to exercise the Web site over a long period of time in order to uncover any defects that occur only after long load or use durations. The number of users should be on the high end of the load requirement that still operates at an acceptable response time. The hardware configuration should properly service the required number of users at that response time.

  Once the number of users and the hardware configuration have been defined, the following factors should be considered for reliability testing:

  —Virtual user sessions

  —Database size in records, such as 10K, 100K, 500K, 1M

  —Test-run length, in days

  —*Think time* of simulated users

  —Image retrieval: Functionality with and without image retrieval

  —Functionality performed with and without the use of SSL

Once the test plans have been completed, the test procedures, or scenarios, and scripts, which define the various parameter settings that apply, including the number of users, think time values, and the use of image retrieval, can be created.

Test Script Creation

The approach for developing test scripts should be quite similar to that for developing functional tests, as outlined in Chapter 2. A test script should be created for each site operation as described earlier, such as I-Search Catalog by Keyword and I-View Previous Order. In addition, virtual user sessions should be created that tie together the site operations into a simulated site user session. Automated test tools generally include a script recorder that can be used for this purpose. Use it to create the sessions, based on the test planning.

It is also important to have the scripts execute multiple iterations of the test. For example, a script that tests the I-View Item function should loop several times on I-View Item, preferably with different input data.

Most test tools enable test procedures, or scenarios, to be configured with a number of options, such as the number of users, the amount of *think time,* and the use of image retrieval. Using the test plans in the previous section, create all the test scenarios with the necessary parameters for various types of tests.

Test Execution

Once test scripts and scenarios have been created, it is time to execute the tests. Prior to execution, several preparation steps are necessary.

Server Configurations

Each test scenario should be associated with a particular Web system hardware configuration description that outlines, for example, the number of Web server processors and the number of Web servers. The site configuration must be verified and reconfigured when necessary to support each test scenario. It may also be necessary to reconfigure certain network devices when subnetting or other network testing applies.

Fresh Starting Point

Depending on the test, it may be desirable to restart both the client test machines and the Web system servers prior to executing each test. Doing so ensures that no remnants, such as component memory leaks, from previous tests will impact the next test.

Monitoring

A test tool may include built-in monitors for tracking server activity. When the test tool does not have such a monitoring mechanism, the computer platform's monitoring tool, such as Performance Monitor for Windows NT/2000 environments, should be started and set to record performance measures from the necessary machines into a log file.

The operation of performance monitoring software on a machine will impact the performance of the machine. Typically, performance monitoring software can be adjusted to obtain measures at shorter or longer intervals. It is important to properly select a measurement interval that gathers the appropriate information without altering the results of a test. It is usually best to run the tests over a longer period of time so that the monitor can be configured to take readings with a longer interval, such as every 10 seconds.

The Windows NT/2000 Performance Monitor can be configured to collect data from several machines onto a single machine on the network. That machine can then be configured to output these measurements to a comma- or tab-separated file, often referred to as a *performance log*. The contents of a performance log can then be loaded into a spreadsheet file for further analysis and charting. This collective mechanism for obtaining performance measurements provides a convenient way to record measurements over long periods of time.

Warm-Up

It is worthwhile to allow the Web system to operate under simulated load, using the testing tool, for about 20 minutes in order to allow caches and buffers to fill up, prior to the collection (recording) of measurements (Microsoft 2000a, p. 12).

Once test preparations have been completed, the execution of the tests can proceed. Most test tools will record the success or failure outcome of each action within the script together with statistics on response times. The performance data captured during the test is essential for supporting performance analysis; therefore, the data should be copied to another location immediately after each test. It is also important to label the data files containing the performance measurements with the name of the test scenario or scenarios from which they were produced.

Common Pitfalls

There are many common performance and scalability pitfalls that may be encountered during Web system development and testing. During development, performance and scalability *surprises* can be avoided by working with system components within the environment for which they will most likely operate. Common concerns that should be addressed as part of development planning include the following.

- The *database* should be large. Don't wait until the end of an iteration—or time of release—to find out how components perform with large amounts of data.
- *SSL* should be enabled and used while developing Web system components.
- *Multiple servers* should be developed, with at least one physical server for each tier, when possible. Don't assume that it will work in a distributed configuration simply because it works collocated on the same machine.
- *HTTP error codes* must be confirmed to return from the site whenever any problems occur. The system's failure to return error codes may fool a test tool or script into thinking that the test completed successfully.

- *Third-party products,* such as a directory server, reporting server, or payment system, should be incorporated into the Web system architecture only after a prototype component has been load tested against this server, in order to verify whether it will function properly under required user load and system stress levels.

Common concerns for the testing phase, which should be addressed as part of test planning and execution, include the following.

- *Unnecessary processes*—services and programs—should be shut down on all client and server machines. This will allow for more of the system's resources, such as CPU, memory, and I/O, to be allocated to support the operation of tests on the client and processing the requests on the server.
- *Service packs and patches* typically include performance and stability enhancements but also bugs and performance degradations. Make sure that clients and servers are properly configured with the *proper,* not necessarily latest, versions of service packs and patches before testing. To be safe, these items should be the same versions in the development environment and ultimately in the production environment.
- *Network bandwidth* should be sufficient to handle all the requests from the clients. Only then can a particular load level on the server machines be created properly. Insufficient network bandwidth may prevent the machines from being properly loaded. Thus, testing over slow wide area network (WAN) links and modems will probably not result in enough load being placed in the servers. In addition, ensure that other systems and people are not using the network during a load test. Performance testing requires a network with as much free bandwidth as possible. Therefore, remove other traffic from the network, or, possibly, place all the test hardware on a separate subnet.
- *Logging functionality* needs to be disabled or compiled out, if applicable, before test execution. Failure to do so can result in wildly inaccurate performance data.
- *Release builds,* not debug builds, of application components must be verified as installed on the server. A *debug build,* a nonoptimized version of a binary executable file, is typically produced and used during development phases and may also contain debugging information. Debug builds are useful during development but result in slower component performance. The release build, which is used within the production environment, is typically constructed with all the compiler's optimization features turned on, in order to produce smaller, faster-running code.

4.5 Interpreting the Test Results

Interpreting the data gathered during testing is the next step in evaluating the performance characteristics of the system and determining where improvements are possible. In order to properly analyze a Web system's performance characteristics, accurate measurements must be obtained during the load tests. To be effective, 50–100 iterations of the test scripts should be run. Some common performance measurements are listed under Measurements in Section 4.3; approaches for addressing performance and scalability issues in order to increase site performance are addressed in Section 4.6.

Performance Measurement Guidelines

Determining measurements of acceptable performance can be a difficult task. Although there may be no absolutely *correct* value for any particular measurement, the list in Table 4-1 offers some *general* guidelines for determining whether a system load problem exists. Figures for each platform and application may vary.

Table 4-1   Measurement Performance Guidelines

Component	Measurement	Notes
CPU	Percent total processor time	Average utilization should be below a range of 75%–85%.
Memory	Available kilobytes	Actual values are based on the amount of random-access memory (RAM) installed, but available memory should remain approximately the same before and after a test.
Memory	Page faults/second	Actual values will vary, but this indicator should remain very low throughout all tests.
Disk	Percent disk time	Sustained high levels of disk time, on any server, should be avoided.
Web server	• Files/second • Maximum connections • Errors	General indicator of Web server load. Should rise and then remain more or less constant during the test run. General indicator of Web server problems.
Database server	• Transactions/second • Cache hit ratio	General indicator of database load. Actual values will vary by database, but 80%–90% is desirable.*

*"Monitoring Memory Usage," *SQL Server 2000 Books Online,* Microsoft Corporation, Redmond, WA, 2000

Adjustments and additional measurements should be added, when possible, in order to aid in analyzing Web system performance.

Base Performance and Load Tests

Base performance tests seek to examine single operations, or use cases, under optimal conditions with a single user. Load tests are performed against both single operations and the entire system. Single-operation load tests attempt to isolate load-related problems to a specific component, whereas system load tests examine the behavior of the system under simulated real-world conditions.

Based on the measurements gathered during tests, the first thing to examine is the results of the single-component tests under both single-user and load conditions. The following steps describe the evaluation of the results of single-component tests.

1. *Compare the response time of the component to the target response time requirement.* If the response time measurement obtained is greater than the target response time, the component is not acceptable in its current state. Proceed to step 2 and examine the system measurements in an effort to determine the cause.

2. *Examine the system load measurements.* If CPU utilization exceeds the recommended level, the component may suffer from design or implementation inefficiencies. If CPU utilization is low, the component may be awaiting a response from another component in the system. Examine system measurements from other machines, such as the database server, to determine where an inordinate amount of usage is causing the component to wait. If the amount of available system memory decreases during the test, the component may have a memory leak.

Figure 4-2 is a screen shot showing the monitoring of performance measures for a system component that was implemented with an inefficient algorithm. The component used a considerable amount of CPU processor time in order to accomplish its task. This inefficiency made the response time of the particular Web system operation poor.

System load testing with virtual user sessions will assist in evaluating how the system performs under load. The interpretation of these results is based mainly on the target response time of the system under load and the number of users it can sustain at the target response time. Here, it is important to recall the following guidelines.

- Response time is evaluated on a per operation basis, which is typically recorded by the test tool during the execution of a test script. For example, a test script may perform several iterations of the I-Search Catalog by

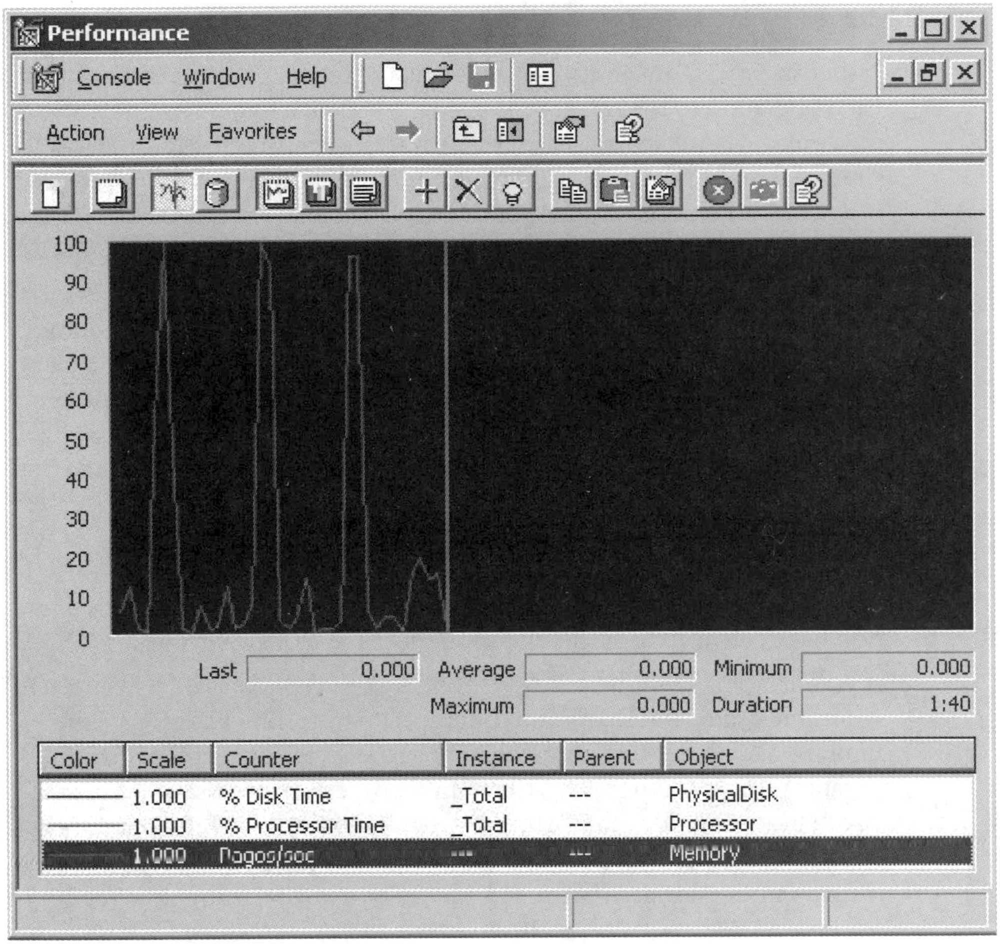

Figure 4-2   Excessive CPU Usage

Keyword and I-View Item operations. The test tool will record the response time for both of those actions during each iteration of the test and will produce an average response time figure for each operation.

- The number of users in each load test should be increased in fixed increments so that measurements can properly chart the degradation of system response to progressively higher levels of load.
- Each load test should be run against several configurations of the site, including single versus multiple Web servers, a different number of processors per server, and any other variations.
- Each load test should be performed on a *base configuration* consisting of one Web server; one application server, if used; and one database server.

The following steps support the evaluation of the results of system load tests.

1. Using the site's base configuration, compare the average response time of each operation to the target response time for each increment of user load. The point where the measured response time meets the target response time of the system represents the maximum user capacity for the base Web system configuration. At this point, the system load measurements on the Web, application, and database servers should be within acceptable limits.

2. Examine the results from a load test performed on a configuration with two Web servers and one application server, if used. When the maximum user capacity of this configuration is approximately twice that of the base configuration, the site is exhibiting linear scaling. When the maximum user capacity is not twice that of the base configuration, a bottleneck has appeared somewhere else within the system. To locate the bottleneck, analyze the load measurements on the application server and database server machines to find excessive system load: CPU, I/O, memory. Correcting the bottleneck condition may require adding an application server or a database server machine to the configuration. After the bottleneck condition has been addressed, the site should be able to achieve linear scaling. If it does not, component or architectural optimization may be necessary.

3. Continue examining maximum user capacity by testing additional configurations in order to project when bottlenecks are likely to appear. An organization may not possess the number of servers necessary to reach a bottleneck condition, so a method of estimation may be required. For example, extrapolation may be necessary to assess the change in performance values associated with the addition of a small number of Web servers, in order to calculate the number of servers at which CPU utilization on a database server has reached its limit. Keep in mind that, as with any extrapolation, the possibility for error is quite large, so it is important to verify the figures with real hardware as soon as possible.

Stress Tests

Once the base component and load tests have been completed, the stress test, which attempts to determine the system's behavior when user load exceeds the system's capacity, must be analyzed. The following considerations should be addressed.

- *User rejections* by the system is one way that it can cope with too much load. Stressing the system during testing should result in an increased number of rejected connections.

- *Error* messages returned to the client Web browser result from component failures as system stress increases.
- *Corruption* of the Web system database can be prevented by examining it after the stress test has been completed to ensure that the database transactions that fail under stress are completely undone, or "rolled back."

Reliability Tests

The reliability test is run over an extended period of time to make sure that the system does not exhibit any defects after substantial uptime and that it continues to perform within the desired response time. Following are some of the important result measurements to examine:

- *Available kilobytes,* which should remain more or less constant over the course of the test. A decreasing value indicates that the system is consuming memory and will eventually begin to *page fault.*
- *Page faults/second* is another gauge for system performance. An increasing or high number of page faults indicates that the system is consuming too much memory and has resorted to swapping memory out to disk as a means to cope with insufficient memory.
- *Errors* experienced during system testing should be examined for possible indication of system reliability problems. A very small number of errors may not represent a significant problem, but an increasing number of errors may indicate that the site is experiencing reliability problems.
- *Database transaction log and table sizes* can grow during extended periods of use. Verify that the transaction log is properly maintained, meaning it is truncated at regular intervals, and that table sizes do not exceed expected limits.

4.6 Improving Performance and Scalability

Once the results of the performance-related tests have been gathered and analyzed, some parts of the Web system may require improvement in order to meet users' response time expectations or so that the system will scale acceptably. This section provides guidance on how to correct common performance and scalability problems.

Architecture

Many technologies can be incorporated into the Web system solution to help reduce server resource use and thereby help improve response time. Some of the more important technologies and design considerations for creating a high-performance Web site are as follows:

- *Inline execution,* which results in reduced system overhead and therefore better response times. ASP/COM+, JSP/EJB, and PHP technologies allow the execution of site functions to occur *inline* with the Web server, typically using threads. Such technology is more efficient than traditional CGI programs, which require the server to start an additional process in order to execute them.

- *CSS,* which can reduce the time needed to transmit a page back to the client, as less data is transmitted. Traditional formatting of HTML pages required a large degree of repeated markup and the use of tables and other layout tricks to produce an acceptable page. CSS can reduce the size of the HTML pages or XSL (eXtensible Stylesheet Language) style sheets by reducing the amount of markup that must be transmitted to the client and by facilitating reuse instead of markup repetition.

- *SSL,* which can be quite expensive in terms of processor time and network bandwidth but improves security. Consider using SSL to encrypt only selected areas of the site, such as user ID and password entry and user payment information. Transmitting large image files over an SSL connection is a particularly performance-expensive operation.

- *HTTP compression,* which reduces the size of data transmitted and thereby improves response time but also puts additional load on the server. It is therefore important to monitor the server when using compression.

- *Page pre-generation,* which saves processing time, as each user request simply retrieves a page instead of invoking business logic and accessing the database (Microsoft 1999a). E-commerce systems typically allow the user to browse a catalog or list of products before committing to the purchase of an item. Even though a good architecture approach would place the product information in a database, these catalog and product pages can be regarded as static information. Because Web servers are good at delivering static HTML and XML pages to users, it is often preferable to pre-generate them on a regular basis by a background process.

- *Database design,* which can be enhanced by optimal use of indexes, stored procedures, and denormalization techniques to speed processing time.

Excessive Use of Resources by Components

During analysis of performance and load test results, some components are commonly viewed as using too many server resources. A component's excessive use of server resources usually results in increased processing time and therefore increased response time experienced by the user. In addition, machine resources needed by other components will be tied up, thus requiring more machines to fulfill the performance objectives of the site. Optimizing a site's resource use is one of the more important tasks in site optimization.

Server resources can be broadly classified as CPU, I/O—primarily disk and network access—and memory. CPU and I/O utilization tend to have the most direct impact on processing time, whereas memory consumption will have an impact mostly when the amount of free memory approaches zero. When memory is no longer available, paging—swapping memory to disk—occurs, resulting in further disk I/O.

Some of the ways to optimize components and reduce their use of server resources follow.

- *Optimize code algorithms.* Excessive CPU use is usually caused by inefficient algorithm design. The performance of inefficient algorithms, especially in loops, can consume a significant amount of CPU. Restructure and optimize code in order to reduce the amount of CPU consumed.
- *Eliminate memory leaks.* A system component will leak memory by allocating memory and then failing to release the memory at a later point. Memory leaks needlessly consume memory and, in some cases, drastically slow down the server, owing to the effects of *paging,* or swapping out those pages of wasted memory to disk in order to make room for other needs. Various tools are available to locate memory leaks down to the source code level.
- *Reduce disk usage.* Physical disks, including RAID (redundant array of independent disks) arrays, are quite slow in comparison to access speed associated with physical RAM. When a system component is demonstrating high levels of disk time, consider loading data into memory and accessing it from there rather than accessing the disk. From a performance perspective, it is always preferable to read from memory rather than access a disk, assuming, of course, that the machine has enough memory to store the data without paging.

Logging can be useful as a rough gauge for determining where processing time is being spent by a system component. Application logs can be used to determine the runtimes of various steps inside a component, which can greatly speed the process of locating a performance problem. Consider the following example: The response time of a use case has been measured as being 1 second too long on average, and one of the components is consuming more than 90 percent of the CPU on average during the base-performance single-user tests. To track down the problem, the logging facility was activated and the test was re-executed. Examination of the application logs after the test show that the component is spending most of its time running a particularly complex algorithm located in a C++ class method. Further examination of the source code reveals that this algorithm is poorly designed and can be optimized to improve the response time.

When implementing a logging mechanism with performance in mind, make sure that the mechanism can place a timestamp on each entry down to at least the millisecond level. It is also important to log often and at major points during code execution so that program execution can be tracked. Following is sample log file excerpt.

```
Date          Time             Message
12/01/2000    20:26:54.721     COM Entrypoint:
                               SearchCatalogByKeyword
12/01/2000    20:26:54.751     querying database
12/01/2000    20:26:54.891     successfully retrieved book
                               list from database
12/01/2000    20:26:54.910     sorting book list
12/01/2000    20:26:56.10      finished sorting book list
12/01/2000    20:26:56.25      SearchCatalogByKeyword ending
```

This trace shows that the component was able to retrieve the book list from the database quickly enough but took more than 1 second to sort the results. In this case, either the sort algorithm could be optimized to run faster, or the database could be used instead of the application code to sort the results. Keep in mind that logging should be disabled or compiled out prior to running any performance tests, as the logging mechanism will consume server resources and therefore have an impact on response times.

Scalability Issues

Increasing a Web system's maximum user capacity is the goal of scalability. Scaling a Web site includes the following considerations:

Web Server Load Balancing[1]

Using more than one Web server within a Web system configuration requires a load-balancing or distribution mechanism with which to direct clients to one of the Web servers. Solutions to this problem range from simple to complex.

---

[1]When load testing against a load balanced Web Site, it may be necessary to "spoof" IP addresses from the load testing client machine if the load balancer uses incoming IP addresses to distribute connections to Web servers. Major load testing tools, such as Mercury Interactive's Load Runner, provide this capability.

- *DNS (domain name server) round-robin,* the simplest form of load balancing, is a feature of most of the popular server platforms and allows them to be configured with multiple IP addresses for a single name, such as www.yoursite.com. Each time a request comes in for the address of www.yoursite.com, the DNS server responds with the next IP address in its list. When it gets to the end of the list, the DNS server will start over at the beginning; hence the name round-robin.
- *Hardware load balancing* is often a better solution than the simple round-robin approach, as the load-balancing algorithms are more complex and can distribute the load to back-end Web servers more efficiently.
- *Windows 2000 NLB,* incorporated into Windows 2000 Advanced Server, is not as efficient as hardware load balancing, but is simple to configure and does not rely on the DNS server to distribute the load.

Application Server Load Balancing

Some EJB application servers, such as BEA WebLogic, have load-balancing capability for distributing requests from the Web servers to application servers. Microsoft Application Center 2000 can load balance requests to back-end COM+ objects on Windows 2000 server machines.

Database Servers

The scaling technique used on a database server is dependent largely on the database vendor. Some databases, such as Oracle and DB2, support clustering multiple servers to increase the maximum number of users. Microsoft SQL Server 2000, on the other hand, does not support clustering to service additional users (clustering is supported to increase availability, however). In order to scale the SQL Server 2000 database, you must either upgrade to a more powerful machine or partition the data across multiple database servers, known as *federated servers,* and direct requests to the most appropriate server in the tier.

Network

The network supporting the Web system may also need to be scaled in order to avoid a network bandwidth bottleneck, which occurs when too many machines are attempting to transmit on the network at the same time. Some of the ways in which a network can be scaled are

- *Switches versus hubs.* If the site is using an Ethernet network, switched Ethernet can improve network performance by providing an isolated connection between hosts on the network. Ethernet hubs use a broadcasting technique, whereby a packet sent by a host is broadcast to all the hosts connected to the hub, even though the packet is destined for only one of them. This broadcasting consumes a significant amount of bandwidth. Switches are much more efficient, as they create an isolated channel between two hosts on the network, allowing them to converse without broadcasting. This kind of scaling is quite cost-effective and does not carry much of an administrative load on the network. For more on switches versus hubs, see Microsoft 2000a, p. 15.

- *Subnetting.* Creating a separate subnetwork for some hosts can reduce the amount of bandwidth used on the network by isolating groups of hosts from one another. Subnetting a network can be complex and may increase the workload for network administrators.
- *Larger Internet connection.* Access to the Web system by a high volume of Web clients can saturate the site's Internet connection, causing more collisions between servers attempting to communicate with their clients on the Internet and clients attempting to communicate with the site's servers. Upgrading the site's Internet connection to a higher-speed capability is one way to deal with this situation.
- *Additional Internet connections.* Alternatively, additional Internet connections can be used to increase the Web system's bandwidth. This also has the added benefit of increasing the availability of the site, as multiple connections can offer redundancy in the event of failure.

Session State

Each user connecting to the site may require some *session state data* to be stored for the duration of the visit. For example, when a user adds an item to the shopping cart, the data associated with the item—SKU, quantity, and so on—must be associated with the user. The data can be associated with the user through

- *Web server sessions,* which store user session data in a *session object,* which is automatically associated with the current user. If the user does not return to the site within a specified timeout interval, the session data is discarded. This ability is available on only some Web servers, such as IIS.
- *Database sessions,* which store the session data in a database table, with the corresponding user's ID used to look up the data when it is needed.
- *Cookies,* which if the session data is small and not security sensitive, can be stored on the client machine. The cookie will be automatically transmitted back to the server when the user accesses a page. Shopping carts are typically implemented with client-side cookies.

Depending on the approach taken, storage of session state data can have a dramatic impact on the ability of the Web site to be scaled. Storing the session state on the Web server effectively *binds* the user to that server, which makes load balancing difficult. The user will have to be directed back to that server for subsequent requests so that the session state data is available. Hardware load balancers can sometimes do this automatically; otherwise, an HTTP redirect must be issued to redirect the client back to the server during the client's initial connection with the server.

Database server sessions are more scalable, as load balancing can be freely used to distribute users among the Web servers. Database server sessions require a bit more work on the development side, as the session data does not automatically expire from the database. In addition, each time the user connects to a Web server, a network connection and query must be made to the database to retrieve the data, which can increase the load on the database server and the network. Cookies, when applicable, are a good solution, as they do not tie up server resources relative to either the database or the Web server and can be set to expire in a number of ways. The transmission of cookies does consume a bit of the bandwidth between the client and the server, as they need to be transmitted to the Web server on each access to a page or other resource.

SSL

Similar to the session state problem, SSL inhibits load balancing of the site. SSL connections have their own kind of state, namely, the *session key,* which is exchanged at the beginning of the secure connection. Both client and server must know the value of this key in order to participate in a secure session. If the user were to be directed to a different server in the middle of an SSL conversation, the new server would not know the session key and, therefore, could not read the client's transmission. Typically, SSL clients are bound to their servers by hardware load balancers or are associated manually through the use of an HTTP redirect.

Background Processing

In some situations, it may not be practical for the Web server or the application server to perform an operation while the client is waiting for a response. Some tasks simply take too long and potentially tie up Web server resources with needless idling, waiting for the task to complete. In these situations, a background processing server may be an effective way to reduce the Web server resource usage. Such a server assumes the processing load from the Web server, which quickly returns a response to the client machine with information that the request has been submitted for processing. Typically, a queuing mechanism, such as MSMQ, BEA's Tuxedo, or IBM's MQSeries, can be used to deposit a request in a queue and then immediately return control to the caller. The client will be notified through another mechanism when the job is complete.

4.7 Analyzing Scalability and Cost

Scalability analysis in the Web environment is the process of determining a site's resource requirements to handle future load within an acceptable response time. This type of planning is especially important when upcoming events may cause additional load on the site. For example, holidays and marketing campaigns can significantly increase the number of users of a Web site.

Using the data gathered during the performance and load-testing activities, it is possible to calculate the required server resources to support a target number of users. For example, Figure 4-3 shows the relationship, called a *scalability curve*, between the number of users on the site and the response time (Chiu 1999). The test producing these results has simulated users by running various types of virtual user sessions. Figure 4-3 also shows the target response time, as specified in the Web system's performance requirements, which in this case is 3 seconds. Using the target ceiling of 3 seconds, the site can accommodate a maximum of approximately 510 users in the listed configuration.

Analysis has revealed that the Web system will soon be required to accommodate a total of 1,800 concurrent users, owing to an upcoming advertising

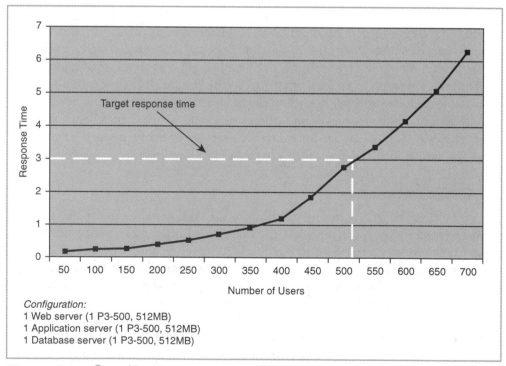

Configuration:
1 Web server (1 P3-500, 512MB)
1 Application server (1 P3-500, 512MB)
1 Database server (1 P3-500, 512MB)

Figure 4-3   Base Configuration Scalability Curve

campaign. To handle this type of load, the site must be properly scaled in order to increase server resources for the additional users and to provide them with response times within the 3-second requirement. In order to reach the target user capacity, the site could potentially be scaled vertically, horizontally, or possibly even functionally. In order to support a decision, performance tests were conducted to reflect the various increases in capacity that would result for each of the three scalability options. The graphs depicted in Figures 4-4, 4-5, and 4-6 summarize the results of these tests.

Figure 4-4 shows the effect of vertical scaling on site capacity. Here, vertically scaling the site by adding processors to the Web and application servers resulted in a user capacity of 650 users, an increase of 140 users. Figure 4-5 shows that the site exhibits the property known as *linear scaling,* as doubling the number of servers in each tier resulted in approximately doubling the user capacity to about 1,050 users. Functional scaling, reflected in Figure 4-6, also offered an increase in capacity, although it fell short of the horizontal, load-balanced solution.

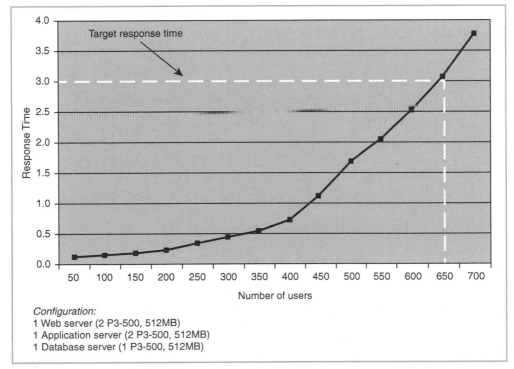

Figure 4-4   Vertical Scaling

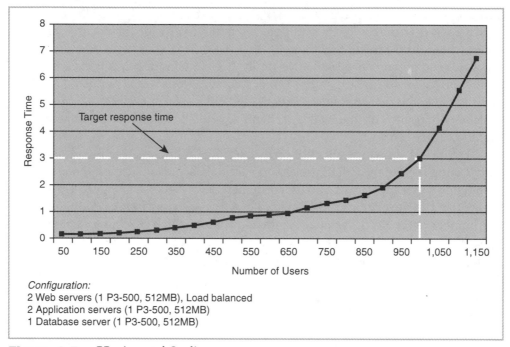

Figure 4-5   Horizontal Scaling

From this analysis, it can be determined that the site can reach its goal of 1,800 users through the implementation of various configurations as follows:

- Horizontal scaling: results in a maximum user capacity of $510 \times 4 = 2,040$
  —Four single-processor Web servers
  —Four single-processor application servers
  —One single-processor database server
- Vertical + horizontal scaling: results in a maximum user capacity of $650 \times 3 = 1,950$
  —Three dual-processor Web servers
  —Three dual-processor application servers
  —One single-processor database server

In order to determine which approach to pursue, the costs associated with each configuration must be considered. Assuming that the cost of a single-processor server is \$4,000 and that of a dual-processor server is \$5,000, the configuration costs for the two scaling options are as follows. The pure horizontal-scaling solution may also have additional administrative costs, as it requires more machines to set up, configure, and monitor.

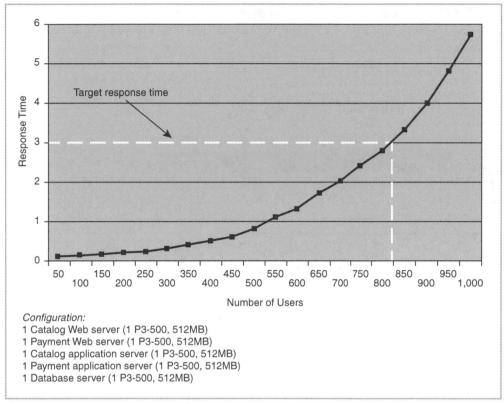

Figure 4-6   Functional Scaling

- Horizontal scaling only: $36,000 ($4,000 × four Web servers, $4,000 × four application servers, $4,000 × one database server)
- Vertical + horizontal scaling: $34,000 ($5,000 × three Web servers, $5,000 × three application servers, $4,000 × one database server)

4.8 TBS Case Study

This section describes the execution of the base performance and single-operation load tests on the I-View Previous Order use case. The tests were conducted in a small lab, using relatively modest hardware:

- One Web server: Dual P3-500MHz, 512MB RAM
- One database server: Single P3-850MHz, 512MB RAM
- 100Mb/sec Ethernet LAN

A load testing tool was used to simulate users accessing the Web server, and both servers were monitored with the Windows 2000 Performance Monitor.[2] The following counters were monitored:

- Web server:
  —Percent processor time
  —Percent disk time

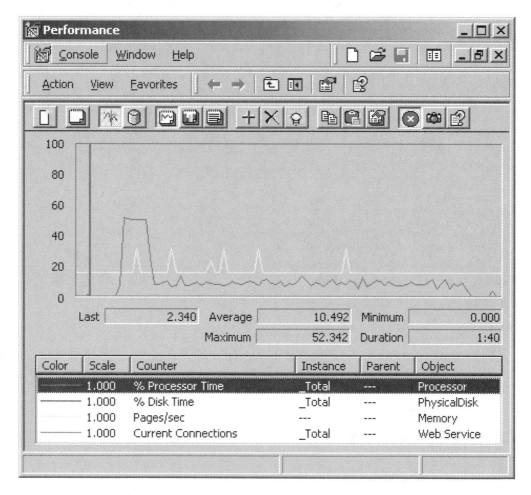

Figure 4-7   Web Server Measurements (Base Performance, First Run)

---

[2]The load testing tool used in this case study example was Mercury Interactive's Load Runner. For more information on Load Runner and other load testing tools, see Chapter 7.

—Pages/second (memory)
—Current connections (IIS)
• Database server
—Percent processor time
—Percent disk time
—Available MB (memory)
—Pages/second (memory)

The first tests performed were for base performance. Recall that this type of test is run with a single user in the base configuration of the site, meaning that each tier implements a minimal number of nodes. Test scenarios for base performance

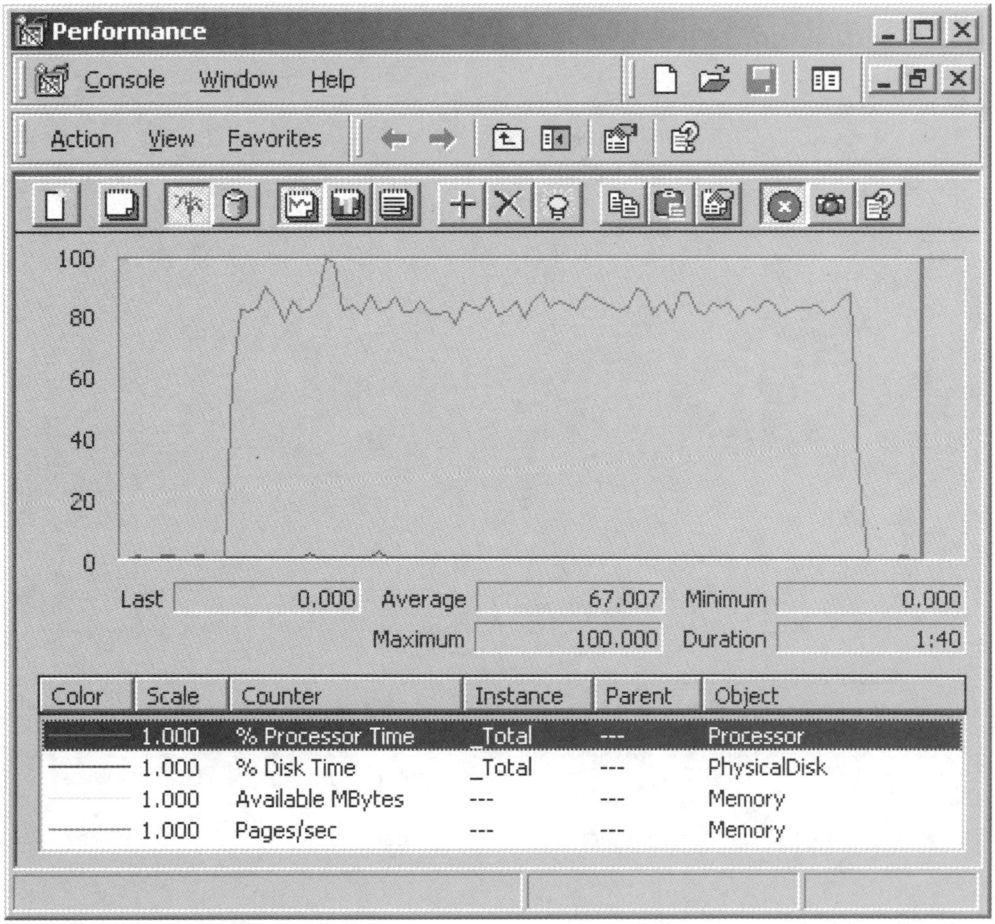

Figure 4-8 Database Server Measurements (Base Performance, First Run)

also vary certain test parameters, such as the number of database records, the use of images, and the use of SSL. The first few tests demonstrated no performance-related issues with I-View Previous Order. Only when the number of database records was increased did the components start to show performance problems.

The first performance captures (Figures 4-7 and 4-8) showed server load with one user, 150K records in the `OrderInfo` table, and 100K records in the `Item` table. Although the average response time for the operation was measured at 0.8 seconds, the performance graphs showed that the database server was experiencing excessive CPU usage during the test and barely any disk or memory use. Although a

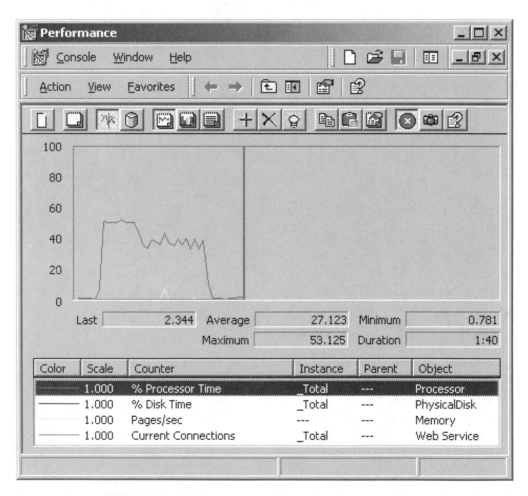

Figure 4-9   Web Server Measurements (Base Performance, Second Run)

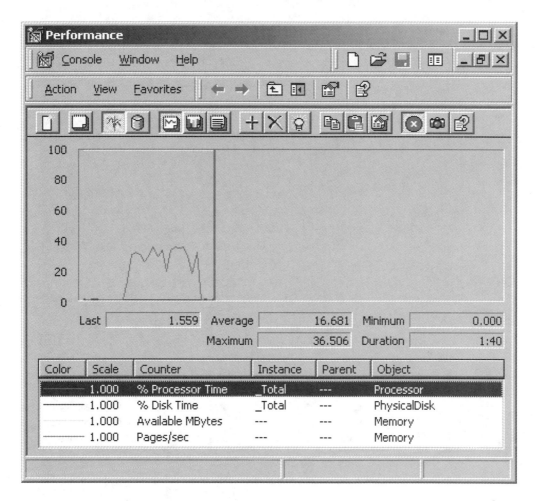

Figure 4-10 Database Server Measurements (Base Performance, Second Run)

large number of records were in the database, the CPU should not be doing a great amount of work for only one user. Investigation of the database revealed that no indexes were created on the OrderInfo and Item tables, resulting in very large table scans being performed on these tables by the database server. After creating indexes on the primary keys of these tables, the performance tests were executed again. This time, the CPU use of both the Web server and the database server were acceptable (see Figures 4-9 and 4-10), as was the response time, 0.26 seconds.

Next, the single-operation load tests, which simply add more users to the base performance tests, were executed against the I-View Previous Order use case. With ten users, the response time was 0.8 seconds per user. Although this figure is

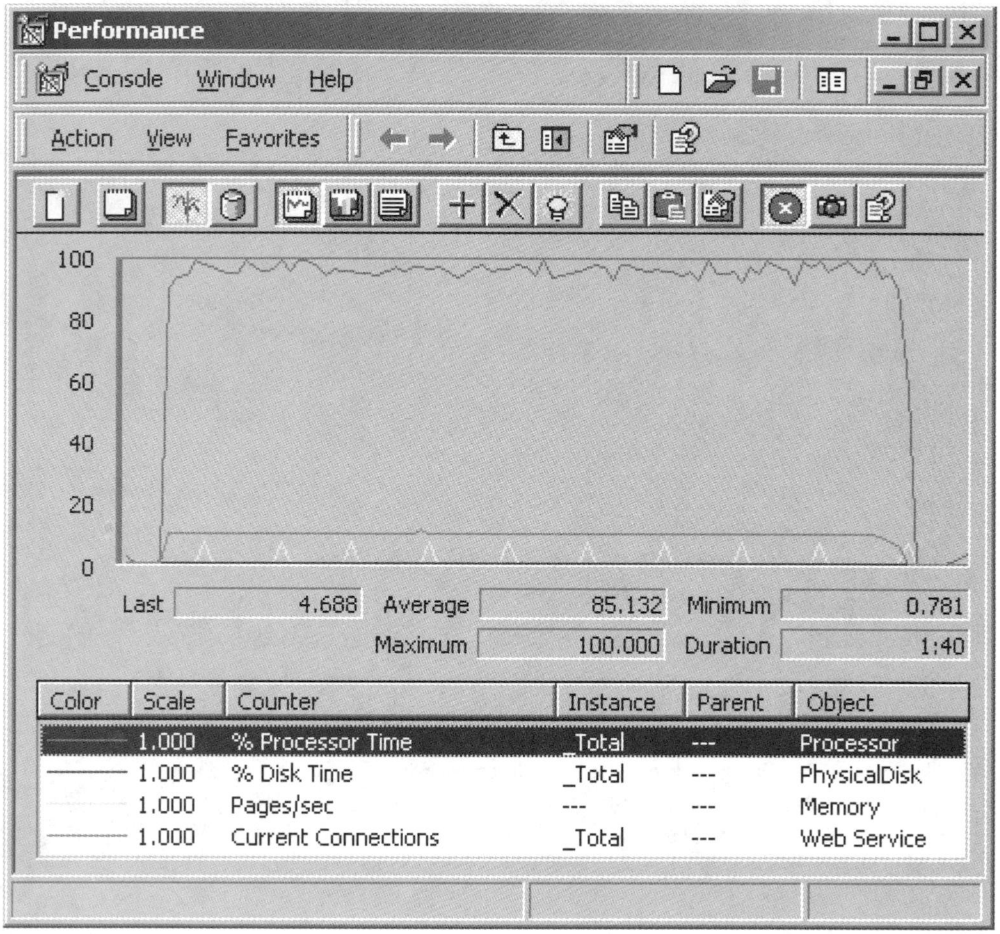

Figure 4-11   Web Server Measurements (Single-Operation, First Run)

acceptable, the CPU use on the Web server is still very high, nearly 100 percent constant (see Figure 4-11), while the database server is within acceptable limits (see Figure 4-12). Therefore, the implementation of the I-View Previous Order components was investigated, revealing that one of the components was making heavy use of C++ STL string operations, which were frequently allocating memory. The component's implementation was optimized to eliminate the allocations, and the tests were executed once again.

Although the CPU use did not drop drastically (see Figure 4-13), it did drop enough to lower the average response time per user to 0.7 seconds, which happens to

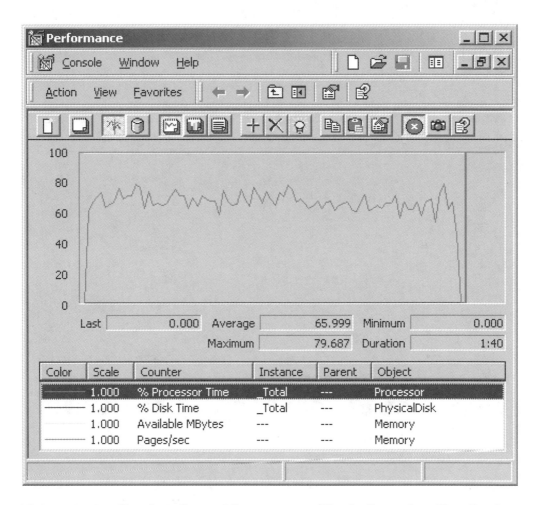

Figure 4-12 Database Server Measurements (Single-Operation, First Run)

be 0.1 second faster than the figure first recorded during the large data set base performance tests with a single user. Further optimization would probably lower the Web server CPU use even more, but the database server CPU appears to be approaching limits here as well (see Figure 4-14).

It is worth noting that according to the TBS nonfunctional requirements specification provided in Appendix C, the TBS system must handle 500 simultaneous *broadband* users with a response time of between 2 and 4 seconds. Further testing showed that with the large number of database records and modest hardware, the I-View Previous Order use case could handle 25 simultaneous users

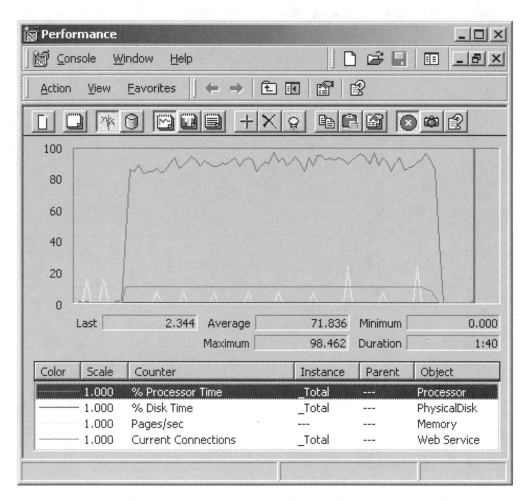

Figure 4-13   Web Server Measurements (Single-Operation, Second Run)

within the response time target of 2–4 seconds. In addition to further component optimization, either vertical or horizontal scaling would need to be applied to achieve the goal of 500 simultaneous users. Given that the tests were performed on smaller, desktop-class machines, vertical scaling to production-class machines would most likely offer the largest capacity increase, although some horizontal scaling would probably need to be performed on the Web server tier as well.

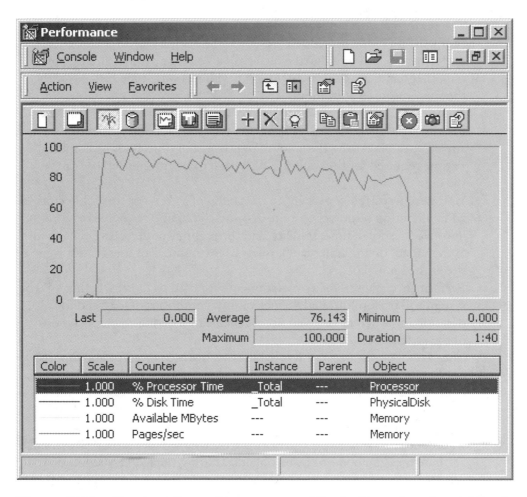

Figure 4-14 Database Server Measurements (Single-Operation, Second Run)

4.9 Chapter Summary

⚠ Ensuring that the Web system is able to service its customers in a timely fashion is critical to the survival of an organization conducting business over the Web. A Web system that feels slow may give customers a negative impression of the business and may give them cause to seek out a competing system.

⚠ Web sites must be able to deal with periodic bursts of user load. The Web site must be able to tolerate, without failure, these peak use times.

⚠ The performance of a Web system is of concern from two perspectives. From an end user's perspective, response time is the basic measure of performance used to judge the quality of a Web site. Administrators, on the other hand, are concerned not only with response time but also with the site's resource utilization.

⚠ Response time performance factors include the amount of time required for a client browser to make a connection to the Web site and transmit any user-supplied data, the amount of processing time, and the amount of time required for the resulting Web page to be transmitted back to the user.

⚠ Web system scalability pertains to the ability of a Web system architecture to add computing resources to a site in order to obtain acceptable or improved response time, stability, and throughput under a particular load. System load, on the other hand, refers to the number of users accessing the site at the same time.

⚠ Performance and scalability requirements are used to judge whether a Web system will perform properly under various conditions of load and for determining whether the Web site is capable of meeting the expectations of the system's customer base.

⚠ The goal of performance and scalability testing is to monitor and report on the site's behavior under various load conditions. The four major types of performance-related tests are base performance, load, stress, and reliability.

⚠ The essential performance and scalability test phases include test planning, script creation, and test execution.

⚠ In order to properly analyze performance characteristics for a Web system, accurate measurements must be obtained during the load tests. Although no absolutely correct value for any particular measurement may exist, the list in Table 4-1 offers some general guidelines for interpreting whether a system load problem exists.

⚠ Once the results of the performance-related tests have been gathered and analyzed, some parts of the Web system may require improvement in order to meet user response time expectations or so that the system will scale acceptably.

⚠ Scalability analysis pertains to the process of determining a site's resource requirements to handle future load within an acceptable response time. This type of analysis and planning is especially important when upcoming events or expectations for significant growth in business over the Web arise. Using the data gathered during performance and load-testing activities, it is possible to calculate the number of additional server resources required to support elevated use levels.

4.10 References

Chiu, Willy. 1999. "Design for Scalability," IBM High-Volume Web Site Team. www7b.boulder.ibm.com/wsdd/library/techarticles/hvws/scalability.html

Menasce, Daniel A., and Virgilio A. F. Almeida. 1998. *Capacity Planning for Web Performance*. Upper Saddle River, NJ: Prentice-Hall.

Microsoft. 1999a. "A Site Server 3.0 Commerce Edition Scalability Case Study." Microsoft Site Server 3.0 Resource Kit. August.

Microsoft. 1999b. "Building High-Scalability Server Farms." Microsoft Site Server Resource Kit. September.

Microsoft. 2000a. "Capacity Planning—Duwamish Online Sample E-Commerce Site."

Rational Software Corporation. 1999. "The Rational Approach to Automated Testing." http://www.rational.com/products/whitepapers/100581.jsp.

chapter 5

Compatibility

Ensuring compatibility across numerous computer configurations involves different software, operating systems, and even devices.

Browser incompatibilities have become a major source of trouble for Web sites over the past few years. Deviations from the HTML standard, as well as varying support for CSS and DHTML across browsers, can make the effort of designing a widely accessible Web system quite difficult. To ensure proper compatibility with a set of target browsers, the system must be designed with a particular level of compatibility in mind from the start.

In a complex Web system, adding support for additional browsers late in the development cycle is generally nontrivial and may require some rather large changes to the site's architecture. For this reason, the Web system requirements should specify, early in the project life cycle, the needed level of browser compatibility. In addition, the use of certain technologies, such as client-side controls or plug-ins, must be carefully considered, as this may result in excluding a wide range of potential browsers and platforms from being able to properly access the system.

Compatibility verification is required to ensure that the Web system displays and behaves as intended when accessed by various kinds of browsers and browser versions. In addition, access to the site should be tested with various operating systems, such as Windows, Mac OS, and UNIX, and possibly even with various hardware and software combinations. As with most types of testing, it is important to repeat compatibility tests following each development iteration, in order to ensure that new compatibility issues have not been introduced.

The appearance and the proper functioning of the Web system are critical to its success. If compatibility problems prevent a Web system from functioning properly, the unpleasant experience will result in lower end user satisfaction and reduced use of the Web system. For e-commerce systems, the primary business goal is to make the system inviting enough that the customer becomes a regular user of the system. Unfortunately, the presence of even one scripting error or deformed table can quickly convince customers that the site, and by extension possibly the business, are not of sufficient quality to warrant their further business.

Before proceeding to discuss compatibility issues and ways to handle them, we need to distinguish between *compatibility* issues and *usability* issues. Many so-called compatibility issues are in fact usability issues. Compatibility refers to whether a technology or an implementation is functioning as intended on all target browsers and platforms. Usability, by contrast, refers to how well something functions. For example, screen size and user connection speed are usability issues; the browser can display the content on various platforms but perhaps not in the best way for the user. Although the site's content makes use of a page width and height that exceeds the user's video resolution, the browser uses scroll bars for the user to navigate to the content that is rendered off-screen. In this respect, the site is *compatible* with the user's video resolution, but the use of scroll bars for navigation reduces the site's *usability*. This chapter focuses on compatibility issues; Chapter 6, on usability.

5.1 Client-side Compatibility Issues

Several compatibility variables reside on the client side of the Web system environment. With each visit to a Web site, a customer is accessing the system through the use of a hardware platform, operating system, browser, and other software components. Although it is possible to support each and every client browser and operating system combination that a Web client may possess, doing so may involve a reduction in site functionality or simplification of some interface elements.

Browser-Related Incompatibilities

A primary compatibility concern on the client side of the Web system equation pertains to browser compatibility. During the 1990s, Netscape and Microsoft battled for dominance in the Web browser market. This competition spawned the continued release of new versions of browser software for which each new release contained additional functionality. Netscape introduced frames as a feature that other browsers did not have.[1] During the mid-1990s, both Netscape and Microsoft advertised browsers and included support for features that the other didn't support. The incorporation of special features, or browser extensions, not supported by other browsers on the market is the root of many Web system compatibility issues.

Modern Web browsers support a number of technologies and languages, all intended to enhance the user's browsing experience. In addition, some technologies, such as CSS, XML/XSLT, and XHTML, provide a means for separating a Web document's content from its presentation. In fact, the state of Web browsers today is the result of a misuse of the original intent of HTML, which had been to divide a document's contents into various sections, such as a title, paragraphs, and links to other documents. The addition and use of browser tags to control the appearance of a document was not the original intent and has led to many problems for Web system compatibility with multiple types of display technologies. This is even more important today, as the popularity of handheld devices and other types of Web access methods increases.

HTML Version

HTML (Hypertext Markup Language) has seen several revisions since the original draft of HTML 1.0 was released in 1992 by the CERN (European Centre for Nuclear Research) team. HTML is defined using the Standard General Markup Language (SGML), a language used to create other languages. HTML was created to mark up documents into various sections for delivery over an Internet connection. One of the first Web browsers, NCSA's *Mosaic*, released in 1993, was based on this specification. A year later, the HTML 2.0 specification was created by the IETF (Internet Engineering Task Force), and Netscape Navigator 1.0 was released shortly thereafter.

The original release of Netscape Navigator also included some extensions to the HTML language, which were referred to as *proposed HTML 3.0* tags. At the time, however, sites that took advantage of these tags could be viewed only with Netscape, which contributed to the dominance of Netscape at that time. A short while later, Microsoft released Internet Explorer and followed the practice of introducing proprietary tags to encourage sites to promote Internet Explorer as the preferred viewer.

Eventually, the W3C (World Wide Web Consortium) organization was formed to bring a standard to the HTML language by working with all the major vendors. The result was HTML 3.2, which contained the extensions developed by

---

[1] For more information, see the Netscape Web site: http://www.netscape.com/newsref/pr/ newsrelease43.html.

Netscape and Microsoft, as well as others. Later, the W3C released the HTML 4.0 specification, which introduced a variety of features, including client-side scripts. Microsoft and Netscape soon released their 4.0 browsers, which made use of the newly released specification. It is interesting to note that the major browsers had supported some form of scripting, such as JavaScript, JScript, and VBScript, well before the HTML 4.0 specification was released, which again contributed to browser incompatibilities.

HTML 4.1, the latest and probably the last specification, mainly corrects a few issues with the HTML 4.0 specification. Internet Explorer 5.x and Netscape 6.0, the latest versions of these products, both implement the HTML 4.1 specification. However, both of these products still fail to implement the complete standard, again contributing to the cycle of incompatibility. In addition, some proprietary HTML extensions are implemented by some browsers but not others.

Because browser versions implement a superset of the HTML specification, typically the one that existed when the browser was being developed, specifying the compatibility of a particular browser version implicitly mandates an HTML version that the site must support. For example, specifying that the site must be compatible with Microsoft Internet Explorer 3.0 means that the site must be able to produce pages that conform to the HTML 3.2 specification. As discussed later, in the section Browser Differences, this can be achieved in several ways.

HTML Rendering

The evolution of HTML has been quite complex and even with the latest releases of the major browsers does not guarantee that a site will look the same on two different browsers claiming to implement the same specification. The primary reason for this is the subtle differences in the way that the browsers render the pages for viewing. For example, many sites have based their display on Microsoft Internet Explorer, designing and implementing pages that display correctly on that browser. Even though these sites are using HTML tags and attributes from the HTML 4.0 specification, which is supported by many browsers, the site may make use of several assumptions about the way Internet Explorer will render the page when presented with certain tags and attributes.

These assumptions break down when the site is viewed with another browser, such as Netscape. Netscape will be able to create all the elements as specified by the site, but they may not display or line up exactly as they do on Internet Explorer, creating an incompatibility. Further, if the site chooses to use some of Internet Explorer's proprietary HTML tags or attributes, Netscape may not be able to render some elements at all.

Cascading Style Sheets (CSS)

About the same time that HTML 4.0 was being developed, the W3C was also working on a proposal for CSS (cascading style sheets). CSS addresses the idea of separating the document's content from its presentation. CSS allows the Web developer to apply *styles* to HTML elements in order to modify the physical appearance of the elements. This provides a mechanism, other than the creation of new HTML tags, to control the way that markup is rendered by a browser. With CSS, the document need contain only the basic content, with a style sheet controlling the way that content is displayed by the browser. The two *levels* of CSS are CSS1 and CSS2. CSS2 added several new features to CSS1, including the ability to precisely position elements and control their visibility.

CSS is another problematic compatibility area. Certain versions of Netscape, for example, do not fully support the CSS2 specification, thus leading to pages that do not properly display on those browsers, even though the pages adhere to the W3C standard.

Handling Browser Differences

Some of the ways in which browser differences can be handled with respect to HTML and CSS processing follow.

Single HTML Page Set

One approach involves the use of a single set of HTML pages that are compatible with all target browsers (Figure 5-1). Also called the *lowest-common denominator* approach, this method is the easiest from a maintenance perspective but requires that the site sacrifice functionality and use of some of the more advanced layout techniques. This approach requires the use of only those HTML and CSS elements that are properly respected by all the site's target browsers, avoiding the use of tags and attributes that do not work properly on those browsers. When it is necessary to support older browsers—those that do not support CSS—it will probably be necessary to use HTML tables to lay out content and to avoid CSS layout techniques. In addition, the use of certain technologies should be avoided altogether. For example, when the site requires compatibility with Netscape Navigator, the use of ActiveX controls should be avoided.

It is important to note that browsers generally ignore elements and attributes that they do not support. This means that it may be possible to use certain features, such as some CSS attributes, to enhance a page for browsers that support CSS and to have those features ignored by browsers that do not support CSS (Graham 2000,

p. 109). As long as it is not necessary to have those features to use the site, down-level browsers will simply display a less attractive version of the site. In some cases, this may be acceptable.

Strict adherence to the W3C HTML specification is required in this approach, as any vendor-specific deviations from the specifications will not carry to other vendors. A useful tool for verifying the level of adherence is the W3C Validator.[2] When provided with a destination URL, such as your Web site, the Validator will examine the site's content to determine the level of W3C HTML conformance.

Multiple HTML Page Sets

Another approach involves the use of multiple sets of HTML pages, one for each type of browser that may be used to access the site. Although some of the site's pages may be compatible with all browsers, some functional areas on the site may require a more complex user interface, in turn requiring that the applicable pages be custom tailored to support particular browsers. In this particular situation, the Web system will need to be able to identify an incoming browser—through the use of ASP, PHP, or another server scripting technology—and then be able to transmit the appropriate page back to the particular client machine. This approach is costly from a software maintenance perspective, as multiple sets of pages must be maintained. At times, however, it may be the only way to produce a complex Web interface on multiple browsers.

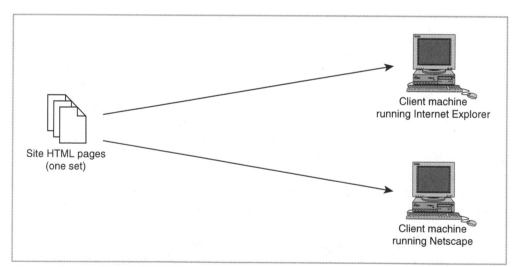

Figure 5-1   Single HTML Page Set

---

[2]This tool is available at http://validator.w3.org.

The following JScript ASP code fragment demonstrates one way this could be accomplished.

```
// the HTTP_USER_AGENT header contains the browser type
// string
var userAgent
    = new String
      (Request.ServerVariables("HTTP_USER_AGENT"));
if (userAgent.indexOf("MSIE") != -1)
{
    // any version of Internet Explorer
    Server.Transfer("page_IE.asp");
}
else if (userAgent.indexOf("Netscape") != -1)
{
    // any version of Netscape
    Server.Transfer("page_Netscape.asp");
}
else
{
    // all other browsers
    Server.Transfer("page_Other.asp");
}
```

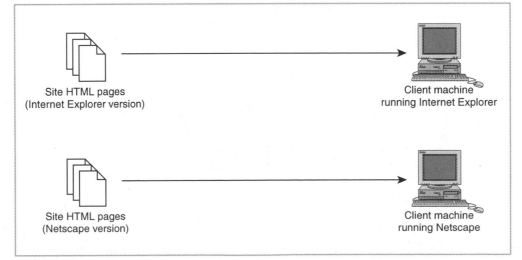

Figure 5-2　Multiple HTML Page Sets

Single HTML/Multiple Style Sheets

If all the target browsers for the site support CSS, a single HTML page can be written and then dynamically linked to the appropriate style sheet for the user's browser (Figure 5-3). This will allow adjustments to fonts and other CSS-controllable differences, while still using a base HTML page. This approach assumes that the HTML elements and structure are compatible with all target Web browsers. Compared to the previous approach, this approach is better from a maintenance perspective, as the same HTML file can be reused across browsers. This approach is limited, however, to CSS-capable browsers.

Following is a JScript ASP code fragment for selecting different style sheets, based on the user's browser. Note that this script will provide a style sheet for Internet Explorer 4.x and 5.x and any version of Netscape but will not provide one for other browsers.

```
<html>
<head>
<%
    // the HTTP_USER_AGENT header contains the browser type
    // string
    var userAgent = new String
        (Request.ServerVariables("HTTP_USER_AGENT"));
    if (userAgent.indexOf("MSIE 4") != -1)
    {
        // Internet Explorer version 4.x
        Response.Write("<link rel="stylesheet"
                            href="IE4.css"
                            type="text/css">
                        </link>");
    }
    else if (userAgent.indexOf("MSIE 5") != -1)
    {
        // Internet Explorer version 5.x
        Response.Write("<link rel="stylesheet"
                            href="IE5.css"
                            type="text/css">
                        </link>");
    }
    else if (userAgent.indexOf("Netscape") != -1)
    {
      // any version of Netscape
```

```
Response.Write("<link rel="stylesheet"
                        href="Netscape.css"
                        type="text/css">
                </link>");
    }
%>
</head>
```

Dynamic HTML Page Set

This approach involves the use of a single set of HTML pages that make use of a script to alter themselves *on the fly.* This approach is similar to the first one but can offer additional capabilities. This approach requires that all the site's target browsers support ECMAScript (see the next section for a discussion of ECMAScript). Each HTML page will contain scripting blocks that output the appropriate HTML markup, depending on the browser, as depicted in the following sample script.

```
<script lang="Javascript">
    if (navigator.appName == "Microsoft Internet Explorer")
    {
        document.write("<marquee>Only Internet Explorer
        supports the 'marquee' tag</marquee>");
    }
```

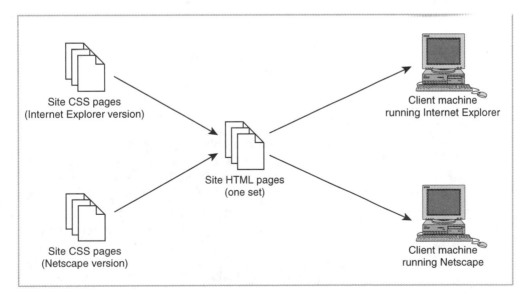

Figure 5-3   Single HTML Page Set/Multiple CSS Style Sheets

```
    else
    {
        document.write("<p>on other browsers we use the
        'p' tag</p>");
    }
</script>
```

This script will cause the document to contain the marquee tag in any version of Internet Explorer, but otherwise the paragraph tag will be used. This method is useful when only a few areas on a page require the detection of the browser through use of a script, as reflected in the example, in order to output different content. When the page requires radically different code and/or markup for each browser, the previous technique is more appropriate.

ECMAScript

Netscape Navigator 2.0 gave Web designers a new feature: the ability to place script code in the HTML page and have the code execute on the client. This capability was provided through the use of *JavaScript*, a scripting language designed for Web page scripting. When Navigator 2.0 was released, this capability was a Netscape-unique feature.

Microsoft also provided scripting capability in the Internet Explorer browser, supporting two languages: VBScript and JScript. VBScript is Microsoft's own scripting language, based on its Visual Basic product. JScript is, with a few minor exceptions, compatible with Netscape's JavaScript. Later, JavaScript/JScript would be standardized into ECMAScript, the scripting language that the past several releases of both browsers support. The ECMAScript language is largely compatible across the major browsers, with a few exceptions.

Document Object Model (DOM)

Another important area of browser compatibility is the Document Object Model (DOM). Critical to client-side scripting, the DOM is the set of *document elements* that the client-side script can interact with to read and to change the contents of the document dynamically, through scripting. This is perhaps the most problematic area of compatibility among the major browsers, as Internet Explorer, Netscape, and other browsers have different scripting "models" for accessing page objects, such as tables and form elements. For example, Internet Explorer's DOM allows document elements to be accessed simply through the use of their ID, such as `CustomerName`. Netscape requires that the element ID be prefixed by the *document* object, which would be represented as `document.CustomerName`. Attempting to access this element by simply using the `CustomerName` ID on a Netscape 4.0 browser will result in a runtime error.

The W3C has also specified a standard DOM, which is being adopted by new releases of the major browsers. Older browsers, of course, will still need special handling in order to adhere to their level of DOM compliance. The use of HTML, ECMAScript, CSS, and DOM is collectively referred to as *dynamic HTML* (DHTML).

The best way to handle the differences between browser DOM versions is to abstract the differences in the DOMs into functions that return the desired objects. For example, consider the following HTML element:

```
<div id="sampleDiv" style="visibility:hidden">This is a
sample DIV element</div>
```

A common Web page practice is to hide and show `DIV` elements in response to user events. A `DIV` element is an HTML element used to divide the document into separate blocks, or divisions, useful for implementing certain types of dynamic behavior, such as hiding and showing parts of the page. For this behavior to work properly for both Netscape and Internet Explorer browsers, a separate script function is required to obtain the `DIV` element object, as the two browsers require different script code in order to access the object. Before this function can be invoked, the script needs to identify the browser in use. Typically, this is established in the `onLoad` event of the body or window, for example, by checking the `navigator.appName` property as outlined in the following sample code:

```
<script lang="Javascript">
      var isIE = false;
      var isNetscape = false;

      function onLoadBody()
      {
            if (navigator.appName ==
                "Microsoft Internet Explorer")
            {
                  isIE = true;
            }
            else
            {
                  // assume netscape
                  isNetscape = true;
            }
      }
</script>
```

This script will initialize the global flags `isIE` and `isNetscape` in order to indicate whether the client is a Netscape or an Internet Explorer browser. Then we can look at changing the `DIV`'s visibility property so that the script can effectively either hide or show the `DIV` element. In this example, both the `DIV` element on the document and the visibility property are accessed differently. The following sample script function uses the flags in order to display the `DIV` element properly in the appropriate browser:

```
function showSampleDiv()
{
    if (isIE)
    {
        sampleDiv.style.visibility = "visible";
    }
    else if (isNetscape)
    {
        document.sampleDiv.visibility = "visible";
    }
}
```

Cookies

Support for HTTP cookies is another area of compatibility concern for a Web site. Originally a Netscape feature, cookies allow for a small piece of *state* to be stored on the client's machine and retransmitted when the user returns to the site. This very useful feature was implemented by other vendors and is now standard on all major browsers. However, some browsers do not, and possibly never will, support cookies, or the user's machine may reside behind a proxy that does not allow cookies to pass through. In addition, the user may have configured his or her browser not to accept cookies or may be using a cookie-blocking software package. For this reason, it is important to perform a runtime check to ensure cookie compatibility prior to attempting to set a cookie.

1. Using a name such as "testcookie," attempt to set a test cookie on the client.
2. Redirect the client to another page and check to see whether the cookie is received on the server.
3. If the cookie is received, the browser—and the network between the browser and the server—is capable of handling cookies, and processing can proceed as normal.

4. If the cookie is not received, another method of handling state must be used, such as a hidden form field.

The following ASP code, written in JScript, performs the previously described sequence of steps. Two files are used: CookieTest_Set.asp, which attempts to set temporary and persistent cookies, and CookieTest_Get.asp, which attempts to read the cookies back.

CookieTest_Set.asp

```
<% @Language=JScript %>
<%
        // set a temporary cookie
        Response.Cookies("TestTemporaryCookie")
                = "temporaryValue";

        // set a persistent cookie and give it a one month
        // expiration time, which isn't much of a concern
        // since we delete it in the second file
        var currentDate = new Date();
        var expirationString
                = (currentDate.getMonth() + 2) + "/"
                 + currentDate.getDate() + "/"
                 + currentDate.getYear();

        Response.Cookies("TestPersistentCookie").Expires
                = expirationString;
        Response.Cookies("TestPersistentCookie")
                = "persistentValue";

        // redirect the browser to a page that will attempt
        // to read the cookies we just set
        Response.Redirect("CookieTest_Get.asp");
%>
```

CookieTest_Get.asp

```jscript
<% @Language=JScript %>

<%
        // check the temporary cookie
        var temporaryCookieValue
                = Request.Cookies("TestTemporaryCookie");
        if (temporaryCookieValue == "temporaryValue")
        {
                // this browser is capable of storing
                // temporary cookies
                // remove the temporary cookie
                 Response.Cookies("TestTemporaryCookie") = "";
        }
        else
        {
                // this browser is incapable of storing
                // temporary cookies
        }


        // check the persistent cookie
        var persistentCookieValue
                = Request.Cookies("TestPersistentCookie");
        if (persistentCookieValue == "persistentValue")
        {
                // this browser is capable of storing
                // persistent cookies
                // remove the persistent cookie
                Response.Cookies("TestPersistentCookie")
                        = "";
        }
        else
        {
                // this browser is incapable of storing
                // persistent cookies
        }
%>
```

Plug-Ins

Netscape Navigator 2.0 introduced the concept of plug-ins, or external programs that are invoked by the browser and can be used to view *foreign* data types as an integral part of a Web page or possibly as an entire Web page. Netscape devised the Navigator Plug-in API to provide a way for vendors to write plug-ins that interact with the browser in specific ways. Microsoft Internet Explorer also supports the Navigator Plug-in API, so most plug-ins will run on both browsers. In fact, most browsers support the Netscape Plug-in API. Plug-ins are platform specific, however. A user with a Microsoft Windows operating system will require the Windows version of the plug-in. A Macintosh user will require the Mac OS version of the plug-in.

Even though the API is supported, the way that plug-ins interact with the host browser raises certain compatibility issues. Some plug-ins operate without problems, but others—that possibly make use of advanced features—may not work correctly. In addition, detecting whether a user has the plug-in installed using client-side script can also be problematic, as the client browser's DOM may be different from what the script is expecting and therefore cause the script to incorrectly report that the user does not have the plug-in.

When the system is intended to support a variety of end user operating systems, it is important to ensure that any browser plug-ins required by the site are available for those operating systems. Because plug-ins are binary components, the plug-in vendor—or the site's developers if the plug-ins are developed in-house—must make a version available for each of the desired operating systems. With an off-the-shelf plug-in, such as the Adobe Acrobat viewer, the vendor must have a version available for the client operating systems. When a plug-in is developed in house, the plug-in must be ported to each target operating system.

Java Applets

Navigator 2.0 introduced another new technology: *Java applets*. Using the Java language and the provided tools, Web developers could now write interactive components that automatically download to the client's machine and execute in the browser. Java applets require a client-side runtime component, called the Java Virtual Machine (JVM). Most major browsers include support for Java, and even those that do not can be enabled to provide Java support through the use of a Java Plug-In.

Several compatibility issues pertain to the use of Java applets. The main compatibility consideration for applets is the level of support required of the client machine's JVM. Several of the compatibility concerns for the use of a JVM on a Microsoft Windows client platform follow.

- Several versions of Microsoft Windows ship with a version of the Microsoft JVM. This JVM is considered to be part of the operating system and may be upgraded by patches or service packs.
- Internet Explorer running on Microsoft Windows uses the operating system's installed version of the Microsoft JVM. Upgrading Internet Explorer, however, may result in an upgrade of the JVM being performed.
- Netscape uses its own JVM, which remains independent of the Windows operating system version of the JVM.

On the client machine, the level of support required to use Java applets depends on the version of the JDK (Java Development Kit) used to build the applet. Because the JDKs are backward compatible, an applet developed with JDK 1.02 will still function properly in a browser that uses JDK 1.1. It also may be possible to use JDK 1.1 to build an applet that is compatible with an earlier JDK version, as long as the code does not use any classes or features that were not available in 1.02.

Note that Microsoft's Visual J++ 6.0 environment is based on the Sun JDK version 1.1.4 but includes various Microsoft-specific extensions that will not function on a non-Microsoft JVM. When using Microsoft Visual J++ to develop cross-browser applets, it is recommended that the developer use only 100% Pure Java code—meaning that it adheres to the Sun Java specification and does not make use of any Microsoft-specific extensions—in the applet. Even then, however, some incompatibilities may result.

Another important consideration for Java applets is the concept of *signatures*. One of the primary goals of the Java applet technology is to provide an operating environment in which the applet cannot maliciously harm files or other information on the client-side computer. However, the ability to access resources on a user's machine is sometimes an important capability. For this reason, applets have been enabled to perform these actions.

In order to operate in this manner, an applet must be *trusted*, or digitally signed by the author, whose signature is verified by a third-party certificate authority. The user can then grant the applet the ability to perform such functions as reading and writing files. Netscape Navigator and Microsoft Internet Explorer have different approaches to the signing process. For example, Microsoft requires that the applet be placed into a CAB (cabinet) file—deployment package—and that file is digitally signed.[3] The Netscape browser makes use of signed JAR (Java Archives) files.[4] When the Web site wishes to deploy a signed applet for use by clients, the client's browser must be detected and the appropriate file (CAB or JAR) downloaded.

---

[3]Microsoft Developer Network, "How to: Make Your Java Code Trusted in Internet Explorer," available at http://support.microsoft.com/support/kb/articles/Q193/8/77.ASP.

[4]Microsoft Developer Network, "How to: Deploying Java in Internet Explorer 4.0 and Netscape 4.0," available at http://www.microsoft.com/Java/sdk/40/kb/179652.htm.

ActiveX Controls

ActiveX controls are an alternative to the active content capabilities of plug-ins and Java applets. ActiveX controls, natively supported by Microsoft Internet Explorer, are similar to plug-ins in that they are platform-specific binary components that must be downloaded and installed on a user's machine. Once installed, a control can be embedded in Web pages and accessed from client-side scripts, just like Java applets. ActiveX controls, like plug-ins, must function appropriately on a given user's operating system and environment and must be built for the user's platform. To date, only Microsoft Windows and Macintosh platforms are supported; Internet Explorer for UNIX does not support ActiveX controls.

Netscape browsers on the Microsoft Windows platform can also run ActiveX controls through the use of specialized plug-ins designed for this purpose. Although they do provide a way to make a site's ActiveX controls cross-browser compatible, these plug-ins may not work with all ActiveX controls; therefore, it is important to carefully test how the control behaves in an ActiveX plug-in.

XML

XML is still a fairly new technology. However, it has quickly become an important technology for Web system development. Like SGML, XML is a language used to define other languages. With fewer features than SGML, however, XML is more "lightweight" but is easier to process, because of its strict requirements.

XML makes it easy to create documents containing any kind of data because it uses tags that make sense for that data. Whereas HTML/XHTML is concerned with marking up traditional documents, XML can be used for much more general tasks. For example, an address list could be represented in XML as follows:

```
<ADDRESSLIST>
    <ADDRESS>
        <STREET>4031 Green Street</STREET>
        <CITY>Columbus</CITY>
        <STATE>OH</STATE>
    </ADDRESS>
    <ADDRESS>
        <STREET>9701 Evergreen Terrace</STREET>
        <CITY>Chicago</CITY>
        <STATE>IL</STATE>
     </ADDRESS>
</ADDRESSLIST>
```

XML data is usually processed with an XML *parser,* a component that provides a set of functions for navigating the XML document from program code. Although a full description of XML is beyond the scope of this book, the preceding XML example illustrates that XML data is represented as a tree structure, with tags for each field of data in the tree. Note that there is no information in the XML data regarding how it should be displayed. Rather, XML's partner technology, XSLT, allows XML data to be transformed into a format suitable for a browser, another program, and so on.

XSLT consists of a set of instructions for navigating and outputting the data from an XML document. One of the more common uses for XSLT is to transform an XML stream into an HTML document for display on a browser. In this case, the XSLT instructions are placed into a *style sheet* containing the instructions and HTML to create a Web page. The XML parser is capable of combining the XML data with the style sheet to produce a full HTML page for display on a browser.

Note that XSLT documents are XML documents, as they conform to the XML language rules. In addition to XSLT, CSS has been enhanced to provide XML capabilities for displaying XML data on browsers. Only Internet Explorer 5.0 and later support XSLT for transforming XML documents, but most major browsers support the CSS extensions for XML.

To take advantage of XML/XSLT with non-XML/XSLT-capable browsers, it is necessary to detect the client's browser on the server. Once the browser is known, the decision can be made to either return a raw XML stream, which the client will automatically render with the XSLT style sheet, or prerender it on the server and return the resulting page.

The following code shows how to make this determination, using JScript code in an ASP page:

```
<% @Language=JScript %>

<%
    // store the path to the XSLT stylesheet
    var styleSheetFile = "sampleStyleSheet.xslt";

    // create a string to hold the XML document and add the
    // XML header
    var XMLDocument = "<?xml version='1.0'?>";

    // build a sample XML data buffer
    var XMLData = "<TESTDATA>";
    XMLData += "    <DATA>123456</DATA>";
    XMLData += "</TESTDATA>";
```

```
// the HTTP_USER_AGENT header contains the browser type
// string
var userAgent
   = new String
     (Request.ServerVariables("HTTP_USER_AGENT"));
if (userAgent.indexOf("MSIE 5") != -1)
{
   // this is an IE browser - it supports XML/XSLT
   // natively. Add the stylesheet header field and the
   // data to the document variable and return it. Note
   // that it is important to set the content type
   // so the client browser knows this is XML.
   XMLDocument += "<?xml-stylesheet
                       type='text/xsl'
                       href='" + styleSheetFile + "'?>";
   XMLDocument += XMLData;

   Response.ContentType = "text/xml";
   Response.Write(XMLDocument);
}
else
{
   // this is another browser of some kind. First, setup
   // the XML Document.
   XMLDocument += XMLData;

   // Now, prerender the XML and return the resulting
   // HTML. To do this,we create two instances of the
   // XML parser, one for the document, and the other
   // for the stylesheet. We then use the
   // "transformNode" function on the document's
   // instance of the XML parser, supplying
   // the stylesheet, which will produce an HTML
   // document.
   var XMLDocumentParser
       = Server.CreateObject("Microsoft.XMLDOM");
   var XMLStyleSheetParser
       = Server.CreateObject("Microsoft.XMLDOM");

   XMLDocumentParser.async = false;
   XMLStyleSheetParser.async = false;
```

```
XMLDocumentParser.loadXML(XMLDocument);
XMLStyleSheetParser.load
    (Server.MapPath(styleSheetFile));

var HTMLResult
    = XMLDocumentParser.transformNode
        (XMLStyleSheetParser.documentElement);

// return the result to the client
Response.ContentType = "text/html";
Response.Write(HTMLResult);
}
%>
```

Because native XML/XSLT rendering is supported only on Internet Explorer 5.0 or later, this script looks for the string MSIE 5 in the HTTP_USER_AGENT header, which is sent by the browser with each request to the server. If the browser is IE5 or later, the script sends the XML data directly to the browser, using the ASP Response object. Otherwise, the XML parser is invoked on the server to render the data into HTML. The resulting HTML is returned to the client.

XHTML

In the ongoing quest to stabilize documents on the Web, the W3C has released the XHTML specification, which is intended to provide an extensible and more rigorous version of HTML. It is, in fact, intended to ease many of the compatibility problems that exist with today's browsers and Web sites. XHTML is an XML-defined language and as such can be processed by XML parsers. XHTML is still quite new, and not well supported, but a few things can be done to help ease the transition to XHTML.

Modifying existing HTML documents and creating new XHTML documents by using the following guidelines will make it easier to take advantage of enhanced XHTML features in the future. Following are the rules for creating a well-formed XHTML document, which can be applied to existing HTML documents without causing compatibility problems with older browsers (Graham 2000, p. 35).

- All element tags and attributes must be in lowercase: <html> rather than <HTML>.
- All tags must be closed; an opening tag must be paired with a closing tag. For example, in HTML, the <td> tag was implicitly closed if a <tr> tag

was encountered. This is no longer legal in XHTML. In addition, empty tags must be closed, as in `<br />`.

- All attribute values must be enclosed in quotes: `<table width="100%">`.

These three guidelines will allow you to create or to upgrade to XHTML documents while retaining compatibility with browsers that predate XML and XHTML. XHTML documents must be returned with a content type of `text/html` to be displayed in any browser.

Fonts

Typically, the most compatible way for the system to specify fonts is to use only common fonts, such as Arial, Courier, and Times New Roman. Because most, if not all, operating systems and browsers support these common fonts, they should be used to ensure the highest degree of compatibility. Font sizes, however, may cause problems, so different CSS style sheets may need to be used, depending on which browser is being used to access the site. When more advanced font support is required, consider the following two alternatives.

- If the target browser is Internet Explorer, font embedding can be used through the CSS `@font-face` attribute to specify a URL for a font file.
- For broader compatibility, create an image file with the text in the appropriate font and display the image instead of text. Provide the ALT attribute on the IMG tag in order to display the text for non-image-enabled browsers.

Colors

Colors are a serious area of concern for Web site compatibility because the user's video settings may not be able to properly recreate a color specified on a Web page or used in an image file. If a color called for by a Web page or an image file is not in the set of available colors on the user's machine, the color will be *dithered,* or created by meshing in a checkerboard-type pattern the two closest colors. Although this is better than no color at all, it is unattractive and should be avoided.

Given the number of color depths—8 bit, 15 bit, 16 bit, and 24 bit—operating systems, browser versions, and browser bugs, only a few colors can be safely used on a Web page without being dithered on any display. Therefore, a choice must be made based on the target browsers and operating systems for the site.

Graphics designers use the *Web-safe palette,* a 216-color palette that contains colors that will not dither on Internet Explorer and Netscape Navigator when run on Microsoft Windows and Apple Macintosh computers. Unfortunately, these colors are not appropriate for UNIX browsers running at less than 24 bits.[5] As such, a choice must be made based on the target platforms.

For many sites, the Web-safe palette will provide compatibility with a large enough user base to be acceptable. Other operating systems and browsers, unable to display the colors directly, will dither them, making the site still accessible but not as attractive. Most graphics tools ship with the Web-safe palette, which can be imported and used for designing Web graphics to provide compatibility with Microsoft Internet Explorer and Netscape Navigator running on Microsoft Windows and Apple Macintosh machines in 8-bit (256-color) or higher modes.

Image Formats

Three major image file formats are available for use on the Web: GIF, JPEG, and PNG. Each of these formats has advantages and disadvantages.

- *GIF:* Originally created by CompuServe for image files, GIF can compress 8-bit (256-color) images without losing any part of the image. The GIF format also supports animation, allowing several GIF images to be stored in a single file and then played back in sequence.
- *JPEG:* Also offering compression, JPEG images can support 24-bit (16.7-million-color) images and also provide a high degree of configurable compression. This compression comes at a price, however, as it is *lossy,* meaning that the image will not be saved exactly as it was created and that some areas will be lost.
- *PNG:* A relatively new graphics format, PNG files compress about 30 percent better than GIF files on average and can store 48 bits of color information. PNG also offers a few additional features, such as cross-platform gamma correction and metadata for searching. The W3C now recommends this image file format.[6] Like GIF files, PNG images are compressed without losing any image data.

The general practice is to use GIF or PNG for smaller, line-art images, such as icons and most Web page graphics, and JPEG for larger, photo-realistic images that can afford some amount of loss and still look acceptable. Using JPEG for icons or similar Web images is not a good idea, as some parts of the image will be lost because of the JPEG compression algorithm.

---

[5]"Which Color Palette: Optimizing Web Graphics," Internet.com Corporation, December 13, 2000; available at http://webreference.com/dev/graphics/palette.html.

[6]"PNG Delivers Higher Quality Graphics for Web Page Design: PNG Fact Sheet," World Wide Web Consortium (W3C); available at http://www.w3.org/Press/PNG-fact.html.

Deciding between GIF and PNG is based mostly on the compatibility requirements of the site. Older browsers do not support the PNG format and thus will be unable to display PNG images, so GIF is the only acceptable choice. As described earlier, GIF images are limited to 256 colors, which is usually desirable if broad compatibility is required. Although the PNG format is supported by recent browser versions, the level of support for the more advanced features, such as gamma correction and transparencies, is lacking and can result in some display problems if these features are used.

Secure Protocols

Secure communication between a Web site and a browser involves the use of SSL, TLS, or PCT; these protocols also have variants and versions, such as 40-bit versus 128-bit SSL. The most popular of these protocols is SSL. The client browser must be able to support the protocol, version, and other variants specified by the Web system in order to support secure communication. This may require that a certain browser version be installed or possibly an operating system service pack or patch.

Compression

Response time—how quickly a site is able to deliver a page to the user over the Internet—is an important usability factor. *Compression* can affect response time by reducing the amount of information that must be transmitted from the server to the user's machine. In order for this to function, the user's browser must support the compression algorithm used by the server.

Only browsers and servers that support HTTP 1.1 can participate in compression. HTTP 1.1 includes a special header that allows the browser to indicate the types of compression, such as `gzip` and the UNIX `compress` format, it supports. The server will select a format that the browser supports, compress the outgoing data, and send it to the client. A non–HTTP 1.1 browser communicating with a compression-enabled HTTP 1.1 server will always receive data uncompressed, as the browser will not indicate to the server that it is capable of receiving compressed data.

5.2 Verifying Site Compatibility

Clearly, a significant number of technology and system configuration variables pose potential compatibility problems for a Web system. It is important to perform compatibility verification with each release of the site, as changes to site content can result in new compatibility problems. The first step in the process is to reduce the compatibility effort and *define the scope*.

Scope

The scope of the compatibility verification is derived from the platforms and browsers specified in the site's nonfunctional requirements specification, combined with such additional constraints as client machine video color depth and the presence of a client-side firewall. The number of client compatibility combinations may be extremely large, however, and the scope of the compatibility effort is limited by the system's budget and schedule. As a result, it is worthwhile to perform a risk analysis to determine the most prevalent client platforms and browsers in the site's target user base. These more common platforms and browsers can be regarded as critical to the site's success and therefore receive a higher priority in the compatibility test effort.

Determining the most prevalent client platforms and browsers can be difficult. If a Web system is already "live," information retrieved from the Web server log or help desk log provides a historical record of the specific browser types that have accessed the system to date. If not enough is known about the intended audience of the Web system or if the audience is extremely broad, it is often useful to refer to public Web sites that provide statistics on the industrywide prevalence of popular operating systems, browsers, and other user-controlled settings, such as video color depth. Based on available statistics, the compatibility test effort can be tailored to address a majority of the most prevalent system combinations that will be used to access the site. Experience has shown that only the largest, most mission-critical projects typically have devoted time and attention to the performance of compatibility testing, testing more than a handful of configurations (Gerrard 2000).

Compatibility Table

Once the risk analysis has been performed, a *compatibility table* that details the combination of browsers, platforms, and other settings that must be included as part of the compatibility tests can be created. Table 5-1, a sample compatibility table, identifies the versions of operating systems, browsers, and end user computer settings that must be tested for compatibility. Note that the development of a compatibility test matrix and the exercise of defining the various configuration variables and potential configuration combinations is of primary use when an organization does not have a specific and narrowly defined user base.

Our sample compatibility table features three columns that must be validated to work with the site, but other columns can be added when necessary. For example, a column for printer types could be added if the site places a focus on printing Web content. Note that the hardware platform is included in the operating system column, as the most common compatibility target is the operating system, not the

Table 5-1   Sample Compatibility Table

Operating System	Browser	Color Depth
Windows 95, 98, ME, NT 4.0/Intel, 2000	Internet Explorer 3.x–5.x Netscape 4.x–6.x Opera 5	8 bit 16 bit 24 bit
Mac OS 7.1–9.1		
Linux/Intel x86 Linux/PPC		

particular processor type. Also note that not all browsers are available for all the operating systems listed, so some combinations will not be applicable.

Environment

The test environment must be able to support compatibility testing across several system component configurations, operating systems, and browsers. One approach involves multiple operating system installations on a single test machine. For example, one machine could be configured with five operating systems: two versions of Windows NT, Windows 98 second edition, Windows 95 A and B, and Windows 2000. For best results, these operating systems should be installed on separate partitions, using one of many available partition management utilities.

An additional configuration concern involves the installation of versions of the same browser, such as Internet Explorer 4.0 and 5.0, on a single machine. Multiple versions of Internet Explorer cannot be physically installed on the same machine, as the installation process upgrades the previous version. With Internet Explorer 5.0, however, Microsoft has provided a compatibility mode that allows Internet Explorer 5.0 to emulate Internet Explorer 4.0 for testing purposes.[7] Unfortunately, Internet Explorer 3.0 must be installed into a separate operating system instance. Netscape browser versions are much more tolerant of multiple installs.

One way to be able to test multiple browser configurations is to create a backup image of the foundation test environment, using a drive-imaging tool, such as Symantec Ghost. These tools are available to clone hard disks or individual partitions, in order to copy certain software from one computer to another and to be

---

[7]More information on compatibility mode can be found in article #Q197311 in the Microsoft Knowledge Base located at http://support.microsoft.com.

able to monitor error-checking and image-comparison output in order to ensure that hard disk or partition images are an exact duplicate of the original image.

Another option, when budget allows, is to set up several computers for different configurations. Even within this setup, several decisions are required. You may decide to have a ratio of the machines set up with the most popular configurations and to use some computers where they can be changed among the less popular browser/operating system combinations. If you do not have access to additional computers and cannot afford to buy them, you might be able to rent a computer lab or get a short-term lease on a number of computers. Commercial sources for computer lab outsourcing are provided in the section Outsourcing.

Verification Strategy

Once the environment has been established, the compatibility tests can be performed, using a combination of operating systems, browsers, and other settings identified from the compatibility table. For each combination identified, the following two steps must be performed.

1. *Execute the functional tests.* In order to verify that the site functions as intended on all platforms, the functional tests discussed in Chapter 2 must be executed on each combination of browser, operating system, and other settings. On many platforms, this may be as simple as reinstalling the automated testing tool, if used, and replaying the test scripts. Other platforms, such as Mac OS, may not support the tool, so the test will have to be performed manually, or using a different tool. As described in Chapter 1, it may not be realistic to test so many combinations of functionality, operating systems, and browsers. Therefore, a compatibility risk assessment must be performed to prioritize the compatibility risks and to generate a subset of functional tests.

2. *Visually inspect each page.* Although it can identify behavior problems with the site, the testing tool probably will not be able to determine whether there are issues with fonts, colors, HTML rendering, and so on. Therefore, it is important to visually inspect each page to ensure that it displays properly on each combination.

As documented in Chapter 7, a few online resources are available for verifying compatibility with different browsers and HTML levels. Although these tools are useful, there is no substitute for true compatibility verification through the execution of functional tests and visual inspections on a browser and operating system installation.

Outsourcing

Given the complexity, the types of tools that may be applied, and the technologies involved with compatibility validation and verification, an organization may wish to use an outside company to perform the testing. Fortunately, several companies are available to perform Web compatibility testing. When considering and ultimately selecting such a company, you must verify that the testing company can support your specific requirements.

If you have special needs, such as an obscure operating system or a browser that supports the blind, you will want to verify that the consulting firm has a specialty in the particular area. Also, if the Web system has a legal responsibility for end user accessibility, you again need to verify that a company is chosen that has relevant experience in this area.

Following are several sources of assistance in compatibility testing:

- *Browser compatibility chart.* A chart outlining compatibility measures between browsers, including Java and JavaScript support, use of frames, use of plug-ins, and support for XML is available online.[8]
- *Compatibility testing services.* A company called TTCX provides a host of testing services, including hardware and device compatibility testing, functionality testing, and audio and graphics hardware testing.[9] Another company that provides testing services is Emergent Information Technologies, which has worked with some major corporations and with Agilent on the development of a low-cost logic analyzer.[10]
- *Compatibility testing for Macs.* Three independent labs, Compatibility Labs, feature more than 100 Macintosh PowerPC configurations with versions of system software compatible with the hardware. The complete line of Apple products is available, as well as a small sampling of third-party products, including displays, printers, scanners, and removable media drives. These labs promote compatibility with Apple products, both released and unreleased.[11]

5.3 TBS Case Study

One of the requirements for the Technology Bookstore is that it must be compatible with Microsoft Internet Explorer 4.0+ and Netscape Navigator 4.0+, Windows and Macintosh platforms, and 8-bit color displays. This sec-

---

[8]Available at http://webreview.com/wr/pub/1999/10/29/feature/index3b.html.

[9]Visit TTCX at http://thetestcompany.com.

[10]Visit Emergent at http://www.emergent-it.com/home.html.

[11]For more information, see http://www.devworld.apple.com/labs.

tion provides several compatibility evaluation examples for the I-View Previous Order use case.

HTML Rendering

Web browsers render Web pages differently. Certain elements, although still valid HTML, will be rendered differently, if at all, on various browsers. The I-View Previous Order interface (Figure 2-9) was viewed on several different browsers to ensure that it was displayed properly. On Microsoft Internet Explorer, the browser used in development, the page displayed correctly. Netscape Navigator, however, did not render the page in the same way (Figure 5-4). The separator line underneath the word Order was missing when the Netscape browser rendered the page.

Inspection of the page source determined that the line was created with the following HTML:

```
<table width="100%">
      <tr height="1" bgcolor="gray">
            <td>
            </td>
      </tr>
</table>
```

This is the "empty table" approach: a markup trick used to hide content or to create certain effects on Web pages. Unfortunately, Netscape ignores empty tables, so the element is missing when viewed on Netscape browsers. As it turns out, a predefined element exists in HTML for the purpose of drawing horizontal lines: the <hr>, or "horizontal rule" element. Replacing the <table> element with the following markup resulted in a compatible page:

```
<hr size="1" />
```

CSS

Although the I-View Previous Order interface displays properly on different browsers, a walkthrough of the markup revealed that colors and text alignment elements were embedded directly into the HTML. Although this functions properly on graphical browsers, TBS would like to use proper page-implementation techniques and allow for the future possibility of access by newer, handheld Web devices and different types of browsers. Because the display-related elements are relatively simple, they can be factored into a CSS <style> element. For example,

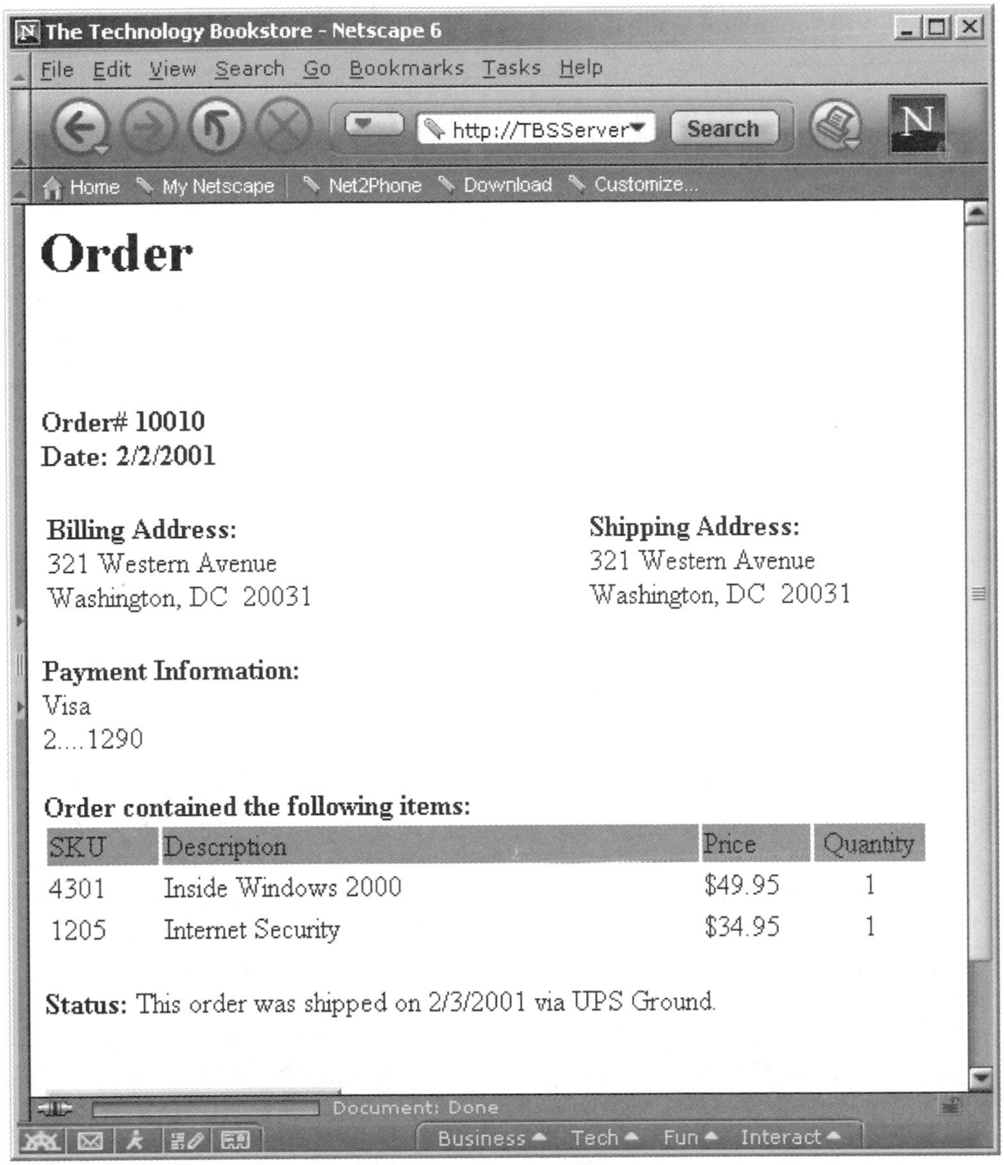

Figure 5-4 I-View Previous Order on Netscape Navigator

consider the following portion of the `<table>` element used to display the header row for the order line items:

```
<tr bgcolor="#90EE90" align="left">
      <td width="60">SKU</td>
      <td width="300">Description</td>
      <td width="60">Price</td>
      <td align="center" width="60">Quantity</td>
</tr>
```

This markup was rewritten using the following elements:

```
<style>
.headerRow { background-color:#90EE90; text-align:left; }

.quantityColumn { text-align:center; }
</style>

<tr class="headerRow">
      <td width="60">SKU</td>
      <td width="300">Description</td>
      <td width="60">Price</td>
      <td class="quantityColumn" width="60">Quantity</td>
</tr>
```

As you can see, the attributes for color and text alignment were factored out of the table and into the `<style>` section. This also allows the possibility of using the "quantity column" style in the data rows of the order item list, thus promoting reuse, as the text alignment attribute will not be repeated on each quantity element of the item data rows. Unfortunately, the `<td>` "width" attributes could not be factored into the `<style>` section, owing to incompatibilities with the 4.x versions of the Netscape browser.

Colors

The previous example improved the header row of the order item list table with CSS. The header row of this list uses a color specification to give the header row an appearance different from that of the data rows. Testing the I-View Previous Order page on different color depths revealed that the color specified, "#90EE90" is not part of the Web-safe palette and resulted in dithering, and therefore a different appearance, on various platforms. To resolve this situation, the color was changed to `"#3399FF"`, which is a member of the safe palette. This color is displayed properly on all color depths and browsers.

5.4 Chapter Summary

⚠ The conduct of compatibility tests is required to ensure that the Web system functions as intended when accessed by various kinds of browsers, versions of the same browser, and different operating systems.

⚠ A primary compatibility concern on the client side of the Web system equation pertains to browser compatibility. The major browser compatibility issues are HTML tags, HTML rendering, CSS, ECMAScript, DOM, cookies, plug-ins, Java applets, ActiveX controls, XML, XHTML, security, colors, and fonts.

⚠ The evolution of HTML has been quite complex and even with the latest releases of the major browsers does not guarantee that a site will look the same on two different browsers claiming to implement the specification. The primary reason for this is the subtle differences in the way that the browsers render the pages for viewing.

⚠ Implementation of the DOM standard for support of client-side scripting is perhaps the most problematic area of compatibility between the two major browsers, as Internet Explorer and Netscape have different models of the document that the browser is currently displaying.

⚠ The number of potential compatibility test combinations is extremely large, whereas the test effort is limited by such factors as budget and schedule. As a result, it is worthwhile to perform a risk analysis in order to identify the specific Web system components of greatest importance to Web system success and those that are most prevalent within the user community.

⚠ The compatibility test matrix identifies the various versions of operating systems, browsers, end user computer platforms, Web connections, adaptors, and peripherals that can reasonably be expected to be used by a Web system's user community.

⚠ The compatibility test matrix is tailored to reduce the magnitude and scope of the compatibility test effort to one that can be performed within the allocated schedule and with available personnel. In order to tailor the compatibility test matrix, assumptions and generalizations will need to be made about the Web system's target audience.

⚠ A test environment is needed that supports compatibility testing across several system component configurations, including different operating systems and browsers. Test environment configuration approaches include the use of multiple setups on a single computer and the setup of several computers involving different configurations. Given the complexity, the types of tools that may be applied, and the technologies involved with compatibility testing, some organizations outsource compatibility testing.

5.5 References

Graham, Ian S. 2000. *XHTML 1.0 Language and Design Sourcebook*. New York: Wiley.

Graham, Ian S. 2000. *XHTML 1.0 Web Development Sourcebook*. New York: Wiley.

Gerrard, Paul. 2000. "Risk-Based E-Business Testing." London: Systeme Evolutif Ltd.

c h a p t e r   6

Usability and Accessibility

On the Internet, it's survival of the easiest:
If customers can't find a product, they can't buy it.

Jakob Nielsen and Donald Norman[1]

When conducting business via the Internet, organizations do not have the opportunity to greet a customer face-to-face. Instead, the customer's initial and lasting impression of the organization and its offerings is the look and feel of the Web system's user interface. As a result, customer relationship building and maintenance are performed via the customer's interaction with the Web system. The customer relationship is enhanced or crippled by such factors as the ease of navigation on the Web site, the logical placement of buttons on each Web page, the intuitive flow of user actions and screen changes, the use of colors and images, the speed at which the system responds to user-initiated actions, and the perceived value of content displayed on the Web page.

---

[1]Jakob Nielsen and Donald Norman, "Web-Site Usability: Usability on the Web Isn't a Luxury," *Information Week,* January 14, 2000, www.informationweek.com/773/web.htm.

Most online users have experienced at least one Web system they consider to be excellent from a usability perspective. Once a user experiences a satisfying online interaction with a site, that pleasant experience becomes the benchmark and establishes a uniform expectation for evaluating other Web systems. The uniform expectation for the online user is that a Web system must be logical and intuitive and provide a unique and pleasant experience. As a result, a Web system's usability must be given proper attention to ensure that the site is delivering the kind of experience that most online users expect.

Usability is first addressed during the requirements phase and then augmented through the design phase. Therefore, when using the RSI approach, discussed in Chapter 2, to define the «interface» use cases, it is necessary to apply usability principles. If usability has not been considered from the beginning, the cost of substantive usability changes to the system will increase as more of the system is developed.

In order to build usability into the Web system, usability standards must be defined, adopted, and communicated. The project development team needs to be aware of and have access to the usability guidelines. When no standards are in place or in addition to standards, usability can be verified through the development, review, and improvement of a system prototype. Such a prototype, consisting of a first cut at the actual system or a paper design, allows users to enhance the usability of the planned system.

When exercising an application for usability, it is important to evaluate the system against organization- or project-specific usability standards. If such standards do not exist, the software professional should evaluate the system against published commercial best practices, standards, and guidelines. Good references to consult are Nielsen (1998), and those promulgated by the W3C standards-setting body for the World Wide Web.[2]

Usability design should be incorporated into the system through the involvement of end users as part of design reviews and system prototype demonstrations. Before the system goes live, it is necessary to verify system adherence to applicable usability standards. Organizations can consider the significant amount of published documentation on usability when developing their systems. Quite a few books address the subject, and entire studies have been conducted or are under way that provide guidelines for engineering usability into a Web system. An abundance of material describing how to conduct usability studies is available.

---

[2]Available at http://www.w3.org.

6.1 Usability Engineering

Usability engineering consists of the design and objective evaluation of the ease of use for a Web system against defined standards or defined end user expectations. However, objectivity is often difficult to attain and indeed can often be elusive. As indicated later in this chapter, the evaluation criteria applied for Web site usability seldom explicitly distinguish between *value* judgments and *objective* criteria, even when standards are applied.

The simplicity of the Web model, and therefore, its case of use, has greatly contributed to its popularity. Users who have experience on the Web generally do not encounter much difficulty navigating a well-constructed Web system. Even so, those Web systems that are not intuitive and that violate usability principles will frustrate users. As a result, usability evaluation seeks to verify whether the Web system follows mature usability principles.

Usability Design Issues

Usability versus Compatibility

In this book, we define compatibility issues as those that arise on some platforms or browsers that cause the displayed content to differ from that on other platforms or browsers. If the browser renders the content properly and it functions as expected, the content is said to be compatible. Usability, on the other hand, refers to the ease of use and appropriateness of that content. Screen resolution would be considered a usability issue rather than a compatibility issue, therefore. If all required browsers are capable of identically displaying the content at various screen resolutions, usually involving scroll bars, the site is in fact compatible with those browsers. It is not necessarily true, however, that the site is *usable* at lower screen resolutions. It may be, for example, that necessary menu and navigation elements are rendered off-screen at lower resolutions, meaning that the user must scroll to find them.

Usability versus Performance

As discussed in Chapter 4, response time is a key measure of Web site performance. Although response time is both a performance *and* a usability issue, the focus of the discussion in Chapter 4 was on the server-side processing performance evaluation and tuning of components. In this chapter, we are interested in the impact of response time on the user's experience with the site.

Although network interaction between the browser and the Web system—that is, waiting for the next page to load—is the most noticeable aspect of response time, performance issues are also present on the client machine, especially in the presence of client-side dynamic content through scripts and controls. At a lower level, the responsiveness of the buttons and lists in the user interface controls is also important to the usability picture.

A non-network-related user interface response time of 0.1 second is about the limit for having the user feel that the interface is reacting instantaneously. This is based on the speed of transmission of neuronal charges in the human brain, which is, generally, a fixed speed. One second (1.0) is about the limit for the user's flow of thought to remain uninterrupted. According to usability experts, such as Jakob Nielsen, delays longer than this threshold cause the user to consciously notice the delay, resulting in the loss of continuity flow. Ten seconds (10.0) is about the limit for keeping the user's attention focused on the actions that are taking place. When experiencing delays longer than 10 seconds, users begin to think about other tasks and no longer fully concentrate on the task at hand. With these factors in mind, the Web site's interface should contain minimal delays in control responsiveness owing to client-side scripts or other processing.

One of the basic guidelines offered by psychology is that when people expect an action, such as a screen display, to be fast, they become highly annoyed when that action is slow. On the other hand, an individual expecting a screen display to be slow will be more tolerant of the delay. Furthermore, a system user who knows that a slow screen display is possible will be more tolerant when it is delayed. The same result is evident when a user expects a screen display to be fast but is advised, via a screen message, that a delay is possible.

Reaction time in usability is another measure of concern. It takes about 0.1 second, the perceptual limit, for a user to be able to recognize an object on the screen and to discern its use. It takes about 0.25 second for the user to be able to shift his or her gaze and attention from one object to another, such as a roll-over or a pop-up menu. In general, it will take a little over 1 second for an individual to make a simple decision between two competing screen actions, such as the selection of different links.

Another usability factor is the use of keyboard or mouse inputs and the degree to which the system requires an individual to switch between them. Entering characters via a keyboard typically consumes a little more than 1 second per character, excluding adjustments necessary to correct errors. A single mouse click consumes, on average, about the same amount of time as a keystroke on the keyboard. When the mouse is needed to move the cursor from one place on the screen to another, about 1.5 second is consumed, owing to brain-processing time required to perceive and to interpret screen elements. Each time a user is required to switch from one input device to another, up to 0.5 second is consumed. Usability evaluations need to gauge the number of times a system requires the user to shift between input devices; where possible, recommendations should be made to minimize shifts.

Content Size and Download Times

Content size refers to the size of all data—pages, scripts, images, Java applets, ActiveX controls—that must be transferred from the Web system to the user's local machine. Because each page of the site is, potentially, made up of many files, the total size of this content can be quite large. If the user has a high-speed connection to the Internet, the time to transfer the content will be minimal. But if the user has a slower connection, such as a modem, the wait for the content to be transferred will be much longer, however, which can be a usability issue. Although the correct use of image file formats and HTTP compression can help here by significantly reducing file sizes, it is usually wise to consider users with slower connections during the design and implementation of a Web system's interface.

Problems with content size can manifest themselves in many ways that might require major changes to the site's interface and implementation. For example, a Web list with one or two vertical "screens" of information—requiring the use of the vertical scroll bar—may not present a problem for modem users, but a list with several hundred "screens" will usually take a large amount of time to transfer. An example of this large-list problem is the page of results from a search engine. Typically, the solution to this kind of problem is to introduce a "paging" mechanism, with Previous and Next buttons to navigate the list. Depending on the site's implementation, introducing a paging mechanism can be quite complex and should be considered as early as possible in the development of the site's interface.

Browser Interface Issues

For the most part, the browser's interface is the responsibility of the browser vendor. In some cases, however, parts of the browser's interface and behavior must be considered from a usability perspective.

- *Back/Next/Refresh.* Each of these buttons causes a browser navigation action. In some cases, the browser may attempt to fetch a page from cache or contact the server to reload it. In each of these cases, the site must properly handle the browser's requests. Although it may seem as though this would be handled automatically, reloading a page may interfere with the browser's ability to navigate pages or to properly display content.
- *Cookie, SSL, and other warnings.* Security settings in the browser can result in usability issues. A user can set the browser to prompt when a site attempts to set a cookie, change to an SSL connection, or download a control. If these actions occur frequently, the user will be continually responding to warning dialogs, significantly impacting his or her experience with the site in a negative way.

- *Printing.* The ability to print a page can be quite useful for users. Unfortunately, simply printing a Web page will most likely result in less than appealing printer output. Browsers that support CSS will allow the use of a special style sheet for printers through the `media` attribute of the `<link>` element.

Screen Resolution

As mentioned earlier, the current video mode or screen resolution of the client machine can have an impact on the usability of the site. Although browsers can typically render content regardless of width and height, scroll bars will be displayed to give the user a way to view the off-screen content if the page size exceeds the available screen resolution or size of the browser window. Although this is not always a bad thing, usability concerns can arise when important items, such as menus or other important content, are rendered off-screen, requiring the user to continually scroll the items into view.

Complex Screens

Screen *busyness* refers to how close the elements are to one another. A common guideline promulgated by psychology states that an individual's senses can deal with a factor of seven inputs plus or minus two. This average range of five to nine represents the number of basic units of information that an average person can or will generally hold in short-term memory. This rule of seven plus or minus two is also a good guide for the depth of actions that can be successfully implemented for a Web site.

A Web system must not unduly impinge on a user's ability to quickly grasp screen elements and layout. A key usability concern, therefore, is the amount of time required for a user to be able to respond to a screen display. With regard to the level of Web page complexity and busyness that typical end users tolerate, the standard-setting body for Web systems is the World Wide Web Consortium (W3C).[3]

A somewhat related issue is the use of frames in Web user interface design. Although frames can offer an interesting way to lay out page content, they deviate from the standard Web navigation strategy, which is page based and mostly linear. Frames complicate and deviate from this strategy and generally result in a more confusing and unpleasant interface.

---

[3]Visit the W3C Web site at http://www.w3.org. For information about its Web Accessibility Initiative, which seeks to promote systems that are accessible to everyone, see http://www.w3.org/WAI/.

Content Depth Levels

The level of depth for a Web site is another usability concern. Specifically, the issue is how far down the user must traverse in order to reach the content of interest. As documented in Chapter 7, tools are available to analyze depth levels and to assist in identifying navigational and design problems that exist for a Web site. A depth problem is defined as an instance in which an individual must traverse beyond four levels of depth in order to reach desired content. A usability evaluation, therefore, must initiate functional paths with the purpose of identifying each instance when a user must traverse five or more levels in order to perform a particular action.

It is important to consider the amount of navigation required to arrive at the depths necessary to perform a desired action. The usability concern here is whether a user who has navigated five or more levels to reach desired content is conscious of where he or she is in the system and knows how to get back to a particular Web page of interest. Books that address user navigation concerns are Fleming 1998, and Flanders and Willis 1998.

Internationalization

Given the global accessibility of the Internet, internationalization is an important topic. If your product has to be functional in other countries, internationalization testing is imperative. The most difficult aspect will be to get the proper resources. Someone fluent in the language should properly verify all dialogue and translations. Certain words and phrases, if translated directly, could result in an entirely different meaning, possily even insulting the user.

An excellent Web resource exists to exchange ideas, hints, tips, announcements, and other useful information about programming for international markets.[4] Topics of interest would include coding for Unicode, code pages, international character sets, collation sequences, formatting currencies, and tools for internationalization.

The following Web sites offer to translate Web page text into several different languages:

- AltaVista's Babelfish (http://www.altavista.com)
- Learnout & Hauspie (http://www.lhsl.com)
- Systran (http://www.systransoft.com)
- Transparent Language (http://www.transparent.com/freetranslation.com)

Also useful is the HTML editing tool HTMLed Pro, from Internet Software Technologies, which comes with a multilingual spell checker. The Microsoft Office

---

[4]The official Web page for the i18n-prog@acoin.com list is located at http://www.acoin.com/i18n/i18n-prog.htm.

2000 Command Translator includes more than 4,300 commands with translations into 29 languages. NJStar is a company that provides more information on support for Asian languages.

Usability Guidelines[5]

A successful Web site is as inviting and easy to navigate for the user as possible. Sometimes, in the heat of Web system design and development, usability guidelines are overlooked, or development personnel exercise a creative license that doesn't really work for the end user. Following is a concise list of usability principles that should be reviewed in support of the Web design and usability evaluation effort.

Web Site Efficiency

- Can tasks be performed with keyboard strokes? (This is important for power users.)
- Does the site reflect a clear understanding of how users do their work?
- Are response times fast enough to keep users in a flow state? (This is also addressed as part of performance testing, discussed in Chapter 4.)

Intuitive Work Flow

- Does the work flow take advantage of users' mental models? Or does it conform to the mental model it is building up? (It will be difficult to accommodate all mental models. Applications will set up their own metaphors that attempt to map a mental model to systemic metaphors that the user is familiar with. So, for example, something that looks like a radio dial with volume should move up or down, not left or right, as a general rule.)
- Does it behave consistently throughout?
- Is it visually consistent?

User Support

- Does the Web site allow mistakes to be easily undone? Or does it provide enough confirmatory material to help prevent mistakes in the first place?
- Does it provide advice? Tools? Reference materials?

---

[5]Used with permission. Adapted from story, Derrik, Usability Checklist for Site Developers, Web Design Articles, October 15, 1999, http://www.webreview.com.

User Engagement

- Do users feel in control?
- Do users enjoy their experience?

Ten Rules for Usability

Strive for a quick-loading, well-designed, solidly written, easily maneuverable, thoroughly tested, pleasantly interactive, meaningful, and distinctive Web site.

1. *Be conscious of response time.* Users have a limited amount of patience while waiting for your pages to load, especially home pages. Some studies cite the "8-second rule," meaning that users will allow, on average, 8 seconds for a page to load before giving up on the site. The waiting can go beyond 8 seconds when a message is given to the user to indicate what is happening. A credit card transaction, for example, may take longer to complete than other operations on the site, but as long as a message tells the user to wait 20–30 seconds, the user will generally tolerate this delay.

2. *Show personality.* Your Web site's first screen on someone's browser should portray the business in a distinctive light. *Branding* is the term used to describe how a business or a product distinguishes itself from the competition. Review the Web site and analyze how well the site promotes the good name of the organization or main products.

3. *Design with the user in mind.* Usability should not constrain good design. Good design, on the other hand, should create a very usable site. Don't let project team members get too isolated in their own functional worlds. Designers, writers, marketers, and technicians should have a broad view of the mission and scope of the Web site. Functionality and design should blend together to create a positive user experience.

4. *The site should be easy to learn.* A good site should be like good software; a manual shouldn't be needed in order to use it. Create a logical taxonomy and integrate good navigational tools. Design the site so that people always "guess right."

5. *The site should be easy to navigate.* Someone who gets lost in the middle of a Web transaction will most likely leave. Ensure that the user can get from point A to point B.

6. *Content should have content.* What good is a Web site if the content is useless? Ensure that each page on the Web site has meaningful content.

7. *Write well.* Agree on a standard dictionary and use it. Develop a house style and stick to it. Be consistent. Have an editor read all copy before

posting. Writers should not be the final reviewers of their own words. Ensure that spelling is correct.

8. *Enable visitor feedback.* The Web site needs to give users a way to offer praise, make suggestions, and ask for clarification. Does the Web site tell the user to contact the organization not only through the Web site but also via phone, e-mail, fax, and regular mail?

9. *Give people what they want.* When the mission of the Web site is to sell books, for example, the site needs to show the user how to purchase them. If the Web site pertains to the operation of a visitor center, the site needs to provide people with reasons for visiting a particular attraction. Ensure that the mission is accurately and sufficiently supported.

10. *Don't forget to test.* Formulate the relevant usability testing criteria; then test, test, test. Team members often become too close to the site's functionality and, as a result, lose their objectivity. Show the site to outsiders and document their experiences. Watch users navigate. Note their body language as pages appear on the monitor. Most important, let those users control the mouse.

Appendix A contains a complete set of usability criteria.

6.2 Accessibility

The material in this section is based on the work of Jakob Nielsen.[6] The use of the Internet, together with Web systems that offer commerce, have been a blessing to those who do not have time or the access to conduct activities via the traditional means of physically traveling to a store to make a purchase or to the library to conduct research. In addition, the Internet has been an enabling technology for people with disabilities. Online information provides many advantages over printed media. For example, people with poor eyesight can increase the font size of text to make content easier to read. Also, the text-to-speech conversion for blind users is better for online text than for print copy. Indeed, many disabled users are empowered by computers to perform tasks that would have been difficult for them with traditional technology.

The National Institute on Disability and Rehabilitation Research has a program called the Rehabilitation Engineering Research Center for Access to Computers and Information Systems, which has published a comprehensive set of

---

[6]Adapted and used with permission from Jakob Nielsen, "Accessible Design for Users with Disabilities," Alertbox for October 1996. Available at http://www.useit.com/alertbox/9610.html.

guidelines for accessible Web design.[7] Figure 6-1 shows the symbol displayed on Web sites that support access for people with disabilities. This symbol is made available through the National Center for Accessible Media.[8]

Types of Disabilities

Making the Web more accessible for users with disabilities is largely a matter of applying markup in the way that it was intended. Specifically, HTML was meant to encode *meaning* rather than *appearance*. When a Web page has been coded for meaning, alternative browsers can present that meaning in ways that are optimized for the abilities of individual users and thus facilitate the use of the Web by disabled users. This can be accomplished through technologies such as CSS.

Visual

The most serious accessibility problems on the Web today likely pertain to use of sites by users with visual disabilities. Most Web pages are highly visual. For example, it is quite common to see combinations of background and foreground colors that make pages virtually unreadable for color-blind users.

Textual pages are reasonably easy to access for blind users, as the text can be fed to a screen reader. But this is not the case when tables or other layout techniques, such as DIVs or layers, are used; they can sometimes cause reading to be out of

Figure 6-1 The Web Access Symbol

---

[7]For more information about rehabilitation engineering, see Web site http://accessiblesociety.org/bkgd/rercs.htm.

[8]For more information about the center, see the Web site at http://icdri.org/ncam.htm.

order. Long pages are problematic, though, because it is more difficult for a blind user to scan for interesting parts than it is for a sighted user to perform the same action.

In order to facilitate user scanning, the structure of the Web page should be emphasized by proper HTML markup. This requires the use of an <H1> tag for the highest-level heading, an <H2> tag for the main parts of the information within the <H1> tags, and use of an <H3> tag and lower levels for even finer divisions of the information. Having the Web page properly structured with HTML tags enables the blind user to obtain an overview of the page by having the high-level headings and main parts of the information read out loud. The user can then quickly skip an uninteresting section by instructing the screen reader to jump to the next lower-level heading.

HTML image elements support ALT *attributes,* which can be used to provide alternative text for images, although many Web pages do not make use of ALTs. Some accessibility specialists advocate the use of so-called *described images,* whereby text is provided to verbalize what a person with vision would normally see. For example, text verbalizing the Web access symbol (Figure 6-1) might be described as "a glowing globe with a keyhole."

Some people question the utility of the described image and consider it to be fairly useless on a Web page. Jakob Nielsen, for example, prefers the use of *utility descriptions* that can verbalize the *meaning,* or *role,* of the image with regard to what the image is intended to communicate and what will happen when the image is clicked.

In addition *image maps,* which are typically used for menus, should use ALT attributes for each link option, so a user who cannot see the image can have descriptions of it read as the cursor is moved around. Sighted users would also benefit from having ALT attributes displayed in the appropriate parts of the picture rectangle while waiting for the image file to download. Note that an ALT attribute can describe the meaning of the hyperlink destination in much more user-friendly terms than can a cryptic URL. In general, design rules intended to help users with disabilities often end up being of benefit to all users.

Many users are not completely blind but have greatly reduced vision. These users typically need to have text displayed using large fonts. Fortunately, most Web browsers offer large fonts as a standard feature. In order to support these users, a Web site should avoid encoding information with absolute font sizes but instead use relative sizes. For example, when using style sheets, a Web system should not set the font-size attributes to a number of points or pixels but instead set it to a percentage of the default font size. In that way, the text on the Web page will grow or shrink as the user issues *text-larger* or *text-smaller* commands, and the initial appearance of the page will match the user's preferences.

Providing full support for users with reduced eyesight would require the Web page to look equally well at all font sizes. Adjusting the Web site in this way is generally not practical. A more acceptable solution might involve page presentation whereby each page looks slightly worse at huge font sizes, so long as the basic page layout still works. It is recommended that Web pages be tested using the default font set to include 10, 12, and 14 points in order to ensure that the design is optimal for these common font sizes. Then conduct additional checks using the default 18- and 24-point sizes in order to make sure that the design still works at these accessibility-enhancing sizes.

Auditory

Individuals who are deaf or have other auditory disabilities rarely have problems on the Web, as sound effects are usually totally gratuitous. The usability of a site nearly always remains the same when the sound is turned off. Given the trend for Web sites to make greater use of multimedia, however, this will change. In particular, transcripts of spoken audio clips and videos should be made available in versions with subtitles, which will also benefit users who are not native speakers of the language used in the video.

Motor

Many users have difficulty with detailed mouse movements and may also have problems holding down multiple keyboard keys simultaneously. Most of these issues should be taken care of by improved browser design and should not concern content designers except for the advice not to design image maps that require extremely precise mouse positioning. Client-side image maps will work even for users who cannot use a mouse at all, as the browser should be able to move through the links under keyboard control.

Cognitive

People vary in their spatial-reasoning skills and in their short-term memory capacity. Programmers and graphics designers tend to get uncommonly high scores on tests of spatial-reasoning skills and are therefore good at visualizing the structure of a Web site. Similarly, young people—and that includes most Web designers—have better memories for obscure codes, such as a URL, than older people do.

Simplified Web site navigation helps *all* users and is a requirement for the elderly and those with cognitive disabilities. Individuals who have difficulty visualizing the structure of information can be helped when site navigation is presented in an organized visualization, such as a site map. Users are further aided when a browser updates the display of the site map with the path of the navigation and the location of the current page. Users with dyslexia may have problems reading long pages and will be helped if the design facilitates user scanability through the implementation of proper headings.

Most user interfaces offering a search capability require the user to type in keywords as search terms. Users with spelling disabilities and foreign-language users will often fail to find what they need as long as perfect spelling is required. Therefore, the site's search engine should include a spell checker. It would also be helpful for the search feature to offer more advanced information retrieval support, such as *query by example* and similarity search.

Accessibility Research and Studies

Additional information about accessibility for users with disabilities can be found in Waters (1997). Additional information on accessibility issues and concerns can be obtained by visiting the following sites:

- http://www.usableweb.com
- http://www.webreview.com/2000/03_10/strategists/03_10_00_3.shtml
- http://www.microsoft.com/enable
- http://www.microsoft.com/Usability
- http://www.usabilityfirst.com
- http://www.chesco.com/~cmarion/Academic/UseEng.html
- http://www.iarchitect.com/shame.htm
- http://www.tau-web.de/hci/space/index.html

6.3 Usability Evaluation

The material in this section is based on the work of Keith Instone.[9] One of the most important ways to ensure that a Web system will be well received is to perform usability testing with end users. The evaluation session can be performed using a system interface paper prototype, a code prototype, or, as a last resort, the production Web system. Many usability experts feel that the only valid way to gather usability data is to observe real users interacting with the system or a prototype. Observation is considered the easiest of all the usability evaluation methods, and perhaps that is why it is not commonly used. It can be fairly easy to obtain real usability insights. It can also be relatively inexpensive when you need

---

[9]Adapted and used with permission from Keith Instone, "Usability Matters: Site Usability Evaluation." Available at http://webreview.com/97/10/10/usability.

to involve only a small number of users in order to be able to identify prospective usability problems (Nielsen 2000).

Observational studies are also referred to as *heuristic evaluation*. Heuristic evaluation involves having three to five evaluators study a user interface by looking for violations of common usability principles, such as rules of thumb, or heuristics. The results can be used to flag the need for an immediate redesign of the user interface or one or more particular Web pages. The results can also aid the design and execution of usability tests on the system prior to release to the production environment.

Heuristic Evaluation Criteria

The rules of thumb used are the most important part of a heuristic evaluation. They set the stage for identifying problems and provide the vehicle for finding solutions. Jakob Nielsen, the author of several books addressing usability, originated heuristic evaluation in the early 1990s and has compiled the most comprehensive set of heuristics. He analyzed more than 200 prevalent usability problems and then statistically reduced the set of problems to the 10 most important usability concerns:[10]

1. Visibility of system status

2. Match between system and the real world

3. User control and freedom

4. Consistency and standards

5. Error prevention

6. Recognition rather than recall

7. Flexibility and efficiency of use

8. Aesthetic and minimalist design

9. Help users recognize, diagnose, and recover from errors

10. Help and documentation

Many of Jakob Nielsen's insights into usability came from data about the usability of pre-Web software systems, yet the heuristics guidance is still very applicable. It is important to ensure that usability concerns are consciously incorporated into a Web system. A heuristic evaluation represents a formal exercise undertaken to ensure that each usability concern is reviewed for the system.

---

[10]"Jakob Nielsen Biography." Copyright 2000 by Jakob Nielsen and Nielsen Norman Group. www.useit.com/jakob/.

Gather Opinions

Once the set of heuristic evaluation criteria is sufficiently clear, it is necessary to identify a few end user representatives to assist in an evaluation. They need to be given an overview of the Web system: its mission, intended audience, and basic engineering architecture. Then they need to exercise the Web system. If only a paper prototype of the system exists, the user must review each user interface from the perspective of performing different functional paths. Ensure that the evaluator's first impressions are captured for each screen interface, and document any perceived problems with the user interface.

Once you obtain an impression of the end user's initial perception of the usability of the system, without the aid of instruction, it may be beneficial to provide each evaluator with a site map and a few defined business scenarios. Observe the degree to which the end user is able to navigate more easily on the Web system, having had some experience with the system and now that a site map is available. Does the user navigate more quickly than before? Is the user hesitating on certain screens? Does the user appear to be any less frustrated than before?

The answers to these questions may indicate whether the system's usability learning curve is minimal, indicating that the system interface is relatively intuitive, or whether the degree of system usability improves little with experience on the system. Ensure that evaluator feedback in terms of perceived problems on this second iteration is again captured. Following the heuristic evaluation, each perceived usability problem should be categorized with a usability concern defined with the organizational or industry usability guidance in use.

Merge and Rate

Each heuristic evaluation represents the *opinions* of the individual evaluator. The benefit of the heuristic evaluation exercise becomes apparent once each usability problem has been categorized and the results of the three to five evaluations are combined into a consolidated list of findings that removes duplication. Next, have each evaluator rate the significance of each usability problem reflected in the consolidated list.

Commonly, the evaluator is requested to score the severity of each problem, using a scale of 1 to 5. A value on the low end of the scale generally means that the individual does not consider the finding a problem. A score on the high end of the scale would indicate that the usability concern reflects a catastrophic problem. Once scores from the evaluators have been tabulated, an average rating is calculated for each usability problem in the list.

The list of findings should now be reorganized to reflect usability problem ratings in descending order. After careful analysis and review of the list, draw a line on the list to represent the threshold between the top, catastrophic usability problems and those regarded as less serious. The new list of findings containing the averaged rating score should be given to product or project management for consideration of design changes for the system.

Work toward a Solution

At this point, you have obtained a few people's opinions about what may be wrong with a Web site. But now that you have the problems defined, how do you correct them? Quite often, the most difficult challenge is identifying a problem; the solution is straightforward.

For example, under the "be consistent" heuristic, your evaluators might point out some very specific inconsistencies. Perhaps a Web page contains a list of products displayed in alphabetical order. Perhaps on the first page, each product is prefixed by a bullet, whereas on the next page, no bullets appear. The fix may be as simple as deciding on one of the two formats and changing one of the two Web pages. On the other hand, the decision may be made that this relatively minor bit of inconsistency is tolerable. In either case, the potential problem is reviewed and a conscious decision made to either fix or ignore the problem.

In other situations, the decision about the problem may not be so obvious, and here the value of the heuristic evaluation comes into play. For example, given a large number of consistency problems, the organization may need to define a standard set of conventions for ensuring a consistent Web site. This document might provide rules for the appearance of the Web page site background, the location on the screen of the Home button, and a dictionary of terms.

Objective Usability Criteria

The material in this section is based on the work of Jasper Sprengers.[11] The evaluation criteria applied for Web site usability seldom explicitly distinguish between value judgments and objective criteria. Successful Web system usability reflects a successful user experience with the site, not the opinion or verdict of a Web design expert. No objective method can tell us whether a Web site is really usable unless we have observed a typical Web site user successfully using it. When a Web site suffers

---

[11]Adapted and used with permission from Jasper Sprengers, "Objective Evaluation of Likely Usability Hazards—Preliminaries for User Testing," Edinburgh, Scotland. 1999. Available at http://www.abeleto.com/resources/articles/objective.html. Jasper Sprengers is founder and director of Abeleto Ltd., a consultancy for Web usability development and online learning resources, based in Edinburgh and Amsterdam.

from frequent flaws that are well documented, however, usability problems are more easily identified by a single design expert, and the solutions to the usability problems are often simple to implement.

Objective and subjective design decisions often compete over a single feature, especially when a trade-off between aesthetic effects and ease of use is involved. Consider the example of the use of *blue underlined links.* Graphics Web design experts can argue about the aesthetics, but because they are an established practice, we all recognize them at once as links.

The criteria outlined in the Usability Checklist in Appendix A helps to make a task-based usability evaluation more meaningful and reliable by first solving objective usability hazards. Note that truly objective criteria are a matter of measurable degree. For example, the mere presence or absence of a certain feature, such as providing a copyright notice, may be a criterion in itself.

The conclusion that a certain feature is incomplete or of poor use does not need to be subjective judgment. When the necessary features of an item cannot be objectively defined, the item has no place in the usability evaluation. Two simple guidelines for content and display enable the Web design or test professional to sift through usability criteria in order to determine those that address objective usability hazards.

- *Content* usability criteria address the simple presence or absence of information items, either visible, such as *date last modified* or a *copyright notice,* or as part of document metadata: keywords or document description. Proper coding conventions for HTML, style sheets, and scripts belong to the same group, as they urge the programmer to include certain attributes or suggest a preferred alternative to reach the same visual effect.
- *Display* usability criteria address how visible elements are rendered in countable and measurable terms. Examples of such criteria are:
  —Size of page elements and their relative or absolute position on the page
  —Use of fonts: types, colors, size
  —Length of text units in headings, lines, paragraphs, and pages
  —Hyperlinks to images or text elements and how they are made visible through, for example, underlining, color, and the use of roll-over

Support from the End User

Usability evaluation does not necessarily need a "professional" set of end users. A lot can be accomplished quickly and easily by using end user substitutes, which requires little time, effort, or expense. The main secret is to observe real people doing real tasks (Nielsen and Norman 2000). When necessary, seek to visit prospective Web system customers where they would normally be visiting your Web site.

Even though friends, colleagues, and spouses aren't likely to be exactly like the real customers of the Web system, a lot can be learned by observing them interacting with the system. To gain the most benefit, watch these substitute end users performing real tasks. Observe their behavior as these users answer questions that are of interest to them, search for products, and try to make purchases—real ones.

An important element of the test experience is to watch and observe the behavior of the substitute end user and not to interrupt or offer help in performing functions. Do not offer help, no matter how great the temptation. Also be careful not to ask why the person has done something until after the test session. In fact, you should sit behind the person so you don't distract him or her or get in the way. It is also best to have the user surrogates talk through their thoughts. In other words, let them "think out loud." This is the best way to gather information on how users think as they navigate around the Web site, because they are likely to say the first things that come to their minds.

Some larger organizations use a dedicated *usability lab* having one-way mirrors and video cameras. This arrangement provides users with a semiprivate area in which to work. User sessions performed in the lab are taped for later review by psychologists and usability experts. Some examples of usability labs can be found at the following URLs:

- http://www.cc.gatech.edu/gvu/lab/descriptions/usability.html (Georgia Tech)
- http://www.slis.indiana.edu/hcilab/(Indiana University)
- http://www.microsoft.com/Usability/tour.htm (Microsoft Corporation)

If you need to bring people to your location for the observations, invite one person at a time so that you can observe that person's natural behavior without the bias introduced by the presence and comments of other people. Watch each person perform a set of typical tasks with the site. For example, if a business site is being tested, ask customers to research a product purchase and determine which member of a product line best fits their needs. If an airline Web site is being tested, ask what the users typically do at a travel site; then watch as they try to perform these functions on your Web site.

Although it's best to observe representative customers, tests performed with colleagues, friends, or a spouse are better than no tests at all. If these user substitutes have trouble with the Web site, beware. When a Web site has serious usability flaws, they are likely to be revealed with even simple tests involving substitute end users.

6.4 Automating Usability Evaluation

Jakob Nielsen, a leading industry expert on Web system usability, is skeptical that automated methods for performing usability evaluations can yield valuable results.[12] He argues that having a computer follow links and count the number of clicks is a poor substitute for human evaluation in determining whether users can find what they are seeking. Computers cannot easily assess how much difficulty a user may be having trying to navigate a Web system in order to locate information about or purchasing a product. An automated program can count the time needed for a user to follow the optimal path to the solution, but that's not how the average user behaves. One wrong word in a menu, for example, and the user is lost for 5 minutes or forever.

The value of automated usability evaluation methods that simply count user clicks necessary to arrive at a solution may be misleading. For example, Jakob Nielsen reviewed the usability of a particular Web site where individuals needed to find certain products. The original design provided product pages within three clicks from the home page; a proposed revision to the Web site navigation required one more click. Yet shopping success was seven times higher in the revised design because each of the new steps was completely intuitive.

Even with one more click, the revised design was faster because users didn't have to spend as much time thinking about where to click. More important, the new design enabled people to find the right product much more frequently than they could under the original design. Despite the usability gains of the revised Web site navigation, an automated assessment may have recorded a higher rating to the original design. Whether the screen design and navigation choices make sense is the one thing an automated evaluation program cannot check.

Another usability measure typically computed by automated usability services is *freshness,* as defined by the percentage of pages that are new. However, a determination cannot be readily made about whether a Web site is up-to-date simply by looking at the timestamps on the files. A site can be extremely fresh even if 90 percent of its content is more than a year old. It may be that the site keeps good archives to supplement the current content. For example, probably less than 1 percent of the pages on nytimes.com are *current,* even though it is a daily newspaper and one of the freshest sites in the world. Conversely, a site can be stale even when most of the pages have been edited recently, as may occur when the changes are not the appropriate ones to bring the content up-to-date in ways that matter to users.

---

[12]This material has been adapted and used with permission from "Voodoo Usability," *Alertbox,* December 12, 1999. Available at http://www.zdnet.com/devhead/alertbox/991212.html.

How do you distinguish between two types of old files: good content that should be archived because it is still of value and outdated content that should be removed or updated? The answer is that you can't tell without understanding the content and the way it will be used. Even full natural-language understanding would not be sufficient to allow a computer to make this judgment.

Appropriate Areas for Automation

Response time, HTML validation, and link rot are some of the aspects of usability appropriate for automatic assessment. It is not necessary to see or understand the contents of a Web page in order to measure the length of time it takes to download the page. As a result, an automated program can provide a perfect estimate of response time.

Automated assessment tools can, potentially, be useful in gauging the existence of *link rot*. Link rot refers to Web page links that no longer work because the page is no longer available or has moved to a different URL. The automated program determines whether a Web page is returned when a link has been initiated. Unfortunately, the program cannot ascertain whether the page returned is in fact the page intended by the user when the link was initiated.

The practice of reusing URLs presents a problem for automated assessment methods. For example, some sites assign a document to a different URL when an article has been moved into archives and reuse the old URL for a new article. This is not a sound practice, as it makes it more difficult for other sites to link, and incoming links are the most powerful Web marketing method. When a Web site does change URLs, the link-rot assessment program may report that the link works, even though the link connects to something completely irrelevant.

Accessibility for users with disabilities can be only partly measured by automated assessment methods. Sure, it's possible to have a program check for the use of ALT text for all images, but without natural-language comprehension, the computer cannot determine whether the ALT text will be meaningful to a blind user, for example. In addition, it is sometimes more beneficial that a Web page avoid the use of ALT text for certain images.

The standards that test and quality assurance professionals use to evaluate and test a Web system should be documented. The documented results of usability evaluations and tests need to cite the particular standard that applies. Test professionals performing usability tests can use automated tools geared to checking against the particular standard.

Automated Usability Assessment Tools

Despite our arguments against automated methods for performing usability evaluations, some progress has been made in this area. Although usability testing might not lend itself to 100 percent automation, automation could complement the manual efforts. Some usability tools that have recently become available are documented in Chapter 7. These tools address typical interpretations of usability: friendly appearance, ease of use, ease of learning, user productivity, and the forgiving of user errors. The mission for such tools is to identify areas where users have difficulty operating a system and to define the reasons for the difficulty. Web system professionals can use their tools in order to track and to analyze the actions of end users with the system and therefore flag potential usability issues and the need for corrective action.

Usability Evaluation at Microsoft

A key lesson with regard to usability pertains to letting the customer help design the Web site. Yahoo does that well, and Microsoft has come a long way in this direction.[13] The fact is that most site designers' perspective differs from that of the majority of site visitors. The Web site designer often focuses in terms of the site's coolness. But what customers value most is speed. They want to come to a site, find what they need, and go on with their business. If it takes 10 seconds to download a page, that's too long. It's a goal at Microsoft, in fact, to make everything on its site so easy to get to that visitors can come to microsoft.com and find what they need in either two minutes or within three clicks.

Of course, achieving this goal requires the implementation of another process plus a lot of new technology. A system is needed that lets the organization listen to the customer. For instance, in its extensive usability tests with site pages, Microsoft puts users in front of a PC and asks them to navigate a page while they tell the Microsoft folks what works and what doesn't work. In this way, Microsoft has learned more precisely the type of navigation that people preferred on the microsoft.com site.[14]

Microsoft implements its approach to usability evaluation with several variations, or prototypes, of each Web page in order to see how alternative solutions work. Microsoft also compares how customers do on its site versus on other sites, timing how long the customer takes to successfully complete tasks and then comparing the results with the performance measurements for the customer on other sites. In essence, Microsoft benchmarks itself against leading Web sites and continually monitors how it does on critical tasks.

Microsoft also surveys site visitors regularly, making it easy for visitors to send e-mail with complaints or suggestions. In fact, Microsoft gets 2,000 e-mail messages a day about the site; the company reads and responds, sometimes making changes to the site within 24 hours,

---

[13]Sanjay Parthasarathy, 2000; available at "What I Learned Running One of the World's Largest Web Sites," http://www.microsoft.com/backstage/bkst_column_16.htm.

[14]For more information about the Microsoft approach, see the Web page http://www.microsoft.com/backstage/bkst_column_8.htm.

based on issues that become apparent as a result of the feedback. As a result, satisfaction with the site is way up.

Although Microsoft's approach may appear intuitive, that approach does not always happen in practice. On the Web, organizations appear to have abandoned some of these good practices in order to keep up with the competition. Rushing to add cool new features, the organization does not always think about how the Web site will perform at low network speeds or even what the visitor *really* wants to do.

Microsoft believes that it is important to let visitors literally design a site that best suits them. Amazon.com does a great job of this, with the way the site is personalized for each customer, based on buying habits and past visits to its site. Microsoft is working on incorporating such personalization as well. By using XML, Microsoft will be able to more easily *tag* visitors with data that's particular to them, something that would have been too complicated and data intensive using just plain HTML. Soon, visitors will be able to customize the Microsoft Web site experience, based on where they live, their interests, whether they're gamers or developers, and all sorts of other things. And when visitors request e-mail newsletters, Microsoft will be able to send them customized newsletters.

In the end, Microsoft believes that successful Web site usability is a cultural thing. It is an obsession with doing the right thing to provide a rich customer experience on the Web site. Often that means that you need to make things simpler and reduce it to the bare essence of what the customer wants.

The following books address the subject of usability, including issues and test concerns:

- Larry L. Constantine and Lucy A. D. Lockwood, "Software for Use: A Practical Guide to the Models and Methods of Usage Centered Design," Reading, MA: Addison-Wesley, 1999.
- Alan Cooper, "About Face: The Essentials of User Interface Design," New York, N.Y.: IDG Books Worldwide, 1995.
- Jennifer Fleming and Richard Koman, *Web Navigation: Designing the User Experience,* Cambridge, MA: O'Reilly & Associates, 1998.
- Jeff Johnson, "GUI Bloopers: Don'ts and Do's for Software Developers and Web Designers," San Francisco, CA: Morgan Kaufmann Publishers, 2000.
- Deborah J. Mayhew, "The Usability Engineering Lifecycle: A Practitioners' Handbook for User Interface Design," San Francisco, CA: Morgan Kaufmann Publishers, 1999.
- Jakob Nielsen, "Designing Web Usability: The Practice of Simplicity," Indianapolis, Ind.: New Riders Publishing, 2000.
- Donald A. Norman, "The Design of Everyday Things," New York, NY: Currency/Doubleday, 1990.

- Mark Pearrow, "Web Site Usability Handbook," Hingham, MA: Charles River Media, 2000.
- Jeffrey Rubin, "Handbook of Usability Testing: How to Plan, Design, and Conduct Effective Tests," New York, NY: Wiley, 1994.
- Paul Saffo, "The Inmates Are Running the Asylum: Why High Tech Products Drive Us Crazy and How To Restore the Sanity," Sams, Indianapolis, Ind, 1999.

6.5 TBS Case Study

This section describes some of the ways that the I-View Previous Order interface of the TBS system was evaluated for usability and some of the corrections that were made.

Font Sizes

To allow for viewing by users with differing visual capabilities, including disabilities, it is important to allow the user to adjust the font size of text displayed on the screen. The I-View Order Status interface was evaluated to make sure that the fonts could be resized without adversely affecting the page content and layout. This factor also borders on a compatibility issue, as adjusting the font size may have different side effects in different browsers. As designed, the TBS I-View Previous Order interface (Figure 2-9) properly displays on all fonts sizes, from "smallest" to "largest" on both Internet Explorer and Netscape Navigator.

Titles

The title of the page—both the HTML page title, which is displayed in the window title bar, and the body page title—should accurately describe the content of the page being displayed. The I-View Previous Order interface was written to use The Technology Bookstore as the HTML title and Order as the page title in the body. These titles are not very descriptive to the user and thus were changed to more appropriate titles. It was decided to change the page title in the body to Order Detail and the HTML page title to The Technology Bookstore—Order Detail.

Copyright Notice

I-View Order Status as implemented did not include a copyright notice, a common practice on commercial Web sites, at the bottom of the page. Therefore, the following markup would be added to the bottom of the page:

```
<center>&copy;2001 The Technology Bookstore</center>
```

This code will display the copyright symbol, ©, in addition to the text provided.

6.6 Chapter Summary

⚠ Poor Web system usability results in lost users. A common problem associated with usability is the phenomenon of frustrated customers abandoning online purchases.

⚠ Usability must be consciously designed into the system from the start, and usability standards must be defined, adopted, and communicated. Similarly, software professionals need to be familiar with usability issues in order to properly design and conduct beneficial usability tests.

⚠ Usability design should be incorporated into the system by involving end users as part of design reviews and system prototype demonstrations.

⚠ Usability testing consists of an objective evaluation of the ease of use for a Web system against defined standards or defined end user expectations.

⚠ One of the most important ways to ensure that a Web system will be well received by customers is to perform usability testing, involving potential end users and a paper or code prototype.

⚠ For a Web site to be successful, it needs to be as inviting and easy to navigate for the user as possible. To this end, Web design personnel should incorporate usability principles as part of the Web design effort.

⚠ The goal of usability testing is to incorporate objective usability criteria into the usability evaluation instead of relying on individual tastes in Web design. A quality level of usability pertains to the overall success of the user experience and therefore involves more than speed and ease of navigating a Web site.

⚠ Making the Web more accessible for users with various disabilities is largely a matter of applying markup in the way that it was intended. The various markup languages used as part of Web systems need to be applied in ways that adhere to the separation of content from formatting.

6.7 References

Flanders, Vincent, and Michael Willis. 1998. *Web Pages that Suck: Learn Good Design by Looking at Bad Design*. Alameda, CA: Sybex Inc.

Fleming, Jennifer. 1998. *Web Navigation: Designing the User Experience*. NY: O'Reilly.

Nielsen, Jakob. 2000. *Designing Web Usability: The Practice of Simplicity.* Indianapolis, IN: New Rider.

Nielsen, Jakob. 2000. "Why You Only Need to Test with Five Users." The Alertbox: Current Issues in Web Usability. March 19. www.useit.com/alertbox/.

Nielsen, Jakob, and Donald Norman. 2000. "Web-Site Usability: Get the Right Answers from Testing," *Information Week,* February 14. Available at www.informationweek.com/773/we3.htm.

Waters, Crystal. 1997. *Universal Web Design.* Indianapolis, IN: New Rider.

chapter 7

Tools

What tools do I need to assist in creating a quality Web site?

The best tool for any particular situation depends on an organization's system engineering environment and the engineering methodology. This chapter covers the types of tools that can assist in implementation of the topics discussed in Chapters 2–6. These tools range from the small command line utility to the full-scale software test environment. As with any software product, engineering and test tools come and go. The examples provided here are current as of early 2001. This is a subset of the numerous tools on the market.

Because several tools are available for each aspect of the Web system effort, they should be evaluated against the requirements of the particular organization and project. Evaluation criteria include feature set, platform support, cost, collaborative (multiuse) capabilities, support, and frequency of updates. Some aspects of validation and verification may be well suited to multiple tools for proper coverage of site functionality.

7.1 Engineering

A Web system development iteration includes the specification of system requirements (typically through use cases) and the development of system test cases. The following types of tools are available to assist with these activities:

- *Use case analysis and software design.* RSI use cases can be modeled in any standard use case modeling tool. These tools allow use cases to be drawn and placed onto a use case diagram and related to other use cases. The process of designing software from use cases through the use of collaborations and other models is also an important feature to look for in a modeling tool.
    —*Rational Rose* is the best-known modeling tool, providing the capability to create use case models and other models that cover most of the object-oriented software development life cycle. Rose can also generate code in several languages directly from the models.
    —*Microsoft Visio2000* features many software modeling capabilities, including use cases, class diagrams, and collaborations. Visio's UML Navigator provides a place to manage such entities as use cases and classes for modeling on multiple diagrams.
    —*Embarcadero GDPro* delivers strict adherence to the UML specification, sophisticated multiuse capabilities, and integration with other engineering products.
    —*SOFTEAM Objecteering,* a full-featured UML modeling tool, is available in many editions for various types of development.
- *Test case management.* Tools in this category allow for planning, managing, and analyzing all aspects of the testing life cycle. Some test management tools are integrated with requirement and configuration management tools to simplify the testing life cycle process.
    —*Mercury TestDirector* is a suite of Web-based tools for developing and managing test cases. TestDirector also provides tools for requirements management, defect management, and reporting.
    —*Rational TestManager* features test plan development, management, and organization, including test case execution and analysis. Test Manager is integrated with other Rational tools for defect management and versioning.
    —*Compuware's QADirector* provides a framework for managing the entire testing process—from design to execution to analysis—and is a powerful, extensible test management solution for full life-cycle testing of distributed large-scale applications.
- *Automated testing tools.* One of the key tools for verification of site functionality—in addition to security, performance and scalability, and compatibility—automated test tools provide a way to capture and script user interaction with the Web system. These tools are typically used to embody the test cases for the system, as discussed in Chapter 2. Appendix B provides a full evaluation of the various tools and their features so that the appropriate tool for the project can be selected.

7.2 Security

Many tools are required for the security verification of a Web system. Unfortunately, most of these tools are oriented to small tasks, such as port scanning, or checking the operating system and service configuration of a server for known vulnerabilities. Advanced security verification involves investigating the site's interfaces and components in site-specific ways that cannot be handled automatically by a tool. The following tools can assist in the security process but should not replace a manual analysis and investigation of the site:

- *Port scanning.* These tools attempt to connect to a machine over a network in various ways, looking for potential entry points.
  - *Nmap,* an advanced port-scanning tool, attempts not only to connect to a server on various ports but also to use various types of packets and fragments to bypass firewalls and other filters.
  - *Cisco Secure Scanner* provides port scanning and vulnerability assessment, in addition to security management and documentation.
- *Network monitoring.* These tools capture network packets in transmission across a network, which can greatly assist in ensuring the security of user authentication and confidential data.
  - *Windows NT/2000 Network Monitor,* provided free with the operating system, allows the capture and examination of packets destined to or transmitted from the local machine.
  - *Tcpdump,* a UNIX utility for network monitoring, is a freeware tool provided with most UNIX distributions. The Windows port of this tool is called WinDump.
  - *Ethereal* is a freeware network analyzer for UNIX and Windows.
- *System vulnerability checking.* In addition to the features of a port scanner, system vulnerability checkers investigate the services they find for known vulnerabilities, such as DNS, FTP, and Sendmail service security holes. New vulnerabilities are discovered frequently, so these tools are usually updated on a regular basis to include the latest findings.
  - *SAINT,* an updated version of the original SATAN tool, provides a detailed analysis of computer and network vulnerabilities and is available for UNIX systems.
  - *WebTrends Security Analyzer,* available for Windows NT/2000, scans machines for security problems and can even correct them. Additional features include scheduling and reporting.
  - *PGP CyberCop Scanner and Monitor* has a full set of security scans and checks and can also monitor a Web site in real time to detect attacks as they occur. CyberCop Scanner is available for Windows NT/2000 and

Linux systems; Monitor is available for Windows NT 4.0 and Solaris systems.

—*Symantec NetRecon* provides security vulnerability assessment and reporting for networks and server machines and is available for Windows NT 4.0 machines. Symantec also offers products to monitor a Web system in real time to guard against intrusion.

7.3 Performance and Scalability

Tools in this category allow for performance, load, stress, and reliability evaluation and can be configured to simulate a number of client users simultaneously in order to load the site and measure response time and resource usage. Load testing typically involves various scenarios to analyze how the site performs under various loads. Stress testing involves evaluating the site's behavior under extremely high levels of load to see when and how it fails. Scalability testing involves the addition of server resources to the site and additional load tests to monitor the impact on response time.

- *Performance and load testing* is performed by simulating large numbers of Web users. Typically, these tools operate at the *protocol* level, bypassing the interface to provide a more accurate level of testing. These tools also feature a mechanism to create virtual user scripts and sessions for replay against the Web site. Appendix B provides an evaluation of some of these tools.
  —*Mercury LoadRunner* is a full-featured testing tool that allows the creation and management of protocol-level virtual user sessions, response time, server resource measurements, data-driven tests, and reporting. The "lite" version of this tool is called Astra QuickTest.
  —*Rational Robot* (part of the Rational Suite TestStudio) when combined with protocols and virtual tester licenses, allows for load/performance testing. It is a scalable protocol capture tool with an interface for modeling complex load testing scenarios.
  —*Segue SilkPerformer* provides customizable, flexible performance and load testing for multiple aspects of a Web system. SilkPerformer features an easy-to-use interface and powerful server monitoring.
  —*Emprix/RSW e-Load,* featuring highly realistic load simulation, is capable of high-volume performance and load testing, as well as server performance measurement. The tool is integrated with the Emprix/RSW e-TEST suite and uses the same scripting tools as the other tools in the suite.
  —*Compuware's QALoad* mimics realistic business usage and validates that the system can meet acceptable service levels.

—*Microsoft Web Application Stress Tool (WAST)*, a free tool provided by Microsoft, allows the basic simulation of user load against a Web server through capture/playback and stores the results for later analysis.

- *Performance monitoring.* To measure server resource usage during a load test, it is important to have a performance monitoring tool gather data about how the server is using its CPU, memory, network, disk, and so on, under load from large numbers of users.

  —*Windows NT/2000 Performance Monitor,* provided with the Windows NT/2000 operating system, allows the configuration and monitoring of a large number of performance measurements on a machine. These measurements are recorded over time and can be logged to disk files for monitoring over an extended period of time.

  —*Ksysguard* is a utility that features enhanced monitoring and logging of system performance on Linux systems under KDE2.

  —*GlancePlus for HP/UX,* provided by Hewlett-Packard, is a graphical performance monitoring tool for HP/UX systems.

  —*Windows NT/2000 Task Manager* has a limited-functionality "performance" tab that can be useful for a quick summary of the CPU and memory usage of a Windows NT/2000 system. This tool is also useful for monitoring the load on the machine that is executing the load-testing tool to make sure it does not exceed its resource limitations.

7.4 Compatibility

Ensuring compatibility is more of a manual process than the previously discussed areas. Typically, each combination of browser version, operating system, and other user settings, such as color depth, must be tested individually by installing and configuring the appropriate software.

- *NetMechanic BrowserPhoto* is a subscription-based service, a continuously updated online compatibility lab capable of rendering your site on many different browser and operating system combinations.
- *AnyBrowser.com Site Viewer* is a free service that can simulate the rendering of a site given a URL and a requested HTML specification level.
- *Microsoft Internet Explorer 5.x "Compatibility Mode"* allows the viewing of site content with the Internet Explorer 4.x rendering engine.

7.5 Usability

Usability engineering is a wide-ranging discipline that includes user interface design, graphics design, ergonomic concerns, human factors, ethnography, and industrial and cognitive psychology. As with compatibility, usability testing is more of a manual process of determining the ease of use and other factors of a Web system's interface. However, some tools can assist with this process, although they should never replace human verification of the interface.

- *ErgoLight WebTester* provides navigation analysis, site evaluation, and mechanisms for user feedback.
- *Web Static Analyzer Tool (WebSAT)* analyzes a site to determine the level of adherence to a set of usability guidelines.
- *CAST Bobby (www.cast.org/Bobby)* is a free service that assists in validating the accessibility of a Web site by identifying site aspects that may make it difficult to use by Web users with disabilities.

7.6 Other Tools

- *Version control,* or managing the revisions of design documents, test case files, and source code, is critical for any project.
  - —*Merant PVCS Version Manager* is a full-featured tool for managing version control of project files and is integrated with PVCS Configuration Builder to assist in developing automated builds.
  - —*Rational ClearCase* provides not only version control capabilities but also build management, process configurability, build auditing, and integration with Rational ClearQuest for defect-tracking capabilities.
  - —*Microsoft Visual SourceSafe,* a component of Microsoft Visual Studio Enterprise Edition, provides basic version control and labeling functions.
- *Defect tracking*
  - —*Merant PVCS Tracker* provides customizable defect tracking, including reporting and integration with many software development environments.
  - —*Elsinore Visual Intercept* features project-oriented, customizable, and scalable defect capabilities. The tool is also extensible through the Visual Intercept Developer's kit.
  - —*Rational ClearQuest,* integrated with other Rational tools, provides customizable, workflow-based defect tracking.
- HTML/Link validation
  - —*Rational Site Check* (included with Robot) tests links, active content, and has virus-scanning built in.

—*NetMechanic HTML Toolbox,* a subscription-based service, scans your site and verifies the validity of hyperlinks, HTML markup, spelling, and other issues.

—*W3C Validators (validator.w3.org),* a free service, provides utilities that can analyze HTML and CSS for correctness and verify links.

—*Watchfire Linkbot* is capable of validating Web site content and ensuring that links and other types of references are pointing to valid destinations.

7.7 Chapter Summary

▲ Each aspect of the Web system requires one or more tools to assist in the engineering, validation, and verification of site functional and nonfunctional requirements.

▲ Many tools exist for each of the functional and nonfunctional areas, so it is important for an organization to select tools that meet the needs of the project. Sometimes, it is advisable to have more than one tool for a particular area.

▲ Automated testing tools are useful in many aspects of the Web system effort.

▲ Engineering tools include use case analysis and software design, test case management, and automated testing tools.

▲ Security tools include port scanners, network monitors, and system vulnerability checkers.

▲ Performance and scalability verification can be facilitated through the use of performance monitors and load-testing tools.

▲ Ensuring compatibility is still mainly a manual process, but a few automated tools are available to assist in this process.

▲ Usability evaluation is a manual process best performed by humans. However, some tools are available on the Web for usability analysis.

▲ Tools are also available for version control, defect tracking, and HTML/link validation.

Evaluation Checklists

This appendix provides checklists for each area covered in this book. These lists are intended to serve as a reference point for developers to ensure that important quality concerns have been considered and for testers to devise test cases.

A.1 Functional

The implementation and testing for the items presented in this section vary by the architecture and design of the site. Some examples are given, but research will need to be done by each site individually to determine the best way to address these areas.

- Forms
  —Browser Back and Next buttons: If it is necessary to prevent forms from being resubmitted—as is the case with payment transactions, for example—the form page and response page should be set to expire immediately. This will prevent the user from going back to the form, using the back button, and then clicking the submit button again to resubmit the form.
  —Browser Refresh button: Again, the form response page should be set to expire immediately.
  —Multiple clicks of the Submit button: The UI should restrict the submit button to a single click (through scripting or a server side check) and inform the user that they cannot submit more than once.

- Links
  - —Internal links: The site should use relative links in all pages, where applicable, to help prevent broken links when relocating the site's content. For example:

    ```
    ../images/book_image.jpg
    ../asp/PurchaseItem.asp
    ```

  - —External links: External links may break if the external site relocates content or goes away altogether. Link-checking tools, such as LinkBot, can be used to verify link integrity.
- Error handling: A standard mechanism for handling errors should be implemented, providing a useful message for users and a code for development personnel to diagnose the problem.
- Sessions: If the site is maintaining user sessions, it should expire and destroy the session information after a predetermined period.
  - —If Web server built-in sessions are being used, this functionality is handled automatically. Typically, there is a configuration setting to control the amount of time allowed before the session expires.
  - —If an external mechanism (such as a database) is being used to store the user session data, removal of the data is not automatic. A custom process or mechanism will need to be created to remove the data.
- Transactions and data integrity: Related database update operations should be performed in a single database transaction. This will enable operations to succeed (commit) or fail (rollback) as a whole and not corrupt records in the database. For example, if a "customer" record and an associated "order" record must be updated as a single unit—meaning both updates succeed or fail together—then a database transaction must be used.
- Concurrency: Multiple users should be isolated from one another, especially if performing update operations. This type of isolation is typically implemented through a combination of database transactions and user interface restriction. For example, if a user is attempting to edit a record, the UI could either prevent other users from viewing the record, or report an error if another user attempts to update the record, if the first user changed it.

A.2 Security

- Authentication: Since HTTP Basic Authentication and custom authentication methods are not encrypted during transmission by default, a third party may be able to intercept user authentication data (i.e., the user's ID and password). Therefore, it is critical to use a secure protocol—such as SSL—when transmitting user authentication information.

- Authorization
  —Regardless of authentication method, the server must restrict access to private content at the URL level and not depend on user interface mechanisms to restrict access to pages.
  —Some pages on the site may be available to the user based only on the data they wish to view, such as details for a customer order. In these cases, the server must restrict access to data, and therefore certain pages, that the user does not have permission to view.
- Content attacks
  —System command execution: Avoid invoking operating system commands using user-supplied inputs from Web system components. If doing so is absolutely necessary, make sure that the inputs are filtered for metacharacters, including relative file path references.
  —Server-side file access: If Web system components access server-side files, avoid passing the path or file name to and from the client browser; that is, do not store them in hidden form fields.
  —Buffer overflows: Check all inputs for length constraints prior to using them in a Web system component. It is good practice to do this regardless of how the input is used, as later modifications to components or other components in the system may open up input-length vulnerabilities.
- Database server
  —Data privacy: Highly sensitive user data, such as payment transaction history information, must be protected against access through the site's Web or other servers. This can be accomplished by using a separate, write-only database.
  —Data encryption: With this common technique for protecting database data, data is encrypted prior to being placed in the database and is then decrypted before it is used by a Web system component.
  —Temporary and log files: Sensitive user data must not be written to temporary or log files on any server's disk. Doing so prior to encryption can defeat the act of encrypting the data in the database.
  —Database objects: Make sure that database objects—meaning tables, views, and so on—are accessible only by the special database user(s) used by Web system components. Permission should be revoked from all other users.
  —Database user ID and password: If the Web system component is using a special database user ID and password to access data on behalf of users,

this log-on information should be encrypted in the component's source code and decrypted prior to being used.

—Database schema information: Information about queries, tables, views, or any other database objects should not be passed back and forth between the client browser and the server, as this exposes information about the site's database to users.

- Client computer

  —ActiveX controls: Inputs to ActiveX controls should be checked for length and character restrictions to prevent buffer overflows and other manipulations. ActiveX controls should not accept file names as input. Storing private data on the user's machine through an ActiveX control should be avoided. If doing so is absolutely necessary, encrypt the data.

  —Cookies: Storing private data in a cookie on a user's machine should be avoided. If doing so is absolutely necessary, make sure to encrypt the data.

- Secure communications: Any confidential data transmitted between the user's Web browser and the server should be encrypted during transmission. This can be verified using a network monitoring program.

- Network

  —Firewalls should be in place to block access to Web system machines on ports other than those needed for site operation.

  —A second firewall can be placed between the Web server and other back-end servers, such as database servers, to protect them if the Web server is compromised.

  —Any unnecessary services, such as FTP, mail, DNS, running on a server should be shut down.

A.3 Performance and Scalability

Factors

- Site requirements: Determine an expected or desired number of users that the site must support, together with a desired response time at that number of users.

- Scaling: Ensure that the site supports the addition of server-side resources—through vertical or horizontal scaling—to increase the number of users supported at the desired response times. Ideally, the site should exhibit the property of linear scaling.

- Stress: Under heavy load—exceeding the number of users defined in the site's requirements—the site should gracefully reject users above its maximum without components crashing or corrupting user data.

- Reliability: The site must be able to function for a sustained period of time at the desired response time and user levels without experiencing a degradation in response time or an inappropriate use of server resources, such as disk usage and database table sizes.

Verifying Site Performance and Scalability

Types of Tests

- Base performance: Using a single user, evaluate each use case on its own, in a base configuration of the site, to determine how it performs in optimal conditions. In sites with a high number of use cases, it may not be practical to do this for all use cases, so select the most important ones.
- Load: Perform load evaluation for both single use case and virtual user sessions. Single use case load evaluation allows the investigation of how a single use-case implementation performs multiple-user access. Virtual user sessions simulate access to the site by users following a typical usage pattern.
- Stress: Evaluate the site's ability to cope with an exceedingly large number of users. In this situation, users should be gracefully rejected, and the site should continue to function without data corruption or major errors.
- Reliability: To verify the site's ability to perform as needed over long periods of time, execute the virtual user sessions, with the number of users defined in the site's requirements, for days or weeks. The site's response times should remain constant.

Considerations in Testing

- Number of servers: Vary the number of servers in each tier.
- Server hardware: Use additional processors, larger disks, and so on.
- Database size: Include small and large data sets to evaluate their impact on performance.
- Location of client machines: Execute load tests from both inside and outside the firewall but not at the same time.
- SSL versus non-SSL: SSL can be resource intensive, so disable it to evaluate the effect on performance.
- Image retrieval: To more efficiently load back-end Web system components, disable image retrieval since it can take resources away from other components.

Measurements in Evaluating Performance

- Client machines
  —Number of users
  —Response times

- All servers
  - —CPU: Percent total processor time
  - —Memory: Available kilobytes and page faults/second
  - —Disk: Percent disk time
  - —Network: total bytes/second
- Web servers
  - —Files/second
  - —Highest number of simultaneous connections experienced
  - —Errors
- Database servers
  - —Transactions/second
  - —Cache hit ratio
- Network: Bandwidth utilization

A.4 Compatibility

- HTML/CSS/Script version compliance: Ensure that the site's content conforms to the versions of HTML, CSS, and scripting required by the browsers used to access the site. This also includes browser DOM objects.
- HTML rendering: Verify that site content appears correctly in each browser platform, even if it supports the HTML, CSS, and scripting versions of the site's content.
- Cookies: If using cookies, the site will need to perform a run-time check to verify that the client browser is currently able to receive cookies. The user may have cookies disabled, or they may be blocked by intermediate network servers.
- Plug-ins: If the site is using any plug-ins, they must be available for the operating systems supported by the site.
- Java applets: Different browsers and operating systems provide different levels of support for Java applets. Build and deploy applets that conform to the JVM supported by the site's target operating systems and browsers.
- ActiveX controls: Like plug-ins, ActiveX controls must be available for the end user platform and must be supported by the user's browser.
- XML: Some browsers can support XML data directly, using a style sheet referenced in the XML document to render its contents. To date, only Microsoft Internet Explorer 5 or later has this capability. For other browsers, XML will need to be prerendered on the server into HTML, which is sent to the client browser.
- XHTML: Existing documents can be converted to XHTML, with backward compatibility, by using the following guidelines.

—All element tags and attributes must be in lowercase: for example, `<html>` instead of `<HTML>`.

—All tags must be "closed," meaning that an ending tag is provided: for example, `</html>`. In the case of empty tags, the special syntax `<tagname/>` can be used, such as `<br/>`.

—All attribute values must be enclosed in quotes, as in `<table width="100%">`.

- Fonts
  —Consider using common fonts, such as Courier, Arial, and Times New Roman, to ensure the broadest compatibility among client platforms.

  —When another font is required, consider using an image of the text instead.

- Colors: Use the Web or browser "safe palette" shipped with most graphics design tools. Note that some operating system and browser combinations will still have problems with this palette, because of bugs or other incompatibilities, and may resort to dithering the colors.

- Image formats
  —For icons and other line-art-type images, GIF or PNG image types are the most appropriate.

  —For photo-realistic images, JPEG is appropriate. Note that the JPEG format is "lossy."

- Security: HTTP basic authentication and custom methods can pass through firewalls properly; others may have problems.

A.5   Usability[1]

Four categories are identified, each representing an area commonly having usability hazards. The first two categories address the verbal or visual rendering of information items. The other two address the logical coherence between information items at all levels of the Web site hierarchy—headings, paragraphs, tables, pages—and the case of navigating through these levels.

Categorization is based on areas of common usability hazards, not on a list of HTML elements or content items. A single page element, for example, can present usability problems in as many as three usability category areas. As a further example,

---

[1]Adapted and used with permission from Jasper Sprengers, "Objective Evaluation of Likely Usability Hazards—Preliminaries for User Testing," Edinburgh, Scotland. Available at http://www.abeleto.com/resources/articles/objective.htm/. Jasper Sprengers is founder and director of Abelto Ltd., a consulting firm for Web usability, development, and online resources.

consider a navigation bar rendered as a *clickable* image map. The number of links and the rationale behind the division of topics pertain to the *information architecture* usability category. The ease of using these links is associated with the *user interface*. The choice of words for each link label pertains to a *language* feature. Such words as *cool, hip,* and *stuff* may carry little meaning with a particular user.

Language

This category refers to the choice of words used to present information. Simple advice on how to make a text item easy to understand and how to structure the text is too subjective for the scope of this text. However, spelling, sentence length, and the use or avoidance of certain words do lend themselves to more objective judgments.

- Offensive language: Check that no insulting or derisory language is used, especially when aimed at specific people or institutions. Also make note of text that is negative, which may reflect badly on the organization. Most Web systems are accessible to the general public worldwide, so be considerate and avoid creating a negative image of the organization in the minds of such potential customers. In addition, inflammatory statements may open the organization up to a libel suit.
- Spelling and grammar errors: Does the text contain any spelling errors or grammar mistakes? Blind faith in spell checkers is not a good practice. Critical users will find any spelling or grammar error unacceptable, and may consider the site sloppy. Such views undermine user confidence in the reliability of the Web system, whether justified or not.
- Instructions: Make sure that the system has online instructions. Even though the Web system may appear intuitive, not everyone has the same perspective. In order to avoid user misinterpretation and confusion, provide a mechanism that offers system instructions. Additionally, the accuracy of system documentation should be reviewed for comprehensiveness and correctness.
- Content: Web pages need to be inspected for text that is incomplete, doesn't make sense, or seems to be out of character with text on other Web pages.
- Internet jargon and popular buzzwords: Frequent use of these words may create the impression that the Web system is associated with a particular subculture, which may offend some users. It is generally beneficial that the Web system portray a neutral and objective style when seeking business with the general public.

Layout and Graphics

This category pertains to how elements are visually rendered on the Web page. A particular issue is identified as a layout problem only when it can be remedied through the addition or modification of such visual features as size of elements, colors, and fonts. A long body of text, for example, can pose a layout problem when fonts, bulleted lists, or paragraph breaks could improve it. When a long body of text could be better managed by breaking it into several linked sections, the issue is one of information architecture, our third category. On the other hand, a long body of text becomes a subjective language problem when the text itself needs to be condensed. In some instances, a long body of text can represent a usability issue in all three categories.

- Text: Check whether text is legible for color-blind people; for example, avoid a green-on-red combination. Common default background colors are white and gray. Are nonstandard text colors still legible with other background defaults and on 256-color screens?
- Color: What colors on the screen are the first to attract user attention? Are the most eye-catching colors associated with the most important messages on the screen? Do some text/background color combinations make the text difficult to read? For example, at first appearance, yellow text on top of a purple image of a fractal pattern may appear interesting, but at a closer look, they may be difficult to use.
- Background: Generally, it is best to use little or no background. When used, a background color or pattern must not distract the customer from the content experience desired. For example, a background might be reflected as a single color on the left side of the page, which may contain related content, such as a navigational bar.
- Images
  —Whether it's a screen shot or a small icon that points the way, a picture is worth a thousand words. Sometimes, the best way to inform or to educate the user about something is to simply display an image. However, available Web system bandwidth and memory necessary for transporting and displaying the contents of an image to the customer's screen are precious.
  —Each image displayed on the page needs to be assessed for its value to the customer's online Web experience. Does the image contribute significantly to the user's online experience? Or does it instead contribute more to performance degradation?
  —In general, it is advantageous to avoid the use of large images on a site's home page, as users are more likely to abandon the attempt to access a

site if the initial page takes too long to load. The more quickly the initial Web system page can be displayed to prospective users, the better the chances that they will spend time navigating the system.

- Appearance: The Web system and particularly the home page must have a professional look and feel. The appearance of the Web system makes an important first and lasting impression on the prospective customer. When a system makes abundant use of bold text, large fonts, or blinking text, a prospective customer will not have a pleasurable experience and may exit the system and never return.

- Horizontal scrolling: Make sure that content can always wrap around the window and that a page with fixed-size elements, such as images, is no wider than 800 pixels. Tables should be sized relative to the window size. Does the page require horizontal scrolling at screen/window sizes under 800 pixels? Avoid horizontal scrolling as much as possible.

- Page elements: Can functional or meaningful page elements be mistaken for advertising? Users are less inclined to click on advertising banners, animation, and pop-up windows, even when they are legitimate design elements. If this happens to a vital linking graphic within your site, the effects are serious.

- Large images: Are images larger than 30K being used solely for visual appeal? Large images that take long to load and have a purely decorative function can annoy the user, especially when they are loaded before other relevant content. A top-level image map for navigation purposes may be acceptable when used sparingly.

- Graphics links: Are graphics referenced from another site? This causes delays during downloads and upsets the layout of the Web page when the images are not available. Also note that copyright laws are skirted when referencing another site's images in this way.

- Bullets: Are bullets used properly? They should be used either to clarify the thematic content of a particular paragraph or to reinforce the visual language or thematic content of a page. Use a small set frequently rather than a large set only once.

- Divider bars: Are divider bars used properly? The same criterion applies as for bullets. In addition, their multiple use on one page will make sections appear indistinguishable.

- Animation: Is there any blinking text, scrolling marquees, or animated GIF images? Instead of attracting attention, these features turn users away. Better ways to highlight include using bold text and colored backgrounds.

- Image dimension tags: Are height and width dimension tags used for images? Such tags enable the browser to start arranging elements on the page before the images are loaded, thereby avoiding the need for multiple requests to the server.

- Window size: When presenting short, clearly segmented information intended to attract attention, are pages longer than a single window? Users may not notice that content follows if a small section of the screen is not visible. Although screen sizes vary in both inches and pixel depth, a good standard to work from is 800×600 pixels while making sure that content can always wrap and tables are sized relative to the window size.

- Lengthy pages: Is any Web page longer than four screens? For pages intended to be read at length, an ideal average length is 1.5 screenfuls at 800×600 pixels per screen. Consider a separate document for printing when a document is intended to be read in lengthy detail. Reading from paper is always more comfortable than from a screen.

- ALT links: Is JPEG format used for message-critical images? Not all browsers support JPEG or render it quickly, especially palm devices. For full-color images, however, no other option is available, as GIF images do not support full color. Therefore, it is a good practice to provide ALT text and text links.

- Image download: Is a single image rendered by several image files? Because they require only one request to the server, low-bandwidth connections load one large image faster than they do several small ones. However, to be of benefit, the large image must be either interlaced GIF or JPEG, to enable partial rendering.

- Thumbnail images: Are cropped and reduced thumbnail images provided to link to full-size versions? Thumbnail images should highlight the essential area of an image at a reduced size. This enables a gallery of images to be displayed within a single screen, which will also work well with slower connections.

- Background images: Are background images less than 15K in size? When displayed in 256 colors, the foreground text must still contrast enough to be legible.

- Image size total: Is the total size of images on a page less than 30K? If not, what is the total size? Review the number of images, relevance, sizes, and order in which the images are displayed. Consider using a thumbnail of the image instead or cropping the image to reduce image size. The benefits of a page that loads quickly are nearly always greater than more impressive artwork, given average bandwidth.

- ALT text for images: Is alternative text included for each image in order to support those users viewing without images or those who may be visually impaired? Such an action represents a small effort but a great increase in usability for those with graphics disabled or unavailable.

- Document link: Is there a separate link to a complete document for printing and saving? When content is suitable for reference or printing and it consists of several files, including images, provide a separate document for downloading. When providing long documents that people will want to print or save in one operation, provide a link to a complete print or saveable document rather than trying to cram lots of content into one page.

- Visual scanning: Does the page layout facilitate visual scanning by a user? The page must be structured to help users ignore large chunks of the page in a single glance. This can be achieved by using grouping and subheadings to break a long list into several smaller units. Have important pages been made accessible for users with disabilities, especially visually impaired users? This concern may not be applicable when by its nature the site simply cannot provide a service for users with some disabilities, such as a database of sound fragments.

- Interlaced images: Are image files interlaced? This technique adds more detail to the entire image in multiple passes. It works well for larger images but is less useful for small images.

Information Architecture

A good information architecture results in the clear, intuitive division of tasks and topics on the Web site. A Web site's content and features can be arranged in more than one way in both width—the number of branching subsections—and depth—the number of levels of hierarchy. The careful wording of titles, introductions, and summaries are site features that help emphasize this structure. Objective criteria for proper structuring are rare, because the best arrangement of information items is highly specific to each site and its purpose.

- URL link rot: Have existing pages moved to a different URL recently? This pestering phenomenon is called *link rot*. Although your internal links may work perfectly after a reshuffle, users who expect to be referred to your site simply never reach you. Although it is good practice to check and update outgoing links, do not assume that sites always do so with their links to your site. Check to ensure that a redirect page has been set up at the old address if a URL has moved.

- TITLE tags: Do TITLE tags make sense out of context? These tags display in search results and bookmark lists. They must be identifiable and understandable when read out of context. One common practice is to start every TITLE tag with the name of the organization hosting the site. This practice would be superfluous for page titles within the text body. Content of the

TITLE tag is more important for search engine results than META tags or content of the BODY.

- Site navigation: Does the site have a map? Sometimes, power users know exactly where they want to go and don't want to wade through lengthy introductions. On the other hand, new users may get lost between system pages. In any case, the implementation of a site map and/or the display of a navigational map can help guide the user. Testing and inspection are necessary to verify that the site map is correct. Does each link on the map exist? Does the site have links that are not represented on the map? Is the navigational bar present and consistent on every screen? Is each link positioned on the page in an intuitive location, and does each link work properly?
- Navigation labeling: Are navigation systems labeled systematically? Labeling for a navigation system can be audience, task, topic, or metaphor based. Combining these types can destroy the intuitive coherence of the system and confuse the reader. However, too rigid consistency makes the navigation system less adaptable to changes in content. Creating a new system of labeling may require an entire rearrangement of the site's architecture.
- Page title: Does the title of the page body explain what the page is about? This pertains to titles within the context of the page they describe. Although they can rely more on context and can be longer, they should convey the content of the page at once and unambiguously.
- HTML title: Does the HTML title reflect the textual page title? This does not mean that the two should be identical. Titles in the page's body are read within the context of the page and the entire site. "Online Ordering" is an acceptable title. An HTML title typically occurs within search results and lists of bookmarks. Such titles must make sense out of context. The simple text "Online Ordering" is not enough.
- Hypertext structuring: Is hypertext used to structure large bodies of content? This enables a bird's-eye view of the page. It is also easier to update several short files entirely than change sections from longer ones.
- Link titles: Does the textual context of each link tell users what they can expect from following that link? When creating a hyperlink, the highlighted text should reflect the topic of what you link to; the surrounding text must relate to this topic only secondarily. Links and their context must give the user a good sense of what to expect from following that link. Consider the following sentence and its embedded links:

  Ira Gershwin has written many timeless *lyrics* to *music by his brother George,* which belong to *the best-loved tunes of the early 20th century.*

This is how we would highlight text in order to link to the following topics: *Ira Gershwin* would link to a biography; *lyrics* would link to a text version of the lyrics; *music by his brother George* would link to works for which Ira did not collaborate; *the best-loved tunes of the early 20th century* would link to a CD title.

- Hypertext instruction: Do hypertext links relate to the linked content in a relevant, meaningful, and unambiguous way? Parts of the text selected for linking should directly relate to the linked content and not rely wholly on its content. This is the case for text highlighted as follows: *Click here* to read more about this product. The highlighted text itself does not relate at all to the linked content, and because the general Web user knows how to follow a link, the instruction is superfluous. It would be better for the system to use such text as: *More about this product.* It is important that the length for the link text be appropriate. Text that is too short may go unnoticed or not be understood. Links that are too long are more difficult to read. When the system uses lists of links with similar text, the links should be used to highlight those words or phrases that are different, rather than highlighting the entire phrase.

- Comment mechanism: Does every Web page link to a comment mechanism, such as a *mail to:* or a form? Offering such a mechanism encourages users to help improve the site and also demonstrates the organization's willingness to stay in touch with its customers.

- Page summarization: Do long Web pages have a brief table of contents so that readers know what to expect from the page? Anything that helps people get a clear and quick impression of a larger body of content is good. The page title is the most concise presentation, possibly followed by a few lines of summary text.

- Biographical details: Are the author's biographical details included? This helps to instill a level of trust and credibility. However, check to make sure that all details are concise and relevant.

User Interface

The user interface for a Web site determines the relative ease of navigation through the Web site's content. Any feature designed to facilitate the user quest to quickly and easily perform a business function on the Web site belongs in this category. Aspects of this category are specific to a Web system and are typically of a technical nature. The usability concern for the arrangement of tasks and topics, which also extends to printed media, pertains to the information architecture category.

- Multiple windows: Do links open a new browser window? Users rely heavily on the Back button for navigation, and a new window makes this button inactive. When a second window is minimized, content can load in that invisible window while the user is waiting. More important, users may treat any new window as unwanted advertising and click it away before it has finished loading.
- Hyperlinks: Test to ensure that each Web site reference displayed has been hyperlinked. System users wish to save time and effort when shopping online. It is advantageous to enable customers to simply click on a hyperlink in order to navigate to an associated Web site rather than requiring them to copy and paste a specific Web site address for their browser to act on.
- Internal link rot: Does every internal link work? Internal *link rot* degrades the user experience. Check to make sure that every internal link is working before allowing a Web site to go live.
- Tables: Does the user always need to scroll to the right in order to view the price of an item? Would it be more efficient and intuitive for the price to appear closer to the left-hand side of the screen and for other, less relevant details to displayed to the right? Are the table columns wide enough, or does the text in every row wrap? Are certain rows excessively high because of one entry?
- Wraparound: Web pages need to be inspected to verify that text wrap-around occurs properly. When text on the screen makes reference to an image on the right, make sure that the picture appears on the right. Make sure that widow and orphan sentences and paragraphs don't lay out in an awkward manner because of pictures.
- Response time: Are server response times acceptable? Users do not know what causes an overall slow transfer; nor do they care. Although the cost of upgrading to a fast server is considerable, so is the price of customers lost from frustration with a site's slow behavior.
- Logo: Does every page contain the organization's name and logo? This vital navigational aid informs users that they are still operating on your Web site. This information should be combined with other consistent layout features, and the user selectable logo should link back to the site's homepage.
- Page redirect: Do pages have an automatic redirect feature? This is a good habit for *this page has moved* announcements and a bad habit everywhere else, as it forces users to an undesired location every time they click the Back button.
- Date reference: Are pages dated with absolute reference and in an internationally recognized format? Even pages that do not require regular

updates or archives should tell you when they were last modified. An unambiguous date reference indicates immediately that the value of the information may not be worth reading.

- Directions: Are links labeled with relative directions, such as *return, back, previous,* or *next*? These labels imply that the system knows where visitors came from or that the user is familiar with the structure of your site. Even when pages have a linear relationship, like chapters in a novel, it is better to give absolute references, such as *proceed to chapter 2.*

- GUI widgets: Are graphical user interface widgets used in the standard fashion? GUI widgets may break up the consistency of interaction when they do not perform the same functions when manipulated across all platforms. Radio buttons give you one choice from at least two alternatives. *Check boxes* can occur on their own, whereas a *set* can be entirely checked or unchecked. Although the value for check boxes may be defaulted to one state or another, it should be enabled so that the user can modify the value when necessary.

- Clickable regions: Are *clickable regions* in an image map clearly marked? The system should present the clickable regions within an image map so that they appear like *buttons*. It is also desirable to provide alternative text links elsewhere on the Web page for image map destinations.

- Button text labels: Are graphical navigation buttons used without text labels? Only very large sites can assume that users are sufficiently familiar with their graphical navigation aids. Check to ensure that text labels and ALT text are provided.

- Search feature: Does the search feature enable the user to set the scope of any collection being searched? Does the feature also indicate whether a search is global or local, that is, within a site/country/language? Does the feature also allow the user to specify a maximum number of hits that are returned for display? The ability to sort results is also very helpful.

- Home page return: Does each main logo link to the home page? Such a feature helps to visually bind all pages to the same site and refers users unambiguously to the main page.

- Link colors: Are link colors used in a nonstandard fashion? Evaluate the trade-off between the value of a better look and that of a more intuitive interface. Typically, visited links are darker in color than those that have not been visited. This way, you can have recognizable links that still harmonize well with other colors.

- Large-site navigation: If a Web site has more than 100 pages, check whether a *search* features exists. A search feature provides a considerable usability improvement when the content is indexed properly. The keywords used for searching a local search engine should be different from those contained in the document and those used for global services.

- Bottom-page navigation: If a page is longer than one and a half screens, check whether a possibly simplified navigational header is at the bottom of the page. The presence of the navigational feature prevents users from having to scroll upward to proceed to other major locations. When the page is part of a linear succession, it is especially helpful to include a reference to previous and following pages/chapters.

- Site title: Does every page contain a recognizable title header in the text body? Not every user notes the TITLE tag of the document. A recognizable page title with consistent layout in the text body reminds users that they are still at your site and relates the purpose of that page.

- Multipart documents: When reviewing multipart documents, check whether document and chapter headings are provided that link back to higher levels of the hierarchy. Consider the long document as an integral subsection of the site, with a separate set of navigation features.

- Image size notice: Are links to large files explicitly mentioned with size? When downloading files for saving, a user's computer will state the file size and estimated download time. However, it is a good practice for the system to reflect this information on the Web page as well. For links to pages with large embedded graphics files, it is even more important.

Test Tool Evaluations

Anyone who has contemplated the implementation of an automated test tool has quickly realized the wide variety of options on the market in terms of both the kinds of test tools being offered and the number of vendors. The best tool for any particular situation depends on the system engineering environment that applies and the testing methodology that will be used, which in turn will dictate how automation will be invoked to support the process.

This appendix evaluates major tool vendors on their test tool characteristics, test execution capability, tool integration capability, test reporting capability, performance testing and analysis, and vendor qualification. The following tool vendors evaluated are Compuware, Empirix/RSW, Mercury, Rational, and Segue.

Table B.1 Test Tool Characteristics: Capture/Playback and Script Creation

Criterion/Feature	Compuware	Empirix/RSW
Ease of Use		
Intuitive and easy to use for users new to automated testing tools	QACenter—Yes Performance Edition—Yes	eTest Suite—Yes Uses Visual Scripts which require no programming.
Intuitive and easy to use for users new to this particular tool but who have used others	QACenter—Yes Performance Edition—Yes	eTest Suite—Yes Maintainable Visual Scripts, fully extensible programming
Easy to install; tool may not be used if difficult to install	QACenter—Yes Performance Edition—Yes	eTest Suite—Yes No proxy servers or special configurations
Tasks can be accomplished quickly, assuming basic user proficiency	QACenter—Yes Performance Edition—Yes	eTest Suite—Yes
Easy to maintain automated tests with a central repository whereby users can separate GUI object definitions from the script	QACenter—Yes Performance Edition—Yes	eTest Suite—Yes Use of shared workspace, VBA code shared between scripts
Can vary how designs and documents are viewed (zooming, multipage diagrams easily supported, multiple concurrent views up at the same time); basic windowing	NA	eTest Suite—Yes View test results/data in MDI windows, and switch between
Tool Customization		
Fully customizable toolbars to reflect any commonly used tool capabilities	Performance Edition—Yes	eTest Suite—Not customizable, but common tool capabilities in the toolbar
Tool customizable: fields added, deleted	NA	NA

Mercury	Rational	Segue
Ease of Use		
Astra QuickTest—Yes	Rational Suite TestStudio, Rational Robot—Yes GUI interface, popup icon bars, tool tips and on-line help.	SilkTest—Yes
Astra QuickTest—Yes WinRunner—Yes	Rational Suite TestStudio, Rational Robot—Yes SQA Robot used for both GUI functional & performance tests.	SilkTest—Yes
Astra QuickTest—Yes WinRunner—Yes	Rational Suite TestStudio, Rational Robot—Yes An administrator should be assigned to help set up test asset datastore & license server.	SilkTest—Yes
Astra QuickTest—Yes WinRunner—Yes	Rational Suite TestStudio, Rational Robot—Yes	SilkTest—Yes
Astra QuickTest—Yes WinRunner—Yes	Rational Suite TestStudio, Rational Robot—Yes Scripts are maintained in a central datastore.	SilkTest—Set up so that by default, object declarations are in separate `include` file so script can have minimum code and intuitive steps inside the test cases.
Astra QuickTest—Yes WinRunner—Yes	Rational Suite TestStudio, Rational Robot—Yes Dockable windows, toolbars and other attributes allow interface customization.	SilkTest—Uses format similar to Word's outlining. Can zoom in and out of scoping by clicking on pluses and minuses. Can view many documents.
Tool Customization		
Astra QuickTest—Yes WinRunner—Yes	Rational Suite TestStudio—Yes Toolbars, menu bars and icon bars are customizable.	SilkTest—No
Astra QuickTest—Yes WinRunner—Yes TestDirector—Yes	Rational Suite TestStudio—Yes Three custom fields used to elaborate on any test asset.	Silk Test—Yes Features are customizable, but not the GUI.

(continued)

Table B.1 Test Tool Characteristics: Capture/ Playback and Script Creation *(continued)*

Criterion/Feature	Compuware	Empirix/RSW
Tool Customization		
Fully customized editor with formats and colors for better readability	QACenter—Yes Performance Edition—Yes	eTest Suite—Yes Code editor fully customizable
Tool support for required test procedure naming convention	QACenter—Yes Performance Edition—Yes	eTest Suite—Yes
Platform Support		
Multiple platform support: UNIX, XWindows, Windows CE, Win3.1, Win95, Win98, NT, Win2000, WinME	QACenter—Supports various Windows versions. Performance Edition supports Unix and various Windows. Can also test servers serving content for mobile devices.	Supports Unix and various Windows.
Browser support: all versions of Netscape, Internet Explorer	QACenter—Yes Performance Edition—Yes	eTest Suite—Yes
Cross-browser testing (record on IE, replay on NS, or vice versa) capability	NA	eTest Suite—Yes
Technology support for one or more of HTML, DHTML, JavaScript, XML, Java applications and applets, MFC (C/C++), Visual Basic, PowerBuilder, Delphi, Terminal Emulator, Oracle, SAP, PeopleSoft, Siebel	QACenter—Yes Performance Edition—Yes Supports Java apps and applets in a customer's JVM. Supports HTML, DHTML, JavaScript, XML, SAP, Oracle, PeopleSoft, Siebel	eTest Suite—Yes Supports Java apps and applets w/in Microsoft JVM/Sun JVM. HTML, DHTML, JavaScript, XML, MFC, Visual Basic, Oracle, SAP, Delphi, Terminal Emulator, PowerBuilder, Oracle, PeopleSoft

Mercury	Rational	Segue
Tool Customization		
Astra QuickTest—Yes WinRunner—Yes	Rational Suite TestStudio, Rational Robot—Yes Robot editor is color-coded. Reserved words highlighted—blue, comments—green.	SilkTest—Good editor
Astra QuickTest—Yes WinRunner—Yes	Rational Suite TestStudio, Rational Robot—Yes Names up to 40 characters. Dashes / Numeric okay.	SilkTest—Yes Alphanumeric with no space.
Platform Support		
WinRunner—various Windows Astra QuickTest—supports various Windows. Astra LoadTest—NT XRunner—HP, IBM, Sun LoadRunner—NT, Unix	Rational Suite TestStudio, Rational Robot—Yes Supports UNIX and various Windows	Supports UNIX and various Windows
WinRunner—Yes Astra QuickTest—Yes	Rational Suite TestStudio, Rational Robot—Yes Presently not Netscape 6.0	SilkTest—Yes
WinRunner—Yes Astra QuickTest—Yes	Rational Suite TestStudio, Rational Robot—Yes	SilkTest—Yes
WinRunner—Yes HTML, DHTML, JavaScript, VBScript, XML, Java applets, ActiveX, Visual Basic, PowerBuilder, Delphi, Terminal Emulator, Oracle, SAP, PeopleSoft, Siebel Astra QuickTest—HTML, DHTML, JavaScript, VBScript, XML, Java applets, ActiveX	Rational Suite TestStudio, Rational Robot—Yes HTML, Dynamic HTML, JavaScript, VBScript, ActiveX, Java apps, Java applets	SilkTest: Yes—HTML, DHTML, JavaScript, XML, Java apps and applets, MFC, Visual Basic, Oracle, PowerBuilder, Delphi, SAP

(continued)

Table B.1 Test Tool Characteristics: Capture/ Playback and Script Creation (*continued*)

Criterion/Feature	Compuware	Empirix/RSW
Test Language Features		
Allows add-ins/extensions compatible with third-party controls	TestPartner—Yes	eTest Suite—Yes
Does not involve additional cost for add-ins and extensions	NA	eTest Suite—Yes
Test editor/debugger feature	QACenter—Yes Performance Edition—Yes	eTest Suite—Yes Extensive debugger
Test scripting language flexible yet robust; allows for modular script development	QACenter—Yes Performance Edition—Yes	eTest Suite—Yes Visual Scripts do not require a programming language, but can be extended by using VB. Can use script libraries.
Scripting language not too complex	TestPartner uses VBA for scripting language. Performance Edition uses C, a common language. QARun has its own scripting language.	VB—a common language
Scripting language allows for variable declaration and use and for parameters to be passed between functions	QACenter—Yes Performance Edition—Yes Language also supports COM testing	eTest Suite—Yes
A test script compiler or an interpreter used	QARun and TestPartner use an interpreter. Performance Edition—Scripts are compiled for performance benefits.	eTest Suite—Yes Scripts are compiled for performance benefits.

Mercury	Rational	Segue
Test Language Features		
WinRunner—Yes	Rational Suite TestStudio, Rational Robot—Yes Supported via following utilities/functions: object mapping, object data test, definition, Java Proxy API, Custom Control API.	SilkTest—Yes Accomplished via object mapping, dll calls, or by adding an extension via our Extension Kit.
WinRunner—Additional costs for some environments	Rational Suite TestStudio, Rational Robot—No additional costs.	SilkTest—Yes
WinRunner—Yes Astra QuickTest—Yes	Rational Suite TestStudio, Rational Robot—Yes Color-coded editor and debugger to include a compile option, debug run mode, go until cursor mode, step mode, breakpoints and a watch variables window.	SilkTest—Yes
WinRunner—Yes uses TSL (Test Script Language) developed for testing. Astra QuickTest uses VBScript.	Rational Suite TestStudio, Rational Robot—Yes Two scripting languages, both robust and extensible. Users can write functions, create libraries & call external API's. Robot can also be utilized using Visual Basic and Java.	SilkTest—Yes
WinRunner TSL is easy to use, English-like interpreted, procedural language. Astra QuickTest uses VBScript also interpreted language.	Rational Suite TestStudio, Rational Robot—SQABasic is a VB-like language. VU is C-like language used for performance testing.	SilkTest—Not complex. Object Oriented language structure with ability to use functions. Very much like C++, not as rigid as Java.
WinRunner—Yes Astra QuickTest—Yes	Rational Suite TestStudio, Rational Robot—Yes	SilkTest—Yes Strong feature of SilkTest.
Mercury Interactive tools use interpreted languages.	Rational Suite TestStudio, Rational Robot—Yes SQABasic scripts compiled and then interpreted at runtime. VU scripts are compiled to an executable format.	SilkTest—Yes Compiler used for performance, manipuate the actual objects, and exercise actual AUT code.

(continued)

Table B.1 Test Tool Characteristics: Capture/ Playback and Script *(continued)*

Criterion/Feature	Compuware	Empirix/RSW
Test Language Features		
Interactive test debugging: allows viewing variable values, steps through the code, integrates test procedures, or jumps to other external procedures	QARun—Limited TestPartner—VBA full debugger Performance Edition—Limited	eTest Suite—Yes VBA debugger combined with Visual Script debugger.
Allows recording at the widget level (object recognition level)	NA	eTest Suite—Yes Objects are recognized at the DOM level.
Allows for interfacing and testing of external .dll and .exe files	TestPartner—Yes Performance Edition—Yes	eTest Suite—Yes Interface to call any external program or .dll
Published APIs: Language Interface Capabilities	TestPartner—Yes	eTest Suite—Yes Capability is called e-PI
Tool is not intrusive: source code of application needs to be expanded by inserting additional statements or dlls for the application to be compatible with the tool	QACenter—Yes Performance Edition—Yes	eTest Suite—Yes
Allows for data-driven testing	QACenter—Yes Performance Edition—Yes	eTest Suite—Yes Wizard driven
Allows for automatic data generation	QACenter—Yes Performance Edition—Yes	eTest Suite—No
Allows for adding timers for timing transaction start and end	Performance Edition—Yes QACenter—Yes QALoad—Yes	eTest Suite—Yes

Mercury	Rational	Segue
Test Language Features		
Mercury Interactive tools offer full debugging capabilities.	Rational Suite TestStudio, Rational Robot—Yes Debugging to include a compile option, debug run mode, go until cursor mode, step mode, breakpoints and a watch variables window.	SilkTest—Yes
WinRunner—Yes Astra QuickTest—Yes	Rational Suite TestStudio, Rational Robot—Yes Object recognition is available and customizable.	SilkTest—Yes Strong feature of SilkTest.
Mercury Interactive tools—Yes	Rational Suite TestStudio, Rational Robot—Yes External dll and exe files can be called from within test scripts. Also a GUI script can detect if a dll or exe is loaded. Also has file existence and file compare verification.	SilkTest—Yes
Mercury Interactive tools—Yes Published APIs.	Rational Suite TestStudio, Rational Robot, Rational TestManager—Yes	SilkTest—Yes Extension Kit allows direct communication with app.
Mercury Interactive tools do not require any modification of the application under test.	Rational Suite TestStudio, Rational Robot—Yes Specific environments like Delphi require code insertion (running the Enabler utility) to achieve object recognition.	SilkTest—Yes Tool is not invasive.
Mercury Interactive tools—Yes	Rational Suite TestStudio, Rational Robot—Yes Both GUI and VU scripts can be augmented to handle data variation.	SilkTest—Yes Object oriented feature implemented to support data driven testing.
Mercury Interactive tools—Do not support data generation but allow for automatic retrieval and import of real test data.	Rational Suite TestStudio, Rational Robot—Yes Datapools can be created for use with GUI or VU scripts.	SilkTest—Yes
WinRunner—Yes Astra QuickTest—Yes	Rational Suite TestStudio, Rational Robot—Yes	SilkTest—Yes

(continued)

Table B.1 Test Tool Characteristics: Capture/ Playback and Script Creation *(continued)*

Criterion/Feature	Compuware	Empirix/RSW
Test Language Features		
Allows for adding comments during recording	QACenter—Yes Performance Edition—Yes	eTest Suite—Yes
Allows for automatic or specified synchronization between client and server	QACenter—Yes Performance Edition—Yes	eTest Suite—Yes
Allows for verification of object properties Allows for object data extraction and verification	TestPartner—Yes	eTest Suite—Yes All properties of DOM objects
Allows for database verification	Performance Edition—Yes	eTest Suite—Yes Via ODBC functions in VB.
Allows for text (alphanumeric) verification	QACenter—Yes	eTest Suite—Yes
Allows for wrappers (shells) whereby multiple procedures can be linked and called from one procedure	QACenter—Yes	eTest Suite—Yes
Allows for automatic data retrieval from any data source—RDBMS, legacy system, spreadsheet—for data-driven testing	TestPartner—Yes	eTest Suite—Yes Via ODBC in scripts or dump to .csv file format to populate a databank
Allows for use of common spreadsheet for data-driven testing	QACenter—Yes Performance Edition—Yes	eTest Suite—Yes Supports .csv format

Mercury	Rational	Segue
Test Language Features		
WinRunner—Yes Astra QuickTest—Yes	Rational Suite TestStudio, Rational Robot—Yes Comments may be added during recording.	SilkTest—Yes
WinRunner—Yes Astra QuickTest—Yes	Rational Suite TestStudio, Rational Robot—Yes Wait States for GUI playback For VU scripts, synchronization is automatic.	SilkTest—Yes Can automatically connect to a particular agent, or use a script to connect. Can change from one particular agent to another.
WinRunner—Yes Astra QuickTest—Yes	Rational Suite TestStudio, Rational Robot—Yes	SilkTest—Yes
WinRunner—Yes Via ODBC and native database connectivity. Astra QuickTest—Yes via VBScript functions.	Rational Suite TestStudio, Rational Robot—Yes Via ODBC functions in SQABasic	SilkTest—Yes Via database Tester 4Test functions.
WinRunner—Yes Astra QuickTest—Yes	Rational Suite TestStudio, Rational Robot—Yes	SilkTest—Yes
WinRunner—Yes Astra QuickTest—Yes	Rational Suite TestStudio, Rational Robot, Rational TestManager—Yes Uses either shell scripts (Robot), LoadTest v2000 schedules, TestManager v2001 Suites.	SilkTest—Yes
WinRunner—Yes	Rational Suite TestStudio, Rational Robot—Yes Via ODBC in scripts or dump to `.csv` file format. SQABasic can also read `.csv` files directly. Also can use `.csv` files to create datapool source data.	SilkTest—Yes Database Tester functions used to supply an ODBC hookup, or can script parsing for any files.
WinRunner—Yes Astra QuickTest—Yes Both support Excel format.	Rational Suite TestStudio, Rational Robot—Yes Uses `.csv` format	SilkTest—Yes. Scripts can access and manipulate content within all common spreadsheets.

(continued)

Table B.1 Test Tool Characteristics: Capture/ Playback and Script Creation (*continued*)

Criterion/Feature	Compuware	Empirix/RSW
Test Language Features		
Ease of maintaining script when application changes	QACenter—Yes Performance Edition—Yes	eTest Suite—Yes Automatic update of scripts, no recoding required.
Test Tool Database		
Tool database scalability when test repository grows	NA	eTest Suite—Yes Supports MS Access, MS SQL Server, and Oracle
Network-based test repository, necessary when multiple access to repository required	QACenter—Yes	eTest Suite—Yes Shared workspaces
Supports ANSI SQL execution	TestPartner—Yes Performance Edition—Yes	eTest Suite—Yes SQL execution can be done through VB.

Mercury	Rational	Segue
Test Language Features		
WinRunner—Yes Astra QuickTest—Yes Via GUI map or object repository	Rational Suite TestStudio, Rational TeamTest, Rational Robot—Yes Robot editor and debug tools enable easy maintenance.	SilkTest—Yes. `Include` file can be updated whenever objects change in name or nature.
Test Tool Database		
WinRunner & Astra QuickTest do not use a database. TestDirector support for all major database vendors.	Rational Suite TestStudio—Yes For v2001—database repository replaced with an XML—based datastore. Within the datastore, Access database used for queries and reports.	SilkTest—Yes. Doesn't have limitations or slowdowns based on the sheer volume of test code.
TestDirector—Yes	Rational Suite TestStudio—Yes	SilkTest—Yes. Files can be placed anywhere, provided there is network directory access to test code.
WinRunner—Yes	Rational Suite TestStudio, Rational Robot—Yes Via SQL commands in SQABasic.	SilkTest—Yes

Table B.2 Test Execution Capability

Criterion/Feature	Compuware	Empirix/RSW
Test Control Features		
Ability to kick off scripts at a specified time; scripts can be scheduled and run unattended	QACenter—Yes Performance Edition—Yes QADirector allows scheduling for specific dates/times and /or regular time periods.	eTest Suite—Yes Schedules Visual Scripts or sets of scripts to run unattended.
Has a complete graphical palette to design and to schedule test runs based on dates and time, or logic between tests	PE/ QADirector do not have graphical palette.	eTest Suite—Yes
Stateless playback: Application does not have to be in a preset state before script playback	Inclusion of File—AID/CS allows PE to test application DBMS states. QADirector allows for setup, execution and restore	eTest Suite—Yes
Centralized execution and control	QADirector supports access, execution, review of results from a central location.	eTest Suite—Yes e-Test console provides centralized monitoring of all application activity.
Standalone test execution automation	QACenter—Yes Performance Edition—Yes	eTest Suite—Yes
Distributed Test Execution		
Distributed test control, synchronization, execution	QACenter—Yes QADirector supports distributed execution where app is tested as it runs in production Performance Edition—Yes	eTest Suite—Yes
Execution of manual or automated tests via a browser for anywhere/anytime test execution, with Web-based test management	Manual test execution is web-based. Web interface is underway for other features.	eTest Suite—No
Supports synchronization of multitest threads	For QADirector tests can be parallel or singular Performance Edition—Yes	eTest Suite—Yes

Mercury	Rational	Segue
Test Control Features		
TestDirector—allows scheduling. LoadRunner has built-in schedulers for load scenarios.	Rational Suite TestStudio, Rational Robot—Yes Robot script checks the time, LoadTest v2000 & TestManager v2001 scheduled to run at a specific time.	SilkTest—Yes No separate tool required
TestDirector—Yes	Rational Suite TestStudio, Rational Robot—Yes Suite creation in TestManager v2001 is all graphical.	SilkTest—No
WinRunner—Yes	Rational Suite TestStudio, Rational Robot—Yes Robot GUI scripts can locate any window, by using window set context to locate a window to begin script playback. VU scripts are completely stateless.	SilkTest—Yes Any script can be run at any time
TestDirector—Yes	Rational Suite TestStudio, Rational TestManager—Yes	SilkTest—Yes
WinRunner—Yes Astra QuickTest—Yes	Rational Suite TestStudio, Rational Robot, Rational TestManager—Yes	SilkTest—Yes
Distributed Test Execution		
TestDirector—allows for local or remote test execution control via networks.	Rational Suite TestStudio, Rational TestManager—Yes	SilkTest—Yes
TestDirector—Yes. All parts of TestDirector can be accessed via a browser.	Rational Suite TestStudio—Not currently	SilkTest—No No web front end at present. One could be created, since tool can run from the command line.
WinRunner—Yes	Rational Suite TestStudio—Yes	SilkTest—Yes

(continued)

Table B.2 Test Execution Capability *(continued)*

Criterion/Feature	Compuware	Empirix/RSW
Distributed Test Execution		
Headless back-end server testing	Performance Edition—Yes QADirector tests can be routed to any server or workstation attached to the network.	eTest Suite—Yes
Allows for test execution across LANs and WANs	Performance Edition—Yes QADirector supports a central repository that can be accessed via the network.	eTest Suite—Yes
Test results analysis: automatic creation of test results log	QACenter—Yes QADirector supports both pass/fail as well as drill down. Performance Edition—Yes	eTest Suite—Yes
Multiplatform testing support	Performance Edition—Yes QADirector supports Unix, Windows and OS/390	eTest Suite—Yes Supports Unix and various Windows.
Test Suite Recovery Logic		
Unexpected error recovery: Can handle error recovery and unexpected active windows, logs the discrepancy, and continues playback (automatic recovery from errors)	QACenter—Yes Performance Edition—Yes	eTest Suite—Yes
Can restore the application to its initial state or provides ways for the application to be restored	QACenter—Yes Performance Edition—Yes QADirector—Yes	eTest Suite—Yes

Mercury	Rational	Segue
Distributed Test Execution		
WinRunner—Yes	Rational Suite TestStudio, Rational TestManager—Yes	SilkTest—Yes
TestDirector—Yes	Rational Suite TestStudio, Rational TestManager—Yes	SilkTest—Yes Network connectivity needed to the particular machine with the SilkTest agent.
WinRunner—Yes Astra QuickTest—Yes Visually displayed for ease of scanning.	Rational Suite TestStudio, Rational TestManager—Yes Test results are viewed from TestManager. Defects and enhancements may be reported directly from the Test Log via ClearQuest integration.	SilkTest—Yes
Mercury Interactive tools provide support for over 28 different platforms.	Rational Suite TestStudio, Rational TestManager—Yes Supports Unix and various Windows	SilkTest—Yes
Test Suite Recovery Logic		
WinRunner—Yes Astra QuickTest—Yes Via exception handler.	Rational Suite TestStudio, Rational Robot—Yes Error recovery for script failures and verification point failure. Also unexpected active window handler can be set. When fatal error is encountered, trap feature can be used to obtain a stack trace, module lists, restart Windows or run a procedure.	SilkTest—Yes
WinRunner—Yes Astra QuickTest—Yes	Rational Suite TestStudio, Rational Robot—Yes	SilkTest—Yes

(*continued*)

Table B.2 Test Execution Capability *(continued)*

Criterion/Feature	Compuware	Empirix/RSW
Test Management		
Supports test execution management	QACenter—Yes Performance Edition—Yes QADirector—Yes	eTest Suite—Yes Through e-Manager
Supports industry standards in testing process (SEI/CMM, ATLM, ISO)	QACenter—Yes Performance Edition—Yes QADirector—Yes	eTest Suite—Yes
Application requirements management support integrated with the test management tool	QADirector—Integrates with Reconcile/DOORS for RM Performance Edition—NA	eTest Suite—No
Requirements management capability supports the trace of requirements to test plans to provide requirement coverage metrics	QADirector Integrated with Reconcile—Yes	eTest Suite—No
Test plans can be imported automatically into test management repository from standard text files	QADirector—Yes Performance Edition—NA	eTest Suite—No
Tool can be customized to organization's test process	QADirector supports various testing methodologies. Performance Edition—NA	eTest Suite—Yes
Supports planning, managing, and analyzing testing efforts; can reference test plans, matrices, product specifications, in order to create traceability	QADirector—plan and report test activity. Performance Edition—NA	eTest Suite—Yes e-Manager and d-Tracker provide the ability to track and manage the testing process
Supports manual testing	QADirector—provides manual test creation. Performance Edition—NA	eTest Suite—Yes
Supports the migration from manual to automated scripts	QADirector—can replace manual tests with automated testing scripts Performance Edition—NA	eTest Suite—No

Mercury	Rational	Segue
Test Management		
TestDirector—Yes	Rational Suite TestStudio, Rational TestManager—Yes	SilkTest—Yes
TestDirector—Yes	Rational Suite TestStudio, Rational TeamTest, Rational TestManager, Rational Unified Process—Yes	SilkTest—Yes
TestDirector—has built-in requirements management. Also integrates with 3rd party RM tools like TBI Caliber, DOORS and RequisitePro	Rational Suite TestStudio, Rational Robot—Yes TestManager can utilize RequisitePro or Rational Rose. Other RM tools used via the creation of Test Input Adapters using TestManager's open API.	SilkTest—No
TestDirector—Yes	Rational Suite TestStudio, Rational Robot—Yes Requirements can be traced to Test Cases within a Test Plan in TestManager.	SilkTest—No
TestDirector—Yes	Rational Suite TestStudio—Yes Via RequisitePro integration.	SilkTest—Yes
TestDirector—Yes	Rational Suite TestStudio, Rational TeamTest, Rational TestManager, Rational Unified Process—Yes	SilkTest—Yes Built-in test plan functionality can be customized to process.
TestDirector—Yes	Rational Suite TestStudio, Rational TestManager—Yes	SilkTest—Yes Via use of extensive results files with collapsability features and through using test plans.
TestDirector—Yes	Rational Suite TestStudio, Rational TestManager—Yes	SilkTest—Yes Specify manual tests via a test plan or using `Agent.Display()` method within a script.
TestDirector—Yes Generates commented script for ease of recording business processes.	Rational Suite TestStudio—No	SilkTest—Yes Can replace manual tests with scripts to perform steps for you.

(continued)

Table B.2 Test Execution Capability *(continued)*

Criterion/Feature	Compuware	Empirix/RSW
Test Management		
Can track the traceability of tests to test requirements	QADirector—Integrates with Reconcile/DOORS for RM Performance Edition—NA	eTest Suite—No
Has built-in test requirements modules	Reconcile provides full RM Performance Edition—NA	eTest Suite—No
Tool can check for duplicate defects before logging newly found defects	QADirector—Yes Performance Edition—NA	eTest Suite—Yes
Allows for measuring test progress	QADirector—Yes Performance Edition—NA	eTest Suite—Yes
Allows for various reporting activities	QADirector—Yes Also supports 3rd party report generators & reports to the web Performance Edition—NA	eTest Suite—Yes
Allows for tracking of manual and automated test cases	QADirector—Yes Also provides file/data mgmt Performance Edition—NA	eTest Suite—No

Mercury	Rational	Segue
Test Management		
TestDirector—Yes	Rational Suite TestStudio, Rational TestManager—Yes viaTestManager coverage reports.	SilkTest—Yes
TestDirector—Yes Also integrates with 3rd party RM tools	Rational Suite TestStudio, Rational TestManager—Yes Via RequisitePro	SilkTest—No
TestDirector—Yes	Rational Suite TestStudio, Rational ClearQuest—Yes	SilkTest —NA Does not support defect tracking.
TestDirector—Yes	Rational Suite TestStudio, Rational TestManager—Yes	SilkTest—Yes
TestDirector—Yes	Rational Suite TestStudio, Rational TeamTest, Rational TestManager—Yes	SilkTest—Yes
TestDirector—Yes	Rational Suite TestStudio, Rational TestManager—Yes TestManager is 100% test case centric to allow for manual & automated implementation.	SilkTest—Yes

Table B.3 Tool Integration Capability

Criterion/Feature	Compuware	Empirix/RSW
Interface to software architecture/modeling tool	Does not have direct integration	Does not have direct integration
Integration to unit testing tools	QADirector—Yes With TestPartner, TrueTime, ActiveAnalysis, TrueCoverage, BoundsChecker.	eTest Suite—Supports unit testing of Middleware Objects.
Interface to test management tool	QADirector—Yes With Reconcile & TrackRecord	eTest Suite—Yes
Interface to requirements management tool	QADirector—Yes With Reconcile & DOORS	eTest Suite—No
Interface to defect tracking tool	QADirector—Yes With TrackRecord	eTest Suite—Yes
Interface to configuration management tool	QADirector—Yes Version control tests within CM tool of choice	eTest Suite—No

Mercury	Rational	Segue
Mercury Interactive tools—Yes	Rational Suite Enterprise, Rational Suite DevelopmentStudio, Rational Suite TestStudio, Rational TestManager—Yes Rational Rose model elements can be used as test inputs using TestManager v2001. Can generate scripts from UML models in Rose.	SilkTest—No
Mercury Interactive tools—Yes Such as McCabe tools.	Rational Suite Enterprise, Rational Suite DevelopmentStudio—Yes Rational Quality Architect v2001 (EJB & COM)	SilkTest—Unit testing supported by SilkTest.
Mercury Interactive tools—Yes WinRunner, LoadRunner, Astra QuickTest and Astra LoadTest integrate with TestDirector.	Rational Suite TestStudio, Rational TestManager—Yes	SilkTest—Yes
TestDirector—Yes Integrates with 3rd party RM tools	Rational Suite TestStudio, Rational TestManager—Yes TestManager fully integrates with RequisitePro and Rational Rose. Other RM tools integrated via the Test Input Adapter API.	SilkTest—No
Mercury Interactive tools—Yes Built-in defect management tool. Also integrate with ClearQuest and PVCS Tracker	Rational Suite TestStudio, Rational TestManager—Yes Test Log is integrated with ClearQuest	SilkTest—Yes
TestDirector—Yes Built-in interface to MS Sourcesafe, PVCS Version Manager and ClearCase	Rational Suite TestStudio—Yes ClearCase LT shipping with testing products v2001 and beyond	SilkTest—Yes

Table B.4 Test Reporting Capability

Criterion/Feature	Compuware	Empirix/RSW
Summary-Level Reporting		
Error filtering and review features	Performance Edition—Yes	eTest Suite—Yes
Metric collection and metric analysis visualization	Performance Edition—Yes Metric collection & reporting	eTest Suite—Yes
Test Report Presentation		
Predefined reports can be modified and new reports created	Performance Edition—Yes Reports modified & created	eTest Suite—Yes
Most widely used views can be created and made public for others to view at their leisure with automatically updated information	Performance Edition—Yes Fields & views customizable	eTest Suite—Yes HTML output to web. Complete flexibility with Web Reporter.
Generate graphs and reports from test results	Performance Edition—Yes Library of graphs/reports	eTest Suite—Yes
Graphs and reports fully customizable, supporting more than just limited modification, such as allowing choice of axis labels	Performance Edition—Yes	eTest Suite—Yes
Reports are exportable to HTML, `.csv,` or `.txt` files	Performance Edition Outputs to HTML format	eTest Suite—Yes

Mercury	Rational	Segue
Summary-Level Reporting		
TestDirector—Yes	Rational TestManager—Yes Users create Test Log filters and sort the log items	SilkTest—Yes
TestDirector—Yes	Rational Suite TestStudio, Rational TestManager—Yes	SilkTest—Yes
Test Report Presentation		
TestDirector—Yes Document Generator provides full customization of reports.	Rational TestManager—Yes	SilkTest—Yes
TestDirector—Yes	Rational TestManager—Yes	SilkTest—Yes Ability to view work of others and can control write-abilty through use of permissions.
TestDirector—Yes	Rational TestManager—Yes	SilkTest—Yes
TestDirector—Yes	Rational TestManager—Yes	SilkTest—No
TestDirector—Yes LoadRunner—Yes Automatic HTML report generation setting	Rational TestManager—Yes	SilkTest—Yes

Table B.5 Performance Testing and Analysis Capability

Criterion/Feature	Compuware	Empirix/RSW
Load and Stress Test Features		
All users can be queued to execute a specified action at the same time	Performance Edition—Yes	eTest Suite—Yes
Automatic generation of summary load testing analysis reports	Performance Edition—Yes	eTest Suite—Yes
Ability to change recording of different protocols in the middle of load-recording session	Performance Edition—Yes Can record multiple middleware and protocols during same recording session.	eTest Suite—Yes Can change protocols as long as within the web transaction and can be recorded.
Actions in a script can be iterated any specified number of times without programming or rerecording of the script	Performance Edition—Yes	eTest Suite—Yes With or without variable data.
Different modem connection speeds and browser types can be applied to a script without any rerecording	Performance Edition—Yes	eTest Suite—Yes
Load runs and groups of users within load runs can be scheduled to execute at different times	Performance Edition—Yes	eTest Suite—Yes
Automatic load scenario generation based on load testing goals: hits/second, number of concurrent users before specified performance degradation, and so on	Performance Edition—Yes	eTest Suite—No
Cookies and sessions IDs automatically correlated during recording and playback for dynamically changing Web environments	Performance Edition—Yes	eTest Suite—Yes Never requires programming, entirely automatic

Mercury	Rational	Segue
Load and Stress Test Features		
LoadRunner—Yes Astra LoadTest—Yes	Rational Suite TestStudio, Rational TestManager—Yes Via sync points	SilkPerformer—Yes
LoadRunner—Yes Astra LoadTest—Yes	Rational Suite TestStudio, Rational TestManager—Yes	SilkPerformer—Yes
LoadRunner—Yes for some protocols.	Rational Suite TestStudio, Rational Robot—Yes All protocols can be captured during a single recording session, so "changing" protocols is not necessary. After recording, the multiple protocols can be put into a single script, or, filtering could be used to put a single, or a combination of multiple protocols into a single script.	SilkPerformer—Yes
LoadRunner—Yes Astra LoadTest—Yes A simple runtime setting.	Rational Suite TestStudio, Rational Robot, Rational TestManager—Yes Most other tools require that all user actions be put in a single script——— Rational Robot allows a user session to be split into multiple scripts, each of which can be iterated any number of times via the graphical scheduling mechanism in TestManager.	SilkPerformer—Yes
LoadRunner—Yes Astra LoadTest—Yes A simple runtime setting.	Rational Suite TestStudio, Rational TestManager—Yes	SilkPerformer—Yes
LoadRunner—Yes Astra LoadTest—Yes	Rational Suite TestStudio, Rational TestManager—Yes	SilkPerformer—Yes
LoadRunner—Yes	SiteLoad, Rational Suite TestStudio—Yes (in TestManager via Transactors)	SilkPerformer—Yes
LoadRunner—Yes Astra LoadTest—Yes Does not require programming, entirely automatic.	Rational Suite TestStudio, Rational TestManager, Rational Robot—Yes	SilkPerformer—Yes

(continued)

Table B.5 Performance Testing and Analysis Capability (*continued*)

Criterion/Feature	Compuware	Empirix/RSW
Load and Stress Test Features		
Allows for variable access methods and ability to mix access methods in a single scenario: modem simulation or various line speed simulation	Performance Edition—Yes	eTest Suite—Yes
Ability to have data-driven scripts that can use a stored pool of data	Performance Edition—Yes	eTest Suite—Yes with DataBank Wizard
Allows for throttle control for dynamic load generation	Performance Edition—Yes	eTest Suite—Yes
Allows for automatic service-level violation (boundary value) checks	Performance Edition—Yes	eTest Suite—Yes
Allows for variable recording levels (network, Web, API, and so on)	Performance Edition—Yes	eTest Suite—No
Allows for transaction breakdown/drill-down capabilities for integrity verification at the per client, per session, and per instance level for virtual users	Performance Edition—Yes Offers integrated load testing and server monitoring.	eTest Suite—Yes
Allows for Web application server integration: ColdFusion, NetDynamics, Dynamo, and so on	Performance Edition—Yes	eTest Suite—Yes
Supports workload, resource, and/or performance modeling	Performance Edition—Yes	eTest Suite—Yes
Can run tests on various hardware and software configurations	Performance Edition—Yes	eTest Suite—Yes

Mercury	Rational	Segue
Load and Stress Test Features		
LoadRunner—Yes Astra LoadTest—Yes	Rational TestManager Suite— Yes Any combination of tests is possible.	SilkPerformer—Yes
LoadRunner—Yes Astra LoadTest—Yes	Rational Suite TestStudio, Rational TestManager, Rational Robot—Yes Via Datapools.	SilkPerformer—Yes
LoadRunner—Yes	Rational Suite TestStudio, Rational TestManager—Yes With Transactors (graphical point and click creation) or Shared Variables (hand coded)	SilkPerformer—Yes
LoadRunner—Yes Astra LoadTest—Yes	Rational Suite TestStudio, Rational TestManager—Yes	SilkPerformer—Scripts can be deployed to support these checks.
LoadRunner—Yes	Rational Suite TestStudio, Rational Robot—Yes	SilkPerformer—Yes Allows variable levels and mixing of protocols for a script, user or transaction.
LoadRunner—Yes Astra LoadTest—Yes	Rational Suite TestStudio, Rational TestManager—Yes	SilkPerformer—Yes
LoadRunner—Yes Astra LoadTest—Yes Including ability to record and replay against the applications, and monitor the app server performance during load test.	Rational Suite TestStudio, Rational Robot, Rational TestManager—Yes	SilkPerformer—Yes
LoadRunner—Yes Astra LoadTest—Yes	Rational Suite TestStudio, Rational TestManager—Yes	SilkPerformer—Yes
LoadRunner—Yes Astra LoadTest—Yes	Rational Suite TestStudio, Rational TestManager—Yes	SilkPerformer—Yes

(continued)

Table B.5 Performance Testing and Analysis Capability (*continued*)

Criterion/Feature	Compuware	Empirix/RSW
Load and Stress Test Features		
Support headless virtual user testing feature	Performance Edition—Yes	eTest Suite—Yes
Requires low overhead for virtual user feature (Web, database, other?)	Performance Edition—Yes Exceptionally low overhead	eTest Suite—Yes Small footprint per Virtual User
Scales to 500–1,000 virtual users	Performance Edition—Yes	eTest Suite—Yes
Simulated IP addresses for virtual users	Performance Edition—Yes	eTest Suite—Yes
Thread-based virtual user simulation	Performance Edition—Yes	eTest Suite—Yes Default and most efficient mode of testing
Process-based virtual user simulation	Performance Edition—Yes	eTest Suite—Yes Optional
Centralized load test controller	Performance Edition—Yes	eTest Suite—Yes
Allows for reusing scripts from functional test suite	Performance Edition—Yes Functional/load test scripts can be created at same time. Two use different languages.	eTest Suite—Yes Visual Scripts created during functional testing reused for load testing and monitoring
Support for WAP protocol testing against WAP Gateway or Web server	Performance Edition—Yes	eTest Suite Yes for the web server
Compatible with SSL recording	Performance Edition—Yes	eTest Suite—Yes

Mercury	Rational	Segue
Load and Stress Test Features		
LoadRunner—Yes Astra LoadTest—Yes	Rational Suite TestStudio, Rational TestManager—Yes	SilkPerformer—Yes
LoadRunner—Yes Very high scalability ratings using TurboLoad technology.	Rational Suite TestStudio, Rational TestManager—Yes	SilkPerformer—Yes
LoadRunner—Yes Largest load recorded to date generated more than 1.35M concurrent connections. Astra LoadTest—Yes	Rational Suite TestStudio, Rational TestManager—Yes	SilkPerformer—Yes
LoadRunner—Yes Astra LoadTest—Yes Both use IPSpoofer feature.	Rational Suite TestStudio, Rational TestManager—Yes	SilkPerformer—Yes
LoadRunner—Yes Astra LoadTest—Yes	Rational Suite TestStudio, Rational TestManager—Yes	SilkPerformer—Yes
LoadRunner—Yes Included since some apps require it for accuracy.	Rational Suite TestStudio, Rational TestManager—Yes Each virtual user has it own process space and unimpeded access to all resources within a process. Multi-threaded model supported when needed.	SilkPerformer—Yes Can set any number of virtual users as a universal default parameter or set number within a script.
LoadRunner—Yes Astra LoadTest—Yes	Rational Suite TestStudio, Rational TestManager—Yes	SilkPerformer—Yes
Astra QuickTest—Yes WinRunner scripts used as GUI Vusers in LoadRunner.	Rational Suite TestStudio, Rational TestManager—Yes	SilkPerformer—Yes
LoadRunner—Yes	Rational Suite TestStudio, Rational Robot—Yes	SilkPerformer—Yes
LoadRunner—Yes Astra QuickTest—Yes	Rational Suite TestStudio, Rational Robot—Yes	SilkPerformer—Yes

(*continued*)

Table B.5 Performance Testing and Analysis Capability (*continued*)

Criterion/Feature	Compuware	Empirix/RSW
Load and Stress Test Features		
Compatible with one or more of the relevant technologies: streaming media, COM, EJB, RMI, CORBA, Siebel, Oracle, SAP	Performance Edition—Yes	eTest Suite—Yes
Compatible with one or more of the relevant technologies: Linux, UNIX, NT, XWindows, Windows CE, Win3.1, Win95, Win98, Win2000, WinME	Performance Edition—Yes	eTest Suite—Yes
Performance Monitor Test Features		
Monitors various tiers: Web server, database server, and app server separately	Performance Edition—Yes	eTest Suite—Yes
Supports monitoring for one or more of ColdFusion, Broadvision, BEA WebLogic, Silverstream, ATG Dynamo, Apache, IBM Websphere, Oracle RDBMS, MS SQL Server, Real Media Server, IIS, Netscape Web Server	Performance Edition—Yes	eTest Suite—Yes
Supports monitoring for one or more of the relevant technologies: Linux, NT, UNIX, XWindows, Windows CE, Win3.1, Win95/98, Win2000	Performance Edition—Yes	eTest Suite—Yes
Monitors network segments	Performance Edition—Yes With EcoSystems and Application Expert	eTest Suite—Yes
Supports resource monitoring	Performance Edition—Yes	eTest Suite—Yes
Synchronization ability in order to determine locking, deadlock conditions, and concurrency control problems	Performance Edition—Yes	eTest Suite—Yes
Ability to correlate any metrics from all monitors to identify performance bottlenecks	Performance Edition—Yes	eTest Suite—Yes

Mercury	Rational	Segue
Load and Stress Test Features		
LoadRunner—Yes	Rational Suite TestStudio, Rational Robot—Yes	SilkPerformer—Yes
LoadRunner—Yes Astra QuickTest—Yes	Rational Suite TestStudio, Rational Robot, Rational TestManager—Yes	SilkPerformer—Yes
Performance Monitor Test Features		
LoadRunner—Yes Astra QuickTest—Yes	Rational Suite TestStudio, Rational Robot, Rational TestManager—Yes	SilkPerformer—Yes
LoadRunner—Yes Astra QuickTest—Yes	Rational Suite TestStudio, Rational TestManager—Yes	SilkVision—Yes SilkVision component provides monitoring capability.
LoadRunner—Yes Astra QuickTest—Yes	Rational Suite TestStudio, Rational TestManager—Yes	SilkVision—Yes SilkVision component provides monitoring capability.
LoadRunner—Yes Astra QuickTest—Yes	Rational Suite TestStudio, Rational TestManager—Yes	SilkVision—Yes SilkVision component provides monitoring capability.
LoadRunner—Yes Astra QuickTest—Yes	Rational Suite TestStudio, Rational TestManager—Yes	SilkPerformer—Yes
LoadRunner—Yes Astra QuickTest—Yes	Rational Suite TestStudio, Rational TestManager—Yes	SilkPerformer—Yes
LoadRunner—Yes Astra QuickTest—Yes	Rational Suite TestStudio, Rational TestManager—Yes	SilkPerformer—Yes

(continued)

Table B.5 Performance Testing and Analysis Capability *(continued)*

Criterion/Feature	Compuware	Empirix/RSW
Performance Monitor Test Features		
Ability to detect when events have completed in a reliable fashion	Performance Edition—Yes	eTest Suite—Yes
Ability to provide client-to-server response times	Performance Edition—Yes	eTest Suite—Yes
Ability to provide graphical results and export them to common formats	Performance Edition—Yes	eTest Suite—Yes
Ability to provide performance measurements of data loading	Performance Edition—Yes	eTest Suite—Yes

Mercury	Rational	Segue
Performance Monitor Test Features		
LoadRunner—Yes Astra QuickTest—Yes	Rational Suite TestStudio, Rational TestManager—Yes	SilkPerformer—Yes
LoadRunner—Yes Astra QuickTest—Yes	Rational Suite TestStudio, Rational TestManager—Yes	SilkPerformer—Yes
LoadRunner—Yes Astra QuickTest—Yes	Rational Suite TestStudio, Rational TestManager—Yes Results can be exported to `.csv`.	SilkPerformer—Yes
LoadRunner—Yes	Rational Suite TestStudio, Rational TestManager—Yes	SilkPerformer—Yes

Table B.6 Vendor Qualifications

Criterion/Feature	Compuware	Empirix/RSW
Consulting Requirements		
Maturity of vendor	On the market since 1996	On the market since 1996
Market share of vendor	Growing market share	Growing market share
Vendor Qualifications		
Financial stability of vendor	Profitable company	Former subsidiary of Teradyne. Formed by the combination of Hammer Technologies and RSW Software and funded by Matrix Partners.
Time existed	Since 1973	Since 1996
Vendor Support		
Software patches provided, if so deemed necessary	Yes	Yes
Upgrades provided on a regular basis	Yes Major releases once per year, point releases once per quarter, bug fixes as necessary.	Yes Major releases once per year, point releases once per quarter, bug fixes as necessary.
Upgrades backward compatible: scripts from previous version can be reused with later version	Yes	Yes
Training available	Yes Onsite and public training.	Yes Onsite and public training.
Help feature available; tool well documented	Yes	Yes
Tech support reputation throughout industry	Highly rated technical support.	Highly rated technical support from customer service surveys.

Mercury	Rational	Segue
Consulting Requirements		
Tools have been supporting industry since early 1990s.	Various testing products have been on the market since early 1980s.	SilkTest/QA Partner products on the market since early 1990s.
Considerable market share	Sustaining market share	Sustaining market share
Vendor Qualifications		
Continued/consistent growth pattern over last several years.	Stable/profitable company	Stable/profitable company
Company incorporated in 1989	Since early 1980s	Since early 1990s
Vendor Support		
Yes	Yes	Yes
Yes Built-in updater in the product to check for new patches and features via the Internet.	Yes Every six months.	Yes
Yes	Yes Upgrade and conversion utilities are always provided.	Yes Always within major version releases.
Onsite and public training. Public training facilities around the world.	Yes Rational University Onsite and public training.	Yes
Yes	Yes	Yes
Given prestigious SSPA STAR award last two years for excellence in support.	Yes Service has received many awards	Good Tech support.

(continued)

Table B.6 Vendor Qualifications

Criterion/Feature	Compuware	Empirix/RSW
Vendor Support		
No consulting needed	Consulting not needed	Consulting not needed
Availability of and access to tool user groups	Several discussion forums	Several discussion forums
Licensing		
Allows for floating license	Floating and node-locked licenses.	Floating and node-locked licenses.
Allows for node-locked license	Yes	Yes
Licensing used	Yes	Yes
Licensing rigid	Flexibility is available.	Flexibility is available and is a commercial decision
Pricing		
Price consistent within estimated price range	NA	NA
Price consistent with comparable vendor products	Yes	Yes

Mercury	Rational	Segue
Vendor Support		
Consulting not needed for Astra QuickTest or Astra LoadTest. A QuickStart is recommended for others to obtain maximum return on tool investment.	Consulting generally not needed. Depends on type of testing to be performed.	None needed. Jump start programs available and recommended for teams with tight time constraint.
Complete network of local users groups throughout world.	Several discussion forums	User Groups exist.
Licensing		
Completely flexible licensing from pay-per-use to engagement based to perpetual pricing	Floating and node-locked licenses.	Floating and node-locked licenses.
Yes	Yes	Yes
Yes	Yes	Yes
Completely flexible licensing	Yes	No. Licensing can be based on most need-based models for customers.
Pricing		
NA	NA	NA
Yes	Yes	Yes

appendix c

Technology Bookstore Case Study

This appendix outlines a case study for our fictional Technology Bookstore (TBS) Web system, which supports the online operations of a bookstore retailing chain that specializes in computing and other technology books, as well as hard-to-find and heavily discounted titles and a selection of audio products. The organization responsible for the TBS system has recently decided to expand its sales exposure by implementing a Web-based e-commerce site that will allow users to browse online and order from its catalog. The TBS system must be able to handle increasingly heavy user loads as the TBS Web site grows in popularity and occasionally sponsors large-scale advertising campaigns.

The TBS system is a good example of a typical e-commerce system startup. Here, the main purpose of the site is to enable existing customers and prospective new customers to browse a catalog and purchase items for shipment.

C.1 Functional Requirements Summary

The TBS system functional requirements can be summarized as follows.

- A *catalog* needs to be available to the general public—anonymous users accessing TBS via the Internet. Users must be able to view catalog items alphabetically and be able to use keywords to search for catalog items. For each item returned as a result of a search or viewed in a browse mode, an image of the item, such as a book cover, needs to be displayed together with a short description and the price of the item.

- A *shopping cart* needs to be available to the user at all times. The user must also be able to save the contents of the shopping cart, exit the system without buying anything, and then later return to the system to resume the shopping experience, with the selected items still registered in the shopping cart. Users select items for their shopping carts by clicking a button that appears next to each item image displayed.

- *Secure online ordering* must be available for *checkout* and *purchase* of the selected items. The transaction should be secured by using an encryption protocol (SSL) in order to safeguard any sensitive user data. A user who has placed orders using the TBS system before should be able to log in and see that the system has already filled in some form field information.

- The user's *order status* must be available for viewing by the user's logging in with the user ID and password set when the order was placed.

C.2 RSI Use Cases

Requirement Use Cases

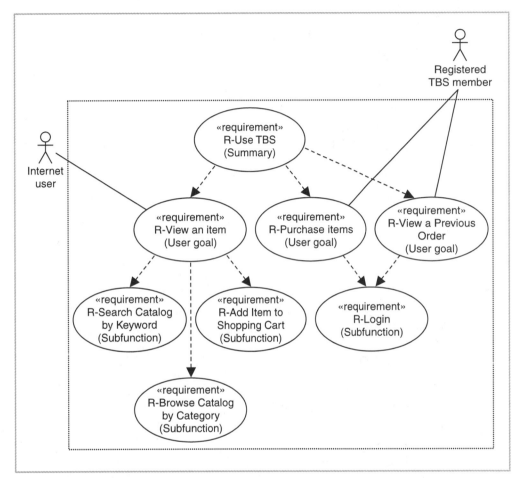

Figure C-1   Requirement Use Case Summary Diagram

«requirement» R-Use TBS

Actor: Internet User
Objective: To locate and possibly purchase items from the
                Technology Bookstore
Level: Summary
Preconditions: None

Main Success Scenario

1. User <u>views items</u> in the TBS catalog.
2. User <u>purchases the items</u> in the shopping cart.
3. User <u>views the order detail</u> to discover the status of the order.

Extensions: None.

Nonfunctional Requirements Additions or Deviations: None.

«requirement» R-View an Item

Actor: Internet User
Objective: View information about an item in the TBS catalog
Level: User goal
Preconditions: None

Main Success Scenario:

1. User selects to <u>browse the catalog by category</u> or <u>search the catalog by keywords</u>.
2. System displays a list of items.
3. User selects an item to view.
4. System displays the item.
5. User selects to <u>add the item to the shopping cart</u>.

Extensions:

2a. No items were found in the category or located by the search.

    2a1. User selects a different category or enters a different set of keywords.

Nonfunctional Requirements Additions or Deviations: None.

«requirement» R-Browse Catalog by Category

Actor: Internet User

Objective: To view the available items in a particular category of the TBS catalog

Level: Subfunction

Preconditions: None

Main Success Scenario:

1. User selects to browse the catalog by category.

2. System displays the available categories.

3. User selects a category.

Extensions: None.

Nonfunctional Requirements Additions or Deviations: None.

«requirement» R-Search Catalog by Keyword

Actor: Internet User

Objective: To view the available items in the TBS catalog by searching with keywords

Level: Subfunction

Preconditions: None

Main Success Scenario:

1. User selects to search the catalog by keywords.

2. System displays a search page.

3. User enters keywords for the search.

4. System presents a list of items that contain the keywords in the title, author, or description.

Extensions: None.

Nonfunctional Requirements Additions or Deviations: None.

«requirement» R-Add Item to Shopping Cart

Actor: Internet User
Objective: To place an item into the shopping cart to possibly be
                  purchased at a later time
Level: Subfunction
Preconditions: The user is currently viewing an item

Main Success Scenario:

1. User selects to add an item to the shopping cart.
2. System displays the current contents, if any, of the shopping cart with the addition of the new item.
3. User selects to modify the quantity of an item in the cart.
4. System updates the quantity and displays the contents of the shopping cart.

Extensions:

1a. System detects that the shopping cart is at its maximum capacity.

    1a1. User removes an item from the cart or purchases the items.

Nonfunctional Requirements Additions or Deviations: None.

«requirement» R-Purchase Items

Actor: Internet User
Objective: To purchase items currently in the shopping cart
Level: User goal
Preconditions: Add Item to Shopping Cart

Main Success Scenario:

1. User selects to purchase items currently in the shopping cart.
2. System prompts user to log in.
3. System displays the contents of the shopping cart and the total cost of the order.
4. User enters billing and shipping addresses and payment information.
5. System displays a final confirmation of the order.

6. User elects to proceed with the order.

7. System processes the order and presents a receipt.

Extensions:

6a. User elects to cancel the order.

   6a1. User is returned to the previous screen.

7a. System detects a problem with the user's address or payment information.

   7a1. User reenters the information.

Nonfunctional Requirements Additions or Deviations: Communication of data to and from the user will occur over a secured connection (SSL).

«requirement» R-Login

Actor: Internet User

Objective: To become authenticated with the system to accomplish higher-privileged tasks

Level: Subfunction

Preconditions: None

Main Success Scenario:

1. System presents login screen.

2. User enters authentication information (user ID, password, and so on).

3. System validates user information.

Extensions:

3a. System detects that user authentication information is invalid.

   3a1. User reenters the authentication information.

Nonfunctional Requirements Additions or Deviations: Communication of data to and from the user will occur over a secured connection (SSL).

«requirement» R-View a Previous Order

Actor: Internet User

Objective: To review the details of a previous order, including
                    its status

Level: User goal

Preconditions: Purchase Items

Main Success Scenario:

1. User selects to view a previous order.

2. System prompts user to <u>log in</u> if user is not already logged in.

3. System displays a list of the user's previous orders.

4. User selects an order to view.

5. System displays the order information, including the status—
   processing, shipped, and so on—of the order.

Extensions: None

Nonfunctional Requirements Additions or Deviations: Communication of
   data to and from the user will occur over a secured connection, such
   as SSL.

Service Use Cases

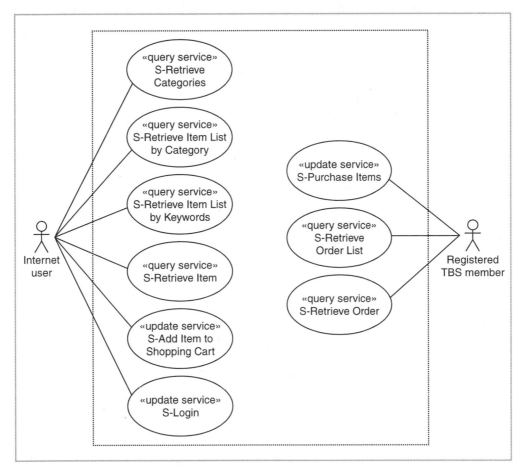

Figure C-2   Service Use Case Model

«query service» S-Retrieve Categories	
Actor:	Internet User
Objective:	To retrieve a list of categories from a parent category
Inputs:	aCategory (parent category, may be omitted, indicating top level)
Outputs:	aCategorySet
Preconditions:	None
Postconditions:	None

«query service» S-Retrieve Item List By Category

Actor:	Internet User
Objective:	To retrieve a list of items from a category
Inputs:	aCategory
Outputs:	anItemSet
Preconditions:	None
Postconditions:	None

«query service» S-Retrieve Item List by Keywords

Actor:	Internet User
Objective:	To retrieve a list of items containing the specified keywords
Inputs:	aKeywordSet
Outputs:	anItemSet
Preconditions:	None
Postconditions:	None

«query service» S-Retrieve Item

Actor:	Internet User
Objective:	To retrieve an item
Inputs:	anItemSkuNumber
Outputs:	anItem
Preconditions:	None
Postconditions:	None

«update service» S-Add Item to Shopping Cart

Actor:	Internet User
Objective:	To add an item to the shopping cart
Inputs:	anItem, aUser
Outputs:	aStatus (OK or Fail)
Preconditions:	None
Postconditions:	anItem is in aUser.ShoppingCart

«update service» S-Login

Actor:	Internet User
Objective:	To become authenticated with the TBS system and thus become a Registered TBS Member Actor
Inputs:	aUserName, aPassword
Outputs:	aStatus (OK or Fail)
Preconditions:	None
Postconditions:	aUser is now authenticated

«update service» S-Purchase Items

Actor:	Registered TBS Member
Objective:	To purchase items in the shopping cart
Inputs:	aUser, anItemSet, aPaymentInformation
Outputs:	aStatus (OK or Fail)
Preconditions:	S-Login has been executed
Postconditions:	anOrder is in aUser.Orders
	aUser.ShoppingCart is cleared

«query service» S-Retrieve Order list

Actor:	Registered TBS Member
Objective:	To retrieve a list of previous orders
Inputs:	aUser
Outputs:	anOrderSet
Preconditions:	S-Login has been executed
Postconditions:	None

«query service» S-Retrieve Order

Actor:	Registered TBS Member
Objective:	To retrieve a previous order
Inputs:	aUser, anOrderNumber (10 chars, [0-9])
Outputs:	anOrder
Preconditions:	S-Login has been executed
	anOrderNumber is in aUser.Orders
Postconditions:	None

Note that in S-Add Item to Shopping Cart, an instance of an Item is added to the user's list of items in the shopping cart. An instance is added *to,* deleted *from,* or updated *in* something. In our case, an Item instance is added to the set of items associated with a User. The User object provides the context within which the Item instance is added and hence its inclusion in the postcondition description.

C.3 Nonfunctional Requirements

The items listed in this specification apply to all use cases in the TBS system, unless otherwise noted in the nonfunctional requirements section of a particular use case. Functional use cases may require additions to these requirements or possibly complete deviations to accomplish their goals. In this case, the particular nonfunctional area is noted in the use case, and the remaining nonfunctional requirements are still applied as they appear in this specification.

- *Security:* Because the TBS system will be handling and storing private user data, such as addresses and credit card numbers, the system needs to be resilient to malicious attacks by Internet users. To accomplish this goal, TBS will apply the following security constraints to system components:
  —*Authentication* via a custom authentication form so that registered users can log on to the system. To protect the user ID and password during transmission, the form contents must be submitted over a secure connection using SSL.
  —*Authorization* restricted to users who are able to authenticate. Most areas of the TBS system are accessible by the general public but will restrict access to components and data intended for registered users. In addition, because some data is specific to a particular user, the TBS

system should not allow a registered user to view data belonging to another registered user.

—*System command execution* limited. Executing an operating system or other utility—by a component's spawning a subprocess—on the TBS server should be avoided, especially when the target utility requires input that was passed in from an Internet user. Any instances of this kind of implementation should be carefully checked to ensure that the utility cannot be manipulated by malicious user input.

—*Server-side file access* limited. Accessing files—other than additional components and pages—on the server's file system should be avoided. If it is absolutely necessary to access files on the server's file system, the use of component inputs in the formation of file names is prohibited.

—*Inputs* checked early. Inputs to system components will be checked as early as possible in the execution of a use case. Most TBS inputs will be checked on entry to a Web system component. To prevent attacks in the form of buffer overflows and input data manipulations, inputs will be checked for both length and acceptable characters. Each «service» use case will specify length and allowable characters in its use case description.

—*Payment transaction history logged:* Any payment transactions conducted through the TBS system must be logged for a period of time after the transaction to account for the dispute period. This data should be write-only.

—*Confidential user data.* Any private user data, such as addresses and telephone numbers, must be encrypted prior to storage in the TBS database. This is necessary to avoid compromising this data in the event of database access by an unauthorized user.

—*Temporary and log files.* Components that use private user data must not place it into a temporary or log file on any server's file system.

—*Database connections.* Web system components needing to access the TBS database will do so using a single-database user ID and password. This connection information must be secured to prevent unauthorized access to the database. To achieve this, the user ID and password will be stored in encrypted form in component source code and decrypted prior to accessing the database.

—*Database object access.* Database tables, views, and other objects will be restricted to the single database user described in the previous item, meaning that insert, select, update, and delete operations should be granted only to the single Web system database user.

—*ActiveX controls.* Any such controls created or used by the TBS site should be capable of handling malicious inputs—meaning excessive length or special characters—and should not read from or write to any files or registry keys, if applicable, on the visiting Web user's machine.

—*Cookies.* TBS components that use cookies to persist state on the user's machine will not store confidential user information, such as address, phone, or payment information, in a cookie.

—*Secure communications.* Any transmission of private data between the user's machine and the TBS servers should be done over a secure channel. Each «requirement» use case that deals with the exchange of private data will note in its use case description that a secure channel is necessary.

—*Network servers.* The TBS system will use a double-firewall approach, exposing only the HTTP and HTTPS ports from the Web servers to Internet users and exposing only the database access ports from the database servers to the Web servers.

- *Performance and scalability:* The TBS system requires the following performance and scalability behavior:

  —*Response time:* For the initial release of TBS, the system should support a peak load of 500 concurrent users in a base configuration and have the following response times: dial-up (28.8K–56K modem), 5–8 seconds; broadband (DSL, cable, T1): 2–4 seconds.

  —*Scalability:* The TBS system should support the addition of servers to the deployment configuration to increase the number of concurrent users while maintaining the previously specified response times.

  —*Stress:* Under extreme load conditions, the TBS system should gracefully reject users once the limits of the server resources have been encountered. Note that this will most likely be at a point exceeding 500 users. Between this point and the 500-user mark, TBS will experience response time degradations that are acceptable. At the point of maximum load, application components must remain stable—not crash—and data remain intact. This is especially important because TBS deals with purchasing transactions, which cannot be allowed to partially complete or fail.

  —*Reliability:* The TBS system will be taken down for maintenance once a week. Therefore, the system must continue to operate at peak load for the entire period of uptime without a degradation in response time or system resource usage.

- *Compatibility:* The TBS system must be compatible with the following software and platforms:

  —*Browsers:* Microsoft Internet Explorer 4.0 and later and Netscape Navigator 4.0 and later. This includes comparable versions of the AOL Web browser.

—*Platforms:* TBS should be accessible by all Microsoft Windows PC operating systems, including but not limited to Windows 95, 98, 2000, and ME. On Macintosh platforms, Mac OS 8.0 and later should be supported.

—*Colors:* Windows or Mac OS platforms running 8-bit (256-) or better color depth must be able to properly display all TBS images and pages. To accomplish this goal, the Web safe-color palette will be used on all images and HTML/CSS color specifications.

—*Image files:* TBS will use two types of image files formats: JPEG for high-resolution images, such as item photos, and GIF for icons and other non-photo-quality images. The Web safe-color palette will be used in creating and editing all images.

—*Secure communications:* Secure communications must take place over SSL to ensure broad compatibility.

- *Usability:* The primary goal of the TBS system is to sell products and so should make this function as easy as possible for the end user. In addition, colors, fonts, and other Web page elements should be viewable by most users, and the site should support as many accessibility features for disabled users as possible. For a complete list of the TBS usability guidelines, refer to the usability checklist in Appendix A.

C.4 Platform and Technologies

TBS is built entirely on the Windows 2000 platform. The production servers for TBS are multiprocessor Intel-based machines, with several machines functioning as Web servers and two database servers running SQLServer 2000. As the TBS customer base—and therefore its load—increases over time, the number of nodes in the Web tier can be increased to handle the additional load, and database data can be partitioned across multiple database servers when necessary. Web server machines are configured with Windows 2000 Network Load Balancing, which automatically spreads incoming connections across the Web server nodes.

The following technologies comprise the TBS system:

- *DHTML (HTML + CSS + scripting):* TBS uses DHTML technologies in its Web interface to provide an appealing look and a certain level of interactivity on the pages.
- *XML/XSLT:* The content of the TBS system is well suited for XML representation, as each item can be broken down into a number of data fields, such as stock number, price, title, and description. XSLT style sheets are used to render the XML data into pages, which provides a high degree of separation between the display of the site and the content.

- *Active Server Pages (ASP) on IIS:* These *dynamic* pages are used primarily to invoke functions on back-end components, which return XML strings from their functions. The ASP page either will send this XML buffer directly back to the browser, in the case of Microsoft IE5.0 or later, for rendering on the client, using the XSLT style sheet, or will render it on the server for browsers that do not support XML and return the resulting HTML.
- *COM+ components:* These components contain most of the application logic for TBS, including code that interfaces with the database. When used for retrieval, data is returned purely as an XML buffer to the ASP pages. In the case of updates, the ASP pages pass in several function parameters— shipping address fields, credit card number, and so on—that are used by the COM+ components to do their work. The COM+ components are written entirely in C++ and use a small set of TBS C++ classes to manipulate items and orders. These classes are responsible for interacting with the database for retrieval and storage of TBS data.

C.5 Architecture

Figure C-3 illustrates the TBS system architecture. Incoming customer connections are handled by one of the Web server nodes. The user interacts with Active Server Pages running on the Web server node: they call the COM+ components to work with the databases, using the TBS classes. These classes facilitate the retrieval and update of each item and the user data in the databases.

In the case of retrieval, the COM+ objects return XML strings containing item, order status, and other data to the calling Active Server Page. This data is stored in the primary database. Update operations performed by administrators will also affect data in the primary database, such as price or item stock number changes. Payment information, such as credit card numbers and customer billing information, is stored in the payment transaction log database in an encrypted format.

Some portions of this data are also stored in the primary database so that users can view their orders and to provide prepopulated forms for subsequent purchases. Note that the COM+ objects do not read data from the payment transaction log database and do not have direct access to the database tables. Updates are performed through stored procedures only. Transactions are processed by a separate system, not shown, at regular intervals.

The TBS network configuration includes two firewalls. One, referred to as a DMZ, is used to protect the Web servers from the public Internet; a second firewall is used to protect the back-end database machines from the DMZ. Only the Web server machines have access to the database machines. No other machines are allowed through the second firewall.

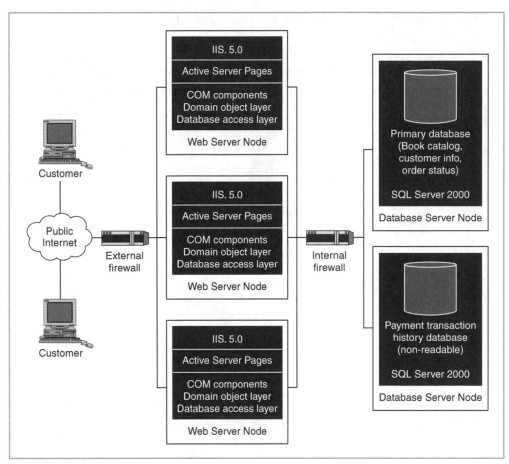

Figure C-3   TBS Architecture

C.6 Developed Components

The main functionality of the TBS system is accomplished through the use of the following ASP scripts:

- `BrowseCatalog.asp`, which displays portions of the book catalog
- `SearchCatalog.asp`, which displays result lists from a keyword search of the catalog
- `AddToCart.asp`, which allows an item to be placed in or updated in the cart
- `ViewCart.asp`, which shows the items currently in the cart

- `Checkout.asp`, which gathers payment and address information from the user and records the order
- `Login.asp`, which authenticates the user with a user ID and password
- `ViewOrdersList.pl`, which displays the list of the orders for the user
- `ViewOrderStatus.asp`, which displays an individual order and its status in the system

Contributing Author Biographies

Several individuals contributed material to this book.

- *Amjad (AJ) Alhait* is the founder of BetaSoft Inc., a software quality assurance consulting company, and the software testing Web site www.qaforums.com. AJ is certified with automated and performance test tools by Mercury Interactive and Segue Software and has nine years of software testing experience. AJ has consulted as a QA manager, architect, and instructor for many of the popular test tools. He also heads local QA user groups in Silicon Valley.

- *Simon Berman* is Director of Product Management at Mercury Interactive, the leading provider of Web performance management solutions. He is responsible for the company's load testing products, including LoadRunner, the company's flagship load and performance testing tool, and has launched initiatives for performance testing of wireless, streaming, dynamic content, and other key Web technologies. Previously, he served as a software engineer at a data communications testing company specializing in the development of network communication protocol analyzers.

- *Mark Collins-Cope* is Technical Director of Ratio Group Ltd., a UK-based training, consultancy, and software development company specializing in object and component technologies (see www.ratio.co.uk). Mark has more than 15 years experience in the software engineering field. His roles have included project management—software development, training course development, consultancy studies, and so on—analysis of requirements, technical architecture, and software design and development.

- *David Daish* is Managing Director of Bluedawn Computer Services Ltd., based in the UK. He has participated in numerous testing projects, including government departments and financial institutions. In recent years, he has provided consultation on test methodologies and practices, including test automation using the Automated Test Lifecycle Methodology. David has 14 years' software development and testing experience.

- *Julie Ferron* is a Senior Quality engineer for Dakota Imaging and has more than 12 years of experience in software quality assurance and testing. Her expertise spans the entire life cycle, from writing requirements and designing test suites to user acceptance testing. She has also supported both federal government and private industry clients implementing the SEI CMM. She has also been a member of the executive board with the Washington, D.C. section of the American Society of Quality.

- *Diane Hagglund* is Director of Product Marketing at Mercury Interactive, a leading provider of Web performance management solutions. She has extensive experience with automated testing for Web applications, including load and functional testing. Diane introduced Mercury Interactive's award-winning Java testing products, launched the Astra family of downloadable Web testing tools, and managed the company's MSP services for hosted load testing and monitoring. She also gained first-hand experience with deploying Web applications when she established Mercury Interactive's first e-commerce site.

- *Dawn Haynes* is an Automated Testing Evangelist for Rational Software. Over the past five years, she has ensured the success of Rational's testing customers through direct support, on-site consulting, and training. She has more than 9 years of experience in manual, functional, and performance testing of software systems on both Windows and UNIX platforms.

- *Jenny Jones* is the QA Lead at IDC in Framingham, Massachusetts. She has performed software engineering since completing a master's degree in mathematics and is pursuing an MBA degree. Jenny has been a featured speaker at many conferences, including Grace Hopper Women in Technology, International Software Quality Management, and LOMA's Distributed Technology Conference.

- *Bruce R. Katz* is a Staff Quality Assurance Engineer in the Rational Suites Business Unit of Rational Software Corporation. He is responsible for researching and implementing strategic and tactical quality assurance initiatives, including best practices and process improvement, as well as new tools, technologies, and techniques. He previously was a content developer for the Rational Unified Process, has more than 15 years of software quality assurance experience supporting both Fortune 500 and start-up companies, and is a Certified Quality Analyst.

- *Carl Nagle* is a Test Automation Engineer for SAS Institute Inc. He has been developing test automation solutions for both hardware and software testing on various platforms since 1988. He is enjoying the growing practical application and continued development of data-driven testing frameworks for SAS and its framework development partners.

- *Jonathan Rende* is Vice President of Product Management for testing tools at Mercury Interactive. He is responsible for the company's functional and load testing and test management solutions. His testing expertise is built on more than ten years' experience in the software industry in development, product management, and marketing.

- *Kevin Sturgeon* is the Director of Worldwide Sales Engineering for Empirix. Over the past several years, he has consulted with many Fortune 1000 and other companies on improving the design, quality, and scalability of their e-business applications. He has more than ten years in software quality assurance and related fields.

- *Tim Van Tongeren* is a Senior Quality Assurance consultant for CDI Corporation working with WorldCom. He has performed all phases of software development while working for several Fortune 500 companies in the telecommunications and finance industries. Since 1998, Tim has focused on the Web testing area.

Index

Also Available from Addison-Wesley

Automated Software Testing

Introduction, Management, and Performance

By Elfriede Dustin, Jeff Rashka, and John Paul

0-201-43287-0 • ©1999 • Paperback • 608 Pages

With the urgent demand for rapid turnaround on new software releases—without compromising quality—the testing element of software development must keep pace, requiring a major shift from slow, labor-intensive testing methods to a faster and more thorough automated testing approach.

Automated Software Testing is a comprehensive, step-by-step guide to the most effective tools, techniques, and methods for automated testing. Using numerous case studies of successful industry implementations, this book presents everything you need to know to successfully incorporate automated testing into the development process.

In particular, this book focuses on the Automated Test Life Cycle Methodology (ATLM), a structured process for designing and executing testing that parallels the Rapid Application Development methodology commonly used today. *Automated Software Testing* is designed to lead you through each step of this structured program, from the initial decision to implement automated software testing through test planning, execution, and reporting.

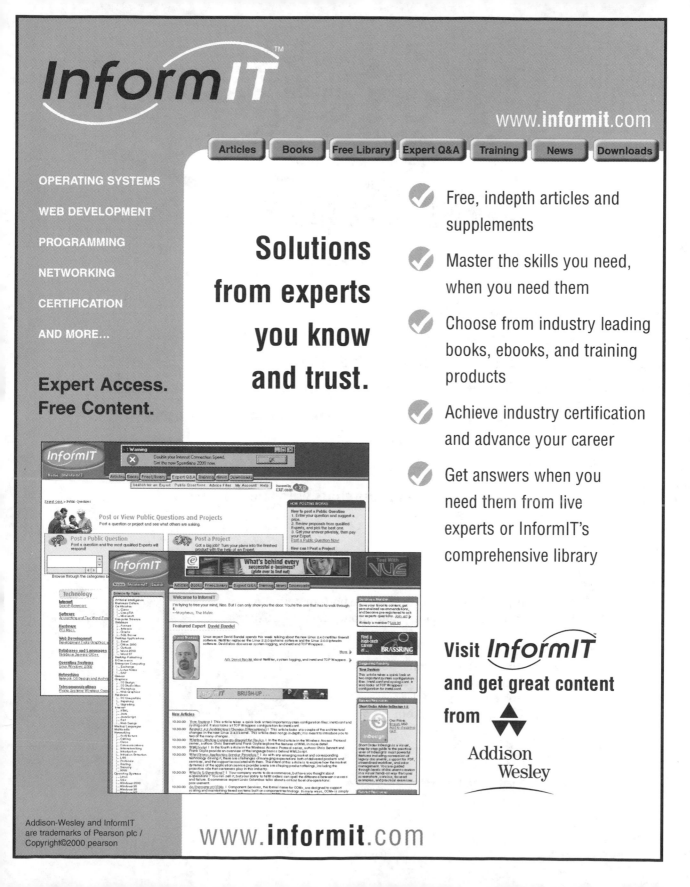